Sir Alan Herbert was born in 1890
and Oxford. Having achieved a fir
joined the Royal Navy and served both at Gallipoli and in France during the First World War. He was called to the Bar in 1918, and went on to become the Member of Parliament for Oxford University from 1935 to 1950.

Throughout his life A P Herbert was a prolific writer, delighting his many readers with his witty observations and social satires in the columns of *Punch*. He was the creator of a host of colourful characters – notably Topsy, Albert Haddock and Mr Honeybubble – and wrote novels, poems, musicals, essays, sketches and articles. He was also a tireless campaigner for reform, a denouncer of injustice and a dedicated conserver of the Thames.

By the time of his death in 1971, he had gained a considerable following and was highly regarded in literary circles. J M Barrie, Hilaire Belloc, Rudyard Kipling and John Galsworthy all delighted in his work, and H G Wells applauded him saying, 'You are the greatest of great men. You can raise delightful laughter and that is the only sort of writing that has real power over people like me.'

A P HERBERT
PUBLISHED BY HOUSE OF STRATUS

GENERAL CARGO
HOLY DEADLOCK
HONEYBUBBLE & CO
THE HOUSE BY THE RIVER
LIGHT ARTICLES ONLY
LOOK BACK AND LAUGH
MADE FOR MAN
THE MAN ABOUT TOWN
MILD AND BITTER
MORE UNCOMMON LAW
NUMBER NINE
THE OLD FLAME
SILVER STREAM
SIP! SWALLOW!
TOPSY MP
TOPSY TURVY
THE WATER GYPSIES
WHAT A WORD

NUMBER NINE

OR

THE MIND-SWEEPERS

A P HERBERT

First published in 1951

This edition published in 2001 by House of Stratus, an imprint of Stratus Books Ltd., Lisandra House, Fore St., Looe, Cornwall, PL13 1AD, UK.

www.houseofstratus.com

Typeset, printed and bound by House of Stratus.

A catalogue record for this book is available from the British Library and the Library of Congress.

ISBN 1-84232-601-5

TO OUR LONG-SUFFERING CIVIL SERVICE

SOME OF THE INTAKE

Number Four	SAMUEL OULD
Number Eight	PEACH MERIDEW
Number Nine	STANLEY BASS
Number Ten	JOY DALY
Number Eleven	ADRIAN HOLT
Number Thirteen	TOM CRAWLEY
Number Fifteen	COSMO LENNOX-EDWARDES
Number Eighteen	LAVINIA GABLE

CHAPTER I

It was 1955. The Russian War had been over for more than two years. All the 'Soviet' aeroplanes had exploded, as predicted by many, the moment they took the air. All the Soviet submarines, through sheer ignorance of the principles of navigation, had collided with each other, gone aground, or steamed unwittingly into rocks, nets, or minefields. Nearly all the inhabitants of all the 'satellite' countries had risen and revolted and stabbed the nearest Russian. The heroic Poles had stopped the Soviet steam-roller at Lemsk and turned it back. British, French, and American troops were in Moscow. And a train was leaving Victoria Station.

'Come aboard!' said the young man, as the porter slammed the door. 'Just made it. Well done, King's Railwayman.' He flung two half-crowns onto the platform and the train rolled out.

Mr Stanley Bass, the only other person in the compartment, glared at the intruder's rump with the indignation proper to an Englishman who has been robbed of his empty carriage. But he could not guess that the rump belonged to an old companion in His Majesty's Navy, Lieutenant the Viscount Anchor. When his lordship turned at last, both the young men stared, as if they had seen a portent. Then they grinned. One said: 'Good God!' The other said: 'You?'

Mr Bass had been a happy officer of the Royal Naval Volunteer Reserve, and had returned reluctantly to the battle of civil life after the war. Anthony was RN and serving still. The two had been shipmates in destroyers – chiefly HMS *Vicious* and HMS *Toad* – for two or three years. They had seen Okelot and Murik together, and *Toad* had made two icy passages to Gdynia, escorting tanks to the grateful Poles. Soon the reminiscences were flowing freely. But little was heard of the heroic encounters they had seen and shared. Occasions were mentioned when one or the other – sometimes both – had taken more gin than a doctor would have advised: and there were references to superior officers who seemed to them to have been inaccurately promoted.

Stanley Bass, though the amateur, had more the authentic look of the Navy than the Royal sailor. He had a broad face, a short nose and a square chin, and a dimpling smile that suddenly changed the picture from severity to gentleness and warm good-humour, like the red light slowly surrendering to amber and green. It need hardly be said that his eyes were blue. Anthony had blue eyes too. He was a little taller, almost too long for the Navy. They must both, one felt, have banged their heads on many a companion-way in His Majesty's destroyers: and perhaps Anthony's slight stoop was the result. The nose, too, seemed long for a sailor. Many good sailors do have long noses: but it is not right. The mouth turned up at the corners when he smiled, and a smile seemed always on the way. You would have said he was twenty-five. But he could look stern enough when moved or angered. Then the lips were thin and tight; a little pucker appeared between the brows: and you would have said he was twenty-seven, with some rich and rough experience behind him. This was correct. His voice was rather high, and sometimes cracked like a schoolboy's in moments of fun, feeling, or excitement. This annoyed him, and he had said once: 'It's like atmospherics on the wireless. Spoils my effects. I shall never be an Admiral.'

'Well,' said Anthony at last. 'Whither bound, old companion?'

'TPQ,' said Mr Bass.

'I beg your pardon?'

'TPQ.'

Lieutenant Anchor rummaged about in his recollections of the International Code, but could remember no signal that seemed to fit the situation. All he could think of, going back to a convoy episode, was PQ – 'I have sprung a leak.'

'Sorry, dear comrade of a thousand victories, but the hoist is "not understood".'

'Test of Personal Qualities. Civil Service Country House. Hambone Hall.'

'What? That plague-point?'

A new light was in Anthony's eyes, though the smile continued.

'Do you realize, you inimitable chump, that you are steering for my ancestral home?'

'Your ancestral home? But I thought you came from Caraway – or somewhere.'

'My father – God bless him!' said Anthony patiently, 'for after all he is an Admiral of the Fleet – is the Earl of Caraway and Stoke. The family name is Adley. Mine is Anchor, being now top son. The family seat is Hambone Hall – or was.'

'But – ?'

'Because it was there that the fifth Earl hit Oliver Cromwell with a hambone. This caused the Restoration.'

'I follow,' said Mr Bass. 'Yes, I quite see that. But why Stoke?'

'I won't go into that. Let there be a little mystery still in the illuminated swamp that we call life. The point, the detonating point *is* – that Hambone Hall was the house of the Adleys – and they have made it a den of Civil Servants.'

'You were turned out?'

'Town-planned – compulsory-purchased – nationalized? God knows what. I was in China, and this is my first leave since the robbery took place. Mother died last year. Dad, of course, is fairly bankrupt, and it seems he wanted the National Trust to take the place over and let him live in the cellar, as most Earls do. But HM's insufferable Gov. wouldn't play. They wanted the whole place for the disreputable researches to which you're bound. So out we went.'

'Where is the Admiral now?'

'At the Lodge by the lake – with sister Prim. Full of steam still, but faintly certifiable, I fancy. He swears he'll be a Commodore of Convoys in the next quarrel though he can't be a day less than a hundred and three. So he keeps his hand in – takes sights over the lake, gets his noon position and morses madly to another sea-farer three miles away.'

'Good stuff.'

'But now,' said his lordship, 'tell me about this beastliness to which you trend. I've only heard the most odious rumours, and Prim's letters are quite unreadable.'

Bass opened a small bag beside him and extracted a printed document: 'Here you are. Operation Orders.'

Anthony read aloud, the pucker appearing:

' "Candidates who reach the qualifying standard in the written examination" – what for?'

'Civil Service. Go on.'

' "And satisfy the Commissioners of their linguistic ability" – have you done that?'

'Um.'

'But you can hardly speak *English*, brother!'

'I have a little café French. The standard is not very high.'

'Well – "will be summoned to undergo a series of tests of *personal qualities*..." – What does that mean? – "The candidates will be assembled in a group of 20–30 at a time at a specified centre, probably near London...".' The pucker deepened. 'My God, to think of the old ancestral becoming a "specified centre"!' He read on: ' "where they will spend 3–4 days and will be provided with accommodation and board free of charge." Any "allowances"?'

'No.'

'Brutal. "During this time a skilled staff will be engaged in *studying their behaviour and character in different situations*" – Gosh! – "both individually and as members of a group… It may be convenient to test Foreign Service candidates at the same time as candidates for the Administrative Class of the Home Civil Service".'

'This' said Viscount Anchor, 'is worse than I thought. Not merely a nest but an *incubator*. With a touch, I take it, of the Gestapo, and the Grand Inquisition?'

'That's about it,' said Bass with a sigh.

'For all I know, some suckling Civil Servant is sleeping in my nursery.'

'Probably two.'

'With microphones in the walls! And you, my poor Stanley, are going into this Hell alone and unafraid?'

'By no means. The wind is definitely up. Of the last lot, I hear, only one got through.'

'Poor devil. I suppose, by the way, there is some honest explanation of your wanting to be a Civil Servant?'

'I don't. I want to go abroad.'

'Ambassador stuff? I'll pass that. But don't tell me that ambassadors have to have the same PQ as those werewolves in Whitehall!'

'Seems so.'

'I don't follow. Ambassadors have to please, and Civil Servants have to persecute – and like it.'

'Well, don't blame me. That's how it is. A girl I know went through it – '

'Girls?' said Anthony. 'Are there *girls* in this quality-contest?'

'Oh, rather. Just a few.'

'As I whizzed down the platform,' said his lordship ruminatively, 'I saw at least two faces which almost caused me to alter course. But "Civil Servant" was *not* stamped upon them. Nor was "Ambassador".'

'Most of them go for the Foreign.'

'But, *Stan*!' Anthony's voice cracked as a new thought struck him. 'With your roving eye, you haven't a hope. Unless the female candidates have the shape of haystacks, the first time you turn your head you'll be ploughed.'

'I know,' admitted the great lover ruefully. 'I shall shut my eyes.'

'Ha!' his lordship laughed incredulously. 'What happened to the intellectual blonde at Southsea?'

'Married.'

'Too bad.'

'Just as well.'

'Well, all this casts a grave new light on the nonsense. I expect they send in delicious houris to catch the unwary. The old home is practically a brothel.'

'Shouldn't wonder,' said Bass gloomily. 'I shan't look.'

'What are these "tests" they talk of?'

'From what Moo says – '

'Moo?'

'Her name's Meriel.'

'I don't follow. Never mind.'

'From what she says they're pretty terrible. They pick a subject out of a hat, and you have to talk about it for ten minutes.'

'My poor Stan, you'll dry up after one.'

'Too right. Then there's the Association Test. They put up words on the wall, and you have to write down what the word suggests in fifteen seconds – '

'Gosh! I know about *that!*' Anthony sat up straight, with a new expression, a rather fierce expression, on his face. 'And, whatever you say, the trick-cyclist says you're a louse.'

'Trick-cyclist?'

'Psy – what-is-it. Psychiatrist.'

'That's right. In the old days, they say, they only had psychologists.'

'What's the difference?'

'God knows. Anyhow, now, it seems, they swarm. Moo had a terror, she said, worst of the lot. One of her words was "Mother". She wrote down "Labour – Pains – Screaming". He said that meant she had a poor sense of responsibility and was ready to put private contentment before – '

'STOP!' said Anthony, in great excitement, it seemed, for he stood up, and the blue eyes seemed to catch a new spark from somewhere. 'What was his name? What was his *name*?'

'O Lord, I forget,' said the astonished Bass. 'Moo did tell me, I know. I think it began with M. Or was it P?'

'It was M. I *know* it was M. It was "Maple" – wasn't it?' The voice cracked with agitation again.

'Maple?' said the wondering Bass. 'By George, I believe you're right. Moo said they used to sing a rude song about "the Maple leaf for ever". Meaning "leave", you see? It's all coming back.'

'Not merely was it "Maple",' said Anthony firmly, almost fiercely, 'it was *Heriot* Maple – God rot his entrails!'

'Heriot Maple? Yes, that seems to ring a tiny gong. Mind you, I never saw the fellow – though I suppose I may.'

'Lord help you if you do!' Anthony subsided into his seat and said, softly, but grimly: 'Well, that settles it.'

'What settles what?' said Bass, bewildered.

'You never knew my elder brother, George? The original Anchor?'

'No, old boy.'

'He was much older than me – ten – twelve years. He was a fine fellow – but not what you might call a knock-about or battling character. Scholar of Magdalen and all that. Must have been a throw-back to the second Earl, who wrote plays and chamber music, whatever that may be. He was a Member of P. and before the war was a junior Minister, or something, doing pretty well. Then they gave him some kind of Regional Commissioner job, up in the North. Useful job – just the thing for him – and quite safe. Too safe, he thought, though he was doing his stuff in the House as well. But there it was – technically, he was "military age": so what does he do but enlist in the Army? He does six months in the ranks. Then, of course, he's hauled out for a Commission and goes to one of these Officer Whatnames. He does all those preposterous antics the Pongoes do – you know, cross-country stuff with live ammunition. That must have been pretty daunting for the poor old chap, for he was never much of a one for running and jumping – to say naught about the live ammunition. But all goes reasonably well till he has his interview with the trick-cyclist.'

'Among other things, they'd done this raving rubbish about words you were talking about – what did you call it?'

'The "Association Test", I think it is.'

'Right. Well, George told me about some of his words – it was the last time I saw him – I happened to have a spot of leave just after he finished the doings. One of his words was COMPLEX. George told me he wrote down "Inferiority – Psycho-analysis – Nonsense". Frank, you see, but no very high marks for diplomacy and tact. Another word was "Bayonet": and George, it seems, wrote something like "Wounded men – blood – screaming – mess". There were a good many other words, but I forget them now. Those were the two that straddled poor George.

'The trick-cyclist, it seems, was in a tough old temper and went to the point at once. "Do you remember, Private Adley," he said – '

'Why Adley? I thought he was Anchor?'

'So he was, but he didn't want to do the Viscount in the Army. So he used the family name. That was old George all over.'

'I never could follow the peerage.'

'You must do some chart-work. Well, this crawling creature says, "Do you remember what you wrote against 'Complex'?" "No," says George. "You wrote 'Inferiority – Psycho-analysis –

Nonsense'. That, for a man of your education, Private Adley, is rather a sweeping statement on rather a big subject. I wonder if you would care to develop it?" "If I may have more than fifteen seconds," says George, "I shall be delighted." That I mark as a fairly penetrating retort. It seems to have hit the psycho-artist between wind and water, for he passed on nastily to the other words. About "Bayonet" he said: "Here you see, you wrote 'Wounded men – blood – screaming'. You did not, I believe, take any active part in the last war. What made you write that?" "I had many friends who were in the war," says George, "and I heard a lot about it."

'I don't know what else took place: but at the end of it all the trick-cyclist said: "I am afraid I shall have to report that, though you have certain high qualities, *you are not fitted to take command of troops in the field.*" '

Anthony paused, as if to let that awful statement sink in. He went on:

'Those were the words that sank poor George. Can you imagine it? Fancy saying a thing like that to a chap who has just given up a safe job to volunteer for the Pongoes! Even if you were sure it was true, can you think of saying it to the chap himself? Nobody can ever tell how he will behave under fire – remember that time when we all found ourselves flat on *Toad*'s bridge, all except Dicky? – but the hope is he'll do better than he thinks. They could have put George in an office – or on the Staff, perhaps: but any day he might have found himself in a scrap – and taking charge too – say an invasion, a retreat, or a tight corner when everybody down to the cooks joins in. How is a chap going to give a good show if all the time he remembers that some cod-fish of an "expert" has said he couldn't command a cow? And how the Hell does the said cod-fish suppose he *knows*? Some chaps look like ghosts, but turn out to have the guts of horses. Remember old Andy? Others look like prize-fighters but could hardly fight a flea. I've heard the Pongoes say the same thing.'

Anthony paused for breath, while Bass surveyed him in some astonishment. He had seldom seen his friend so earnest and angry.

'What happened?'

'Old George took it badly. He thought he'd show 'em. He couldn't show 'em in the Army, because they posted him for office duty or something. How he managed it I don't know – of course, he knew his way round Whitehall – but he got himself transferred to the RAF and volunteered as a rear-gunner. That, as you know, is not a safe job. Even the training, I believe, tore George's hands to bits. He did two trips over France and blazed away a bit. But on the third they got him.'

Bass simply stared at his companion.

'Now the name of the abominable oaf who caused all this was Heriot Maple: and he seems to be in action at my ancestral. I'm sure he is. Not only the name – I recognize the form.'

'Tough show. But I don't quite see' said the fair-minded Bass, 'how you can say it "caused it all". After all, if your brother had taken his advice, he might be alive today.'

'If that fish had kept his flap shut George would have gone into the Army in the ordinary way, and with any luck he would have come through. Millions of Pongoes, after all, do survive. Besides, you seem to forget the insult.'

'Oh, I quite see that, old boy,' said the other hastily.

'George had a grand finale, if you like, but after all, he proved nothing much, except that he had long-distance guts. For all he knew, the trick-cyclist was right – about the infantry, I mean. That's what maddened Dad. There's a black mark on the line. That filthy report is on the records at the War House still. I'm not sure' he went on, ruminative, 'that I ought to tell the old man. As like as not, he'd cruise up to the Hall and strangle the fellow. He was very fond of George. So was I. Young Roderick, bless him, is much less of a magnet.'

Bass said after a small silence:

'You haven't said what settles what.'

'Isn't it obvious, old boy? All the way home I was wondering if there wasn't some way to smoke these vermin out and get the old man back to his quarters. I couldn't think of anything. I can't now. But now that I know about Maple – '

'But you don't know about Maple.'

'Yes, I do. Bet you a fiver. Anyhow,' said Anthony, 'it's war.' The lips set very tight and the chin was noticeable.

'And you, Stanley Bass,' he went on, 'are simply heaven-sent. You will be our spy at head-quarters. You – '

'Hey!' said Bass, in alarm.

'You will pursue and study this Maple. You will find out his habits, dig into his sex-life – '

'Here! Hey! Don't forget I've got to pass an exam.'

'Pass it, by all means, old boy. But keep an eye on this pest. And all the other pests. When they've done with you, you will render a full report. In fact, you'd better come and stay at the Lodge. I shall want a ground-plan of the whole building, ship's routine, bedrooms of the staff, locking-up time, any guard at night, and so on. Have you an electric torch?'

'Yes. But – '

'How's your morse?'

'Pretty rusty, I should think. They don't morse much in the City.'

'Well, mug it up. The old man has a lamp on the top of his mast, and we may have to communicate. Give me a flash from your bedroom tonight.'

'But, steady on, old boy. What do you mean to do?'

'I can't say yet. But we must have our tackle ready. The best thing will be if you regard yourself as an offensive patrol – '

'But – '

'Hallo! We're alongside.'

The train drew up at Hambone Halt. On the little platform about a dozen young men and women eyed each other dubiously. The men, on the whole, were relieved by what they saw. 'If that's the standard,' each one thought, 'I ought to be all right.' The women thought, 'All these spectacled fellows! I haven't a hope.'

'Now for the Specified Centre,' said Anthony. 'I suppose you'll have a communal bus?'

'Moo said she had to walk.'

'Well, I'll give you a lift in the Old Implacable.'

'Don't bother, old boy.' Mr Bass, for the first time in his life, was conscious of an itch to leave his old friend's company.

'Oh, come on. Potter's sure to be here.'

'But you'll have a lot of luggage.'

'Potter can come back for it. Here, give me your bag.'

The masterful fellow marched ahead, and Mr Bass followed, unwitting of his doom, but anxious.

The Old Implacable, when first manufactured, had been classed as a motor-car. Few would have gone so far as that this evening. All the string in the county, all the grey paint in the world, could not much help her battered wings, her broken springs, her rattling doors and immovable windows. But she might be described as the Horseless Wonder, for she still moved across the earth's surface, lurching, rattling, sometimes roaring and frequently boiling, without visible aid. Many legends surrounded her: the favourite was that she was the earliest landing-craft, and the Admiral, as a midshipman, had put her ashore at the siege of Sevastopol. She was of no known 'make'; you could not say that she was a 'Gilbert', a 'Spurling', or a 'Redvers': she had bits of all the cars in history inside her. Even the string that kept her more important parts together was of different sizes and colours. Some was common parcel-string, and some, white drawing-room string, and some, strong tarred stuff from the ship-chandler's near the Monument, where the Admiral got his cordage. At all events, she did move, noisily, across the earth's surface: and she was all the Earl-Admiral could afford.

Potter stood beside her, the only Potter. Well, no, that is not accurate, for Potter was of the numerous, immortal breed of

Chief Petty Officers in the Royal Navy. With no offence to the Sergeant-Majors of the Guards, it may be said that these are about the finest men in uniform, for character, sagacity, technical skill, and knowledge of men. 'Immortal' is too much, perhaps, for it would be unreasonable to expect Providence to supply such men for ever: but if Potter had perished the Admiral at that date could have found his like in many corners of the sea-girt isle.

Ex-Chief Petty Officer Potter was itching to salute the young Lieutenant and lord, but, being compelled to wear the degrading costume of a civilian, could only stand to attention by the Old Implacable and express his emotions by the stiffness of his back and the solemnity of his face. But, for this high occasion, he had pinned on his numerous medals. Potter, these days, protruded below the belt a little more than he liked: but the protuberance was as hard as oak and would hurt a man who hit it. His face, a rich mixture of brown and red, would have done well for a binding of the *Oxford English Dictionary*.

Anthony introduced Bass, put him beside him and took the wheel.

'The Old Implacable again,' said Anthony, with a happy sigh. 'How is she, Potter?'

'Not what she was, Sir. She should be in dock, by rights. Would you rather I drove, Sir?' he added anxiously.

'Not on your life, Potter. This is the moment I dreamed about in China. Hullo, we're off.'

'She seems exactly what she was,' he said, as the engine stopped outside the station. Potter got out and heaved on a lengthy starting-handle. There was a loud roaring noise in the bowels of the car. She shuddered and went back a yard or two.

There was a light, low mist in the valley, and Anthony switched on the lights. Potter inspected them one by one.

'Lights burning brightly, Sir,' he shouted over the roar of the Implacable. 'All's well. But watch your starboard light, Sir. It has a tendency to dim.'

'Why is that?' yelled Anthony through the window.

'It's the string!' shouted Potter. 'Faulty connection!'

'Full ahead both,' said Anthony, putting in the clutch, 'and let us pray.'

Stanley Bass did pray. Afterwards he said that he had a premonition of disaster. Potter, too, said that he was worried about the officer taking the wheel.

For one thing, he did not know about the great motor-coaches which now roared through the green but narrow roads, filling them like a battleship in the Suez Canal. And whenever he tried to tell him the young lord was shouting about something else. ' "Specific Centre!" he'd be shouting,' said Potter, later. ' "Specific Centre!" – and laughing fit to split a cod. I thought perhaps he was on to gunnery – or something of that. Afterwards I hear it's something to do with this madhouse up at the Hall – but how was I to know? "Specific Centre," he shouts, and laughs like a sea-horse.'

The mist was thicker, almost a fog.

'Look out for the coaches, Sir!' poor Potter said, while Stanley Bass prayed again. But Anthony yelled back: 'How's the Admiral, Potter?'

'First-class, Sir!' shouted Potter. 'When I left him he was doing his stars for the twilight position.' And then 'Slow ahead, Sir!' roared the anxious Potter. 'Your starboard light's gone!'

But Potter was too late. 'Round the corner' Anthony pronounced, loudly ironical, 'is the *Specified Centre*!' But round the corner came a vast motor-coach, filling the road as a cork fills the neck of a bottle. The skilful driver, no doubt, could have stolen a foot or two from the ditch and the hedge if he had seen two lights on the approaching little car. But he saw one only. 'Christ!' said Lord Anthony, as he saw the Juggernaut towering ahead. He wrenched the wheel to the left and the Old Implacable, just missing the Juggernaut, came to rest in the ditch against a tree. Her speed was not great, and the impact was not severe. Anthony suffered nothing more than a chest bruised by the wheel. Potter was flung forward, in spite of premonitions and precautions, but his head fell fortunately between Anthony and Bass. Bass, with hands extended, just saved his head; but his knee was under the dashboard.

'Fairly numerous apologies,' said Anthony, as he switched off the engine. 'Personally, I am alive, though discouraged. How are others?'

'All well, Sir,' said Potter.

'Fairly well,' said Stanley Bass. 'The only thing is – I think I've broken a leg.'

'Too bad, old friend,' said Anthony. 'And that, of course, wrecks all our plans.'

CHAPTER II

For some time before the wreck of the Old Implacable, Admiral of the Fleet the 17th Earl of Caraway and Stoke had been preparing to get his twilight position by the stars. By joining two small balconies together he had constructed a modest 'bridge', facing South across the lake. It was nothing to the grand bridge he had had up at the Hall, but it had to do. Here he had his azimuth compass, with which he took bearings of ducks on the lake and low-flying aeroplanes. At one end the signal-halyards ran up to a small yard-arm. Just inside his bedroom window was a chart-table, a chronometer, a morse tapping-key and a capacious flag-locker. He felt it his duty to keep in touch not only with the Naval Code but the International Code: so there were 126 flags neatly rolled in the pigeon-holes. On the small hill across the lake to the SE (SE by S, if you insist) he could see, with a telescope, the signal-yard of Admiral Mole. These two, using Ordnance maps, converted the surrounding country-side into sea, and from time to time fought major naval battles, taking it in turn to be in command. They moved vast fleets and valuable convoys through Kent and Surrey and Sussex and as far West as Hampshire, where the maps ran out. They fought old engagements, won the Battle of Jutland, and hunted down the *Bismarck* in very quick time. The best battles raged for days. All day flags ran up and down (with Potter as Yeoman of Signals), and half the night the neighbours could see the flicker of morse across the lake or in the tree-tops up the hill.

To the South-West, higher than Admiral Mole, he could see the top windows of his old home, the Hall, and the tall mast and yard-arm. Every night, before he turned in, he flashed an insulting signal in that direction, such as:

YOU ARE A LOT OF BASTARDS

But no one at the Hall knew morse.

The Admiral was rather short. He had a trim grey beard; he had bow-legs and walked sturdily with a maritime roll. The eyes, of course, were blue, but very pale, as if long wear and washing had taken the colour out of them. He had a voice like a six-inch gun. The ancient bull-dog, Beatty, too old now even to walk downstairs, lay in a basket near the chronometer, snuffling like the wind in the willows.

Tonight the Admiral had selected the many-coloured Capella, in the West, Regulus in the South, very near the meridian, and the yellow star, Arcturus, bearing 100°. Also, he had taken a sentimental sight of Betelgeuse, too low, for Orion, dear Orion, would soon be seen no more. These four could be seen from the bridge. To complete his 'fix' he proposed to find the altitude of the Pole Star, but for that he would have to go into the bathroom at the back, which he resented. The great bridge at the Hall had commanded all points of the compass. For his noon position, by the Sun, he used an ordinary sextant, bringing down the Sun to the far edge of the lake, with a special allowance for 'dip'. But for the stars he used an averaging bubble sextant, 'a damned new-fangled affair', but still. It took six sights in 58 seconds, averaged them out, and showed the result in a little window. It looked rather like a cinema camera, and while the clock-works were running, it sounded like one. The preparation of this ingenious machine required numerous adjustments, each of which could lead to error: and the Admiral cursed the contrivance continuously.

Tonight he was in a special fret. At the end of his operations he would signal to Admiral Mole 'My position is – '. Admiral Mole, also, when he had done his sums to his satisfaction, would flash 'My position is – '. These 'positions' were never quite correct, so tricky was the bouncing bubble: but if either Admiral got within a mile of the correct position[1] he was delighted. Now and then, one of them would get within a few hundred yards: and then wild wounding boastful signals would wink across the water and the woods.

Lately, Admiral Mole had come through first far too often, and had been far too near: Caraway felt that he was 'slipping'.

It was a nuisance Potter having to meet young Anthony: for Potter acted as 'Tanky', the navigator's assistant, stood by the chronometer and noted the time of each 'sight' to the nearest second when the Admiral cried 'Stop!' – or sometimes 'Bang!'

His daughter Primrose was a fairly willing understudy, but she seemed to have no notion of the importance of navigation, and did not know one star from another. Once she had put down all his altitudes in the wrong columns – given Vega's to Arcturus and so on. He had worked out his sums on that basis; Mole had come through early with a good result: and until he found the error the Admiral thought that he was going mad.

Now he had Capella, Regulus and Arcturus 'in the bag' – pretty good sights, too, he thought, in spite of the rolling mist, and he was after Polaris, the North Star. To get the altitude of Polaris he had to kneel on the lavatory by the window – 'a damned uncomfortable station'. The bubble sextant had no telescope, and the Admiral's eyes were – he had to confess – weaker than they were. Capella, Vega, and Arcturus, fine blazing fires, had shown through the bubble well enough. But the famous Pole Star is not as bright as its fame. The Admiral could not find it. When he did the bubble seemed to have disappeared. 'GOD DAMN!' cried the Admiral.

'WHAT WAS THAT?' cried Lady Primrose Adley, who stood patiently by the chronometer in the bedroom.

'I SAID "GOD DAMN!"

'FATHER?'

'YES?'

'YOU'RE SWEARING AGAIN!'

Silence. The bubble had reappeared: the Admiral had pressed the right lever, and the bubble was illuminated. There, too, rather faint, was the Pole Star. But they were far apart. The Admiral, with the fingers of his right hand, twiddled the wheel which should bring them together. There was a click, and the wheel stopped: the star and the bubble were still far apart.

'GOD DAMN!' shouted the Admiral.

'FATHER!' said Lady Primrose, protesting.

'IF YOU HAD TO HANDLE THIS BLOODY BUBBLE YOU'D SWEAR A LITTLE TOO, MY GIRL!'

It was now clear what was wrong. In the darkness he had set the machine to 30° instead of 50° – or 40°, which would have done as well. The Admiral produced a small electric torch and a magnifying-glass and began to make the necessary adjustment. At once the magnifying-glass fell into the lavatory pan. The Admiral fished it out.

'AND WHY' he yelled, 'THEY HAD TO PUT THIS LAVATORY BY THE WINDOW I CAN'T IMAGINE!'

It occurred to Lady Primrose, waiting patiently by the chronometer, that perhaps the poor architect or housebuilder had not foreseen that one day the bathroom window would be used by an Admiral of the Fleet, anxious to establish the altitude of the Pole Star. But she thought it wiser to keep quiet. Lady Primrose was a gentle creature. The sweet and forgiving expression now on her face was habitual. She was not a beauty, but that kind, understanding expression made her beautiful to the milder, and perhaps the better, kind of man. She was rather short, like her father; and among the Animal Kingdom you would not have put her much higher than a brown squirrel, or perhaps a rather attractive mouse.

She was very fond of her father: but she sometimes wished that he would try to live more of the life of an ordinary land-animal. He often said that he had 'swallowed the anchor': but it did not seem to have been digested. The altitude of the Pole Star seemed to her to be a matter of small importance, and, in spite of many explanations, she had never been able to understand what facts of life depended on it. She was thinking now that it would be nice to see Anthony again, her favourite brother, and that if the Admiral did not soon let her go his dinner would burn. She also tried to compose in her head the speech she would have to make at the opening of the Sale of Work.

The Admiral had now worked the Pole Star nicely into the middle of the bubble. He pressed the little lever and the clockwork began. At the end of the 58 exciting seconds, in which the lighted bubble danced about the Pole Star, he shouted 'STOP!'

This was the signal for Primrose to note and record the exact time by the chronometer. But she had not done this duty for some time, and, coming out of her reverie with a jump, all she did was to answer 'WHAT?'.

'I said "STOP!" ' And he began to read off the figures: 'Fifty. Damn it, I can't see. Fifty – nine and a quarter.'

'What's the matter, Dad?'

The Admiral stumped out of the bathroom, a glow of triumph on his face. 'Fifty – nine and a quarter. Got it?'

'Yes, Dad,' said his daughter, dutifully writing, while the Admiral peered suspiciously over her shoulder.

'No, it's not 59. How *could* it be 59? It's 50 degrees, 9 minutes, and a quarter.'

'Sorry, Dad. It sounded just like fifty-nine.'

'You ought to know by this time that the elevation of the Pole Star is the same angle as the latitude: and your latitude is – I suppose,' he went on, a horrid thought striking him, 'I suppose you do know what your latitude is?'

'No, Dad,' Primrose confessed.

'You're a fine daughter. – Where's the time?'

'The time?'

'The time of the sight. I gave you a hail.'

'Sorry, Dad, I must have been thinking.'

The Admiral nearly made the famous remark of leaders of men: 'You're not paid to think,' but remembered in time that this was his beloved daughter. He looked upon her with reproach and sorrow and said: 'My God, I shall have to start all over again.'

It was at this point that Potter appeared, panting a little.

'Beg pardon, Sir. The Lieutenant's come aboard, Sir.'

'Give him my compliments, and ask him to report to the Bridge.'

'Aye, aye, Sir. Beg pardon, Sir, there's a casualty below.'

'Casualty? But where was the action?'

'The Old Implacable, Sir. Collision. About twenty yards North of the West Gate. Friend of the Lieutenant's. Broke his knee, Sir. Starboard knee, Sir.'

'Damn it! Who was at the helm?'

'Lieutenant Anthony.'

'At this rate,' thought the Admiral, 'I shall never get my position.'

But the need for action overcame his irritation. 'Where is the Sick Bay Attendant?'

'Here, Sir,' said Potter.

'Have the Sick Bay prepared.'

'I'll do that, Dad,' said Primrose, and hurried from the room.

The Admiral frowned slightly at this departure from strict routine.

'Yeoman of Signals?'

'Aye, aye, Sir,' said Potter.

'Make a signal to that new doctor – what's-his-name?'

'Sale, Sir.'

'Carry on. I'll come below and lend a hand with the stretcher.'

'Aye, aye, Sir.'

'Oh, and, Bo'sun?'

'Yes, Sir?'

'Pass the word for an extra tot of rum.'

'Aye, aye, Sir.'

Before he left, the Admiral peered out across the lake towards the stronghold of Admiral Mole. There was no flashing from the forest: but any moment now old Mole might come through. What was to be done? He himself had perhaps fifteen minutes of sums and logarithms and plotting on the chart before him: but he must greet his son and attend to his injured guest.

After a guilty glance at the door, he went to the tapper and began to 'call up' Admiral Mole – with a series of A's – short-long-short-long-short-long. Presently a light glowed steadily in the woods, and he could imagine old Mole cursing as he turned from his calculations.

Slowly he tapped out: '51.8 North 17.30 East'.

He felt a little bad about it. It was cheating, of course. And he had never cheated before.

1 51° 07' N. 0° 18' E.

CHAPTER III

Stanley Bass was safe in bed: and Lady Primrose did what she could while they waited for the doctor.

Meanwhile, there was a fond reunion between father and son.

'Up Spirits!' said the Admiral, and handed Anthony a generous tot.

Anthony apologized about the Old Implacable and explained about Stanley Bass.

'In that case,' said the Admiral, 'I suppose we ought to make a signal to that beastly place and let 'em know what's happened to him.'

'Hold on, Sir. I have a rather meaty report to make. It seems, from what Stanley said, that one of the principal skunks at the Hall is the man Maple – the ineffable squirt who did the dirty on poor George.'

'What? Not the psycho-trypist who made that stinking report?'

'The same, Sir.'

The Admiral, as Anthony had feared, became highly excited. The veins stood out on his forehead and he breathed strongly through the nose.

'Have my Barge alongside!' he exclaimed. 'I'll go at once. I'll put him in irons. By God, I'll flog him round the Fleet!'

'I thought you might feel that way, Sir. And, as soon as I heard the grim intelligence, I made up my mind to declare a small private war myself.'

'You're absolutely right, my boy. Carry on, lad. Make it so.'

'Unfortunately,' said Anthony, 'we've started with a setback.'

'How's that?'

'Young Stanley Bass was to have been my spear-head. I relied upon him to come out on Tuesday or so with a first-class intelligence report.'

'And now he's in dock. Too bad.'

'All, however, may not be lost, Sir, if I may have your co-operation and advice?'

'Go on, boy. And drink up.' He issued another tot, said 'Here's good hunting' and sat down, as straight as a ruler.

'It's a bit of bad luck for young Stanley really: for this may put him out of the running for quite a time.'

'Bit of jam, I should say. He seems too good for the Civil Service, anyhow.'

'Stanley doesn't look at it that way. And, as I put him in the ditch, I feel I owe him an effort. What I thought, Dad, was – well, why shouldn't I do duty for him?'

'You mean – ? Go up there?'

'I don't want to blow any trumpets, Sir, but the Bass brain is not very noticeable: and I believe I might get him through. If so, it seems the least I can do, don't you think, Sir?'

'But you'd be spotted at once!'

'Well, no, Sir. It seems that the crew up at the Hall are not the same set of wets as do the preliminary examination. None of this lot has seen young Bass to date. He's just a name to them. At least, that's the hope.'

'I see,' said the Admiral, dubious for once. 'I don't want you to get into any scandal, young man. Especially in your rightful home.'

'No, Sir. I don't foresee that. And, of course, Sir, while the main object of the Evolution would be wholly al – all – al – '

'Altruistic?'

'That's it, Sir – there is the added point that I should be absolutely in the heart and guts of the enemy.'

'By Gad, yes.'

'I should presumably have actual speech with the principal stoat?'

'Yes.'

'And who knows if I might not in some way encompass and snare the monster?'

The Admiral nodded and grunted fiercely. The doubts seemed to be dispersing.

'In fact, the whole affair does look a little like the finger of Fate – don't you think, Sir?'

'By God, boy, I believe you're right. Plan approved. But I shall want to see your Operation Orders.'

Anthony, surprised and delighted by his father's complacence, delicately led him on.

'Well, Sir, the first thing is, if I'm going up, I shall have to go pretty soon. But I left my gear at the station and the Old Implacable's out of action. What then?'

'I see the point,' said the Admiral, and brooded. 'Ha!' he said at last, suddenly, 'Where's the boy's gear?'

'Here, Sir. One bag.'

'Then there you are! You take his name – you take his bag – you take his clothes. He won't be needing 'em. His hull looked similar. Then there can't be any trouble about wrong markings on your shirts, and so on. That's it, I think.'

'Sir! That's brilliant!' said Anthony, with great enthusiasm, though he had already determined on that particular course of action. 'Then, Sir, there's the question of the doctor. I wonder if you could help us there?'

'The doctor?'

'The doctor. He's a new man, isn't he?'

'Yes. Only seen him once myself. Not a bad chap. Drinks – they say. Has to – because of this Health Scheme.'

'So he doesn't know *me*?'

'No, I suppose not. Ha! That gives me an idea.'

'Yes, sir?' said Anthony, politely, as one waiting to be led out of the wilderness.

'We don't want a lot of newspaper stuff about Bass being a casualty.'

'No, Sir. But there's bound to be some publicity about the wreck of the Old Implacable.'

'Probably. I think you're right. Ha! I have it! We'll give out that *you're* the chap with the broken leg. How's that, eh?'

'I think that's wonderful, Sir.'

'Well,' said the Admiral, 'we seem to be getting on. Let's have another tot. By the way, what about Worthington? I expect he could do with a tot, poor fellow.'

'Bass, Sir,' said Anthony gently. 'I took him one, Sir, before you came down.'

'Ah, yes, I was reporting my position,' said the Admiral, with a twinge of conscience. 'Well, take him another. Poor devil. He little knows how important he's going to be.'

' "Little" is the word, Sir.'

While Anthony was upstairs the Admiral reflected in contentment that after all the old brain was not doing so badly. Still a jump or two ahead of the young ones. It was a pity about that 'position', though, and he felt a little mean. One day he would confess to old Mole, and make a joke of it. That would clear the thing up. The Admiral felt better.

Anthony returned and reported: 'The patient is what they call "comfortable" in hospitals, which means, I fear, in savage pain and swearing horribly. I promised faithfully to ring the Hell-hole for him. And so begins a career of deceit and shame.'

'All strategy' said the Admiral grandly, 'is founded on deceit. You can't do without it.' Even the deception of Admiral Mole, he rather felt, after two powerful tots, was part of the Grand Plan.

'Well, where were we?'

'There's the question of the doctor,' said Anthony, patiently returning to the original point.

'The doctor?'

'Somebody will have to square him. I expect he'll have to sign something, or something.'

'I'll square the doctor,' said the Admiral speciously. 'Leave him to me. I'll make him so drunk he'll sign the pledge.'

'That's fine, Sir. First-class. Then there's Prim.'

The air of invincible confidence departed from the Admiral.

'I will not' he said at last, 'undertake to square your sister Primrose. She has great ideas about the truth, the whole truth, and so forth. Primrose I shall leave to you.'

'Aye, aye, Sir. Then there's Bass.'

'Bass? You mean Worthington?'

'Bass, Sir.'

'Very well. What about him?'

'He may resent my taking his place, Sir. You know how touchy some chaps are. He might try to make a signal to the enemy.'

'(A)' said the Admiral firmly, 'he should be delighted; (B) I see no reason why he should know; and (C)' he concluded, 'Lieutenant Worthington will be under close arrest till you return.'

A bell rang.

'That sounds like the doctor,' said Anthony.

'You'll give me a flash tonight, won't you, my boy? We must keep in touch.'

'Aye, aye, Sir. Unless they put me at the back.'

'Anchor,' said the Admiral. 'This is a good Evolution. You stay here. I'll deal with the doctor.' And he rolled away.

There was no fracture, said the doctor. The ligaments of the knee were torn – a painful but not prolonged affair. Anthony snatched a word with his sister, and the Admiral squared the doctor.

Lady Primrose, as the Admiral had foreseen, was the more difficult. She embraced him fondly and he mischievously pulled her hair, a family jest, for she had always disliked this gesture. She disliked still more the extraordinary instructions he showered upon her, the first time they had met for two years. She was to sneak in at once and remove all the clothes her patient had been wearing. She was not to let him send messages to anyone, and, if he wrote a letter, it must be handed to the Admiral. And she was to tell the world that her brother Anthony was in bed with a broken leg. Finally, having wished upon her the task of nursing a strange man with a broken leg, he was going away for four days. It was really a very disappointing return of long-lost brother.

'It's only for a weekend, darling,' he protested.

'Yes, Anthony,' said the Lady Primrose. 'But lies last for ever.'

'Don't, Prim. You're breaking my spirit.' With Prim's very proper sentiment in his mind Anthony hurried into Stanley's suit, which hung a little loosely round the stomach.

Intending a respectful farewell to the Admiral, he stopped outside the study door. He could hear the Admiral haranguing the doctor: he could hear very little in reply. It was clear from what he heard that the Admiral's imagination, stimulated by the Evolution and perhaps assisted by the rum, was flying high. Suddenly, the Admiral opened the door, made a face at him, and shut it again. The next thing Anthony heard was something about 'Lieutenant Worthington of the Secret Service' and he judged it best to steal silently away.

It was quite untrue that Dr Sale 'drank'. Indeed, from pure fear of 'alcohol' and all the legends about that demon, he was deliberately and thoroughly abstemious. But he had a vice as bad. A pale anxious fellow himself (and slightly deaf), he had a feeling akin to adoration for Strong Men. In his profession (of which he was no mean member) he should have dreamed of being a Harvey, a Pasteur, a Curie or a Fleming. Instead, he wanted to be a Napoleon, a Jellicoe, a Montgomery: he would not have objected strongly if God had made him a Hitler. So, when this famous Admiral (and Earl), brilliant as the Sun (with rum), magnetic as the Moon (with bonhomie), invited the doctor into his illustrious orbit, the doctor swam in like a spent comet.

'Up Spirits!' said the Admiral. 'Drink hearty!' And before the doctor knew what he had sunk two mighty tots. But the Admiral was still three ahead of him.

'How is my son?' he roared.

'Your son, my lord? I don't think I've met him.'

'Fellow in the Sick Bay. You must have noticed him. Damn it, you're mending his leg.'

'But' stammered the doctor, 'he said his name was Bass.'

'Worthington. That's part of the plan.'

'I don't quite understand.'

'Then have another tot. Clears the brain.'

'I'd really rather not, milord.' The doctor's head had begun to swell.

'It's an order,' said the Admiral, and charged the glass again. 'The thing is, what are you going to sign?'

'Sign, Sir?'

'You'll have to sign something, they say. And I want you to get things clear.'

'Yes, my lord.'

'Don't call me milord. Not on the quarter-deck.'

'No, Sir.'

'You see, there are two ways. You could put him in the log as Anchor, or you could put him in as Worthington.'

'He said his name was Bass,' said the doctor, clinging feebly to the only fact that seemed to be firm.

The Admiral opened the door, shut it, and lowered his voice.

'It makes no odds. Lieutenant Worthington belongs to the Secret Service. Naturally he uses a great many names, and, for all I know, Bass may be one of them. But whether he calls himself Worthington, Bass, Sherry or Gin, his real name is Viscount Anchor, and he is my second son and heir. Do you follow?'

'Yes, Sir,' said the doctor feebly.

'Drink up. Did I ever tell you the story of Admiral Random?'

'No, Sir.'

'Well, I will in a minute. Where were we?'

'Viscount Anchor, Sir.'

'Good man,' said the Admiral approvingly. 'Drink up. The point is – don't you go giving a lot of interviews to the Press about Worthington or Bass, or you'll get the lad into trouble, besides assisting the enemy. Signal understood?'

Doctor Sale had heard a great deal about the effects of strong drink on the brain: but he had had no notion that a little rum could produce such confusion as was present in his head that evening. But he said 'Yes, Sir,' and hoped for light.

'Well done,' the Admiral continued. 'Why the boy thinks it necessary to keep it up in his own home I can't tell. Perhaps he got a knock on the head. Did you examine the head?'

'No, Sir. He made no complaints. Only the leg.'

'I should have a look. Can't be too careful. I was going to tell you about Admiral Random.'

'Yes, Sir.'

The doctor lay back in his chair. His head was about to burst, and he thought that for the first time he must be in the condition described as 'intoxication'. But he still felt the same warm admiration for the rugged, dominant man of the sea.

'In one of these wars – ' said the Admiral, 'I forget which – I was in command of a small anti-submarine yacht called the *Proserpine*. One dark night we were lying in a little port in the Shetlands – '

The Admiral paused for reflection. 'Lying,' he thought. 'By Gad, I've never lied so much in one day in my life. This is a true story, all right, but I wasn't in command of *Proserpine*: it was that old fish Fallon. The worst of it is you can tell a story so often, you begin to believe it yourself. Never mind, we've started now.'

Meanwhile, the doctor had closed his eyes and was almost off to sleep.

'It was the kind of place' said the Admiral, 'with four pubs, three chapels, and not much else. You've heard of Admiral Random, of course?'

'No, Sir.'

'Well – I say, have another tot.'

'I'd rather not. To tell you the truth, Sir, I think I must be a little tight.'

'Half-seas over? Ever been tight before?'

'No, Sir.'

'High time you were. You'll know now how other people suffer. Well, Admiral Random was a first-class seaman, but a bit of a psalm-singer. 'Oly 'Orace the Lower Deck used to call 'im. One dark night he comes to me in a high flap with a couple of signals in his hand. "Steam up, Commander?" "Yes, Sir." "U-Boats outside," he says. " Make ready to proceed to sea."

'Well, we ring the bell to get the Liberty men out of the pubs and presently they roll along. There was a fireman called Flood who was always last out of the pubs. Rather a foul mouth he was, and if he didn't like you he always promised to "cut your something lights and liver out". So when we hear somebody on the quay saying "If you aren't something careful I'll cut your something lights and liver out" we know that all the crew's aboard and off to sea we go.

'She was a tiny little ship – I say, are you listening?'

'Yes, Sir,' said the doctor, waking with a start.

'And on the little bridge were only the Admiral, myself, and the quarter-master. Just aft of the bridge is a ventilator funnel going down to the stoke-hold where Fireman Flood is feeding his fires.

'Well, we clear the harbour and steam into the dark night, looking for periscopes and so forth. Suddenly, from down below we hear "CLANG" as the furnace door shuts: and then we hear a voice like a corn-crake singing:

'Nearer, my Gawd, to Thee –
Nearer, my Gawd!
Nearer, my Gawd, to Thee –
Nearer, My Gawd!

I don't know if you're musical, doctor, but that's exactly how he sang it – more out of tune than you'd think that mortal man could manage.'

'How I lie!' thought the Admiral. 'I wasn't even there!' But his unmusical singing had been well done and the doctor was wide awake.

'But up on the bridge the Admiral is delighted, and he says to me: "Did you hear that, Commander Caraway?" "Yes, Sir." "Very fine. A man singing to his Maker as he goes into action." "Yes, sir," I said, though I knew the poker-pusher rather better than the Admiral did. "Very gratifying." There was quiet after that for a bit. Then we heard "CLANG" and the corn-crake went into action again: "Good-morning, Admiral Beatty." "How *are* you, Admiral Jellicoe?" "Well, not so dusty, Admiral Beatty, and thank-you for the kind inquiry." "I tell you what, Admiral Jellicoe, what'll you have, Admiral Jellicoe?" "Well, that's very kind of you, Admiral Beatty, if it's all the same to you I'll have a nice pint of mild-and-bitter." "Now that's a wonderful idea, Admiral Jellicoe. *Two* nice pints of mild-and-bitter, please, Miss. And see they're good measure, please, Miss, if you'll pardon the remark." "CLANG."

'Up on the bridge the Admiral looks rather solemn: and he says "Did you hear that, Commander Caraway?" But just then there's another "CLANG", the corn-crake starts again and we both give ear as if it was the Pope. "Well, Cheer-Oh, Admiral

Jellicoe!" "Here's all-you-wish-yourself, Admiral Beatty! But look here, Admiral Beatty, I've got a little job for you." "A job, eh, Admiral Jellicoe? What sort of a job is that?" "Well, *all* I want you to do, Admiral Beatty, is to go up to the Shetland Islands. And there you'll find a something old bastard called Admiral *Random.*" "Who's Admiral Random, Admiral Jellicoe? Never 'eard of him." "Well, all I can tell you, Admiral Beatty, is that he's the kind of something old bastard who pulls the sailors out of the pubs on a dark night and sends them to sea." "Oh, does he, Admiral Jellicoe? That's bad, ain't it? And what would you like me to do in a case like that, Admiral Jellicoe?" "Well, *all* I want you to do, Admiral Beatty, is to go up to the Shetland Islands and cut out his something lights and liver – see?" "Oh, is *that* all, Admiral Jellicoe? Well, anything *you* say, Admiral, is as good as done. Cheer-Oh, Admiral Jellicoe!" "Good-night, Admiral Beatty." "CLANG!"

'Admiral Random looks at me and says: "You must have heard *that,* Commander Caraway?" "Yes, Sir," I said, "but if I were you I'd take no notice. The man's a bit excited, Sir, going into action: he's a good worker and don't realize that anyone can hear him. I tell you what I'll do, Sir, if I may: I'll send the Engine-Room Artificer down to tell him to keep his conversation to himself."

'Well, I do this, and presently, down the ventilator, we hear the scissor-grinder talking to Fireman Flood. "You shut your something trap!" he says. "What, *me*?" says Fireman Flood, as if he'd been accused of murdering his mother. "I never said a word since the evolution began. All I done was to sing 'Nearer, My Gawd to Thee! Nearer my Gawd!' Of course if the Admiral don't *like* sacred music I won't sing no more. Sorry, I'm sure." '

Admiral Caraway was now thoroughly enjoying himself: but a pallid glazed expression had come over the doctor's face.

'Well, we steam on for a bit, all serene: and Fireman Flood is as quiet as a lamb. But suddenly it's too much for him and we hear "CLANG!" "Good-morning, Admiral Jellicoe." "*Good-*

morning, Admiral Beatty." "How are you, Admiral Jellicoe?" "Oh, well, one mustn't grumble, Admiral Beatty. Just a touch of the 'screws'." "That's bad, Admiral Jellicoe. I wonder what you'd like to take for that?" "Well, do you know, Admiral Beatty, I think I'd like a mild-and-bitter. No, I tell you what, do you mind if I change my mind, Admiral Beatty?" "Certainly, Admiral Jellicoe." "Well, then, I think I'd like a nice Reid's, Admiral Beatty." "Now, that's a wonderful idea, Admiral Jellicoe. Two nice Reid's, Miss, if it's not troubling you too much." "Well, that's all very fine, Admiral Beatty, but what about that little job I gave you?" "What job was that, Admiral Jellicoe?" "Well, didn't I tell you about Admiral Random?" "Why, yes, Admiral Jellicoe, it's all coming back. Wasn't he the something old bastard what pulls the sailors out of the pubs on a dark night and sends them to sea?" '

The Admiral paused, and gazed keenly at the doctor. 'And do you know what happened then? A torpedo struck us and the ship went down with all hands, every man jack of us.'

The Admiral's suspicions were justified. Not even that surprising conclusion drew any comment from the doctor. The doctor was asleep.

The next morning he remembered at least the main purpose of the Admiral's conversation, and a slight sense of guilt made him eager to please the Admiral. He hastened to examine his patient's head, and addressed him respectfully as 'My lord'. Stanley Bass insisted strongly that there was nothing wrong with his head.

'No head-ache, my lord?'

'Not a sign. And, look here, what's all this about lords? I'm not a lord!'

'I know – I know,' said the doctor knowingly, but kindly.

'My name is plain Bass.'

'As you wish, Sir.'

'It's not, a question of "As I wish",' said the patient testily. It's a fact.'

'Very well, Sir.' But it was said as by one humouring a child or imbecile, and the patient did not feel patient. What was all this about? Why didn't Anthony come to see him?

'I want to see Lord Anchor.'

'Oh, of course,' said the doctor, backing out of the door. 'I'll tell him – I'll tell him.'

Stanley Bass felt his head.

CHAPTER IV

Viscount Anchor's sensations, as he walked up through the spacious grounds of his old home, wearing the modest suit and carrying the modest bag of Stanley Bass, were queer. He returned, part trespasser, part burglar, part crusader, as some lonely Abbot might have crept back to a monastery despoiled by Henry VIII. But even the Abbot might have felt less indignation than Anthony: for Henry VIII was after all a King of England, and the robber at Hambone Hall was merely 'the State', a body repulsive to all decent citizens. It is surprising that modern statesmen have not taken more note of this important distinction, especially those wise men who desire to see everything owned and controlled by the nation. Anthony was himself a servant of the State and spent all his days loyally protecting or using State property. But his ship was His Majesty's Ship, and those who ruled his life were the Admiralty, not the Ministry of Armed Vessels. If the White Ensign had been flying over the Hall (or rather had been hauled down at Sunset), if he had heard the bugles sounding 'Colours', the heart of the exile would have softened, might have surrendered. But up the hill, waiting for him, were damnable little men from some Government Department: and his heart was bitter.

The mist had rolled away, and in the first light of the moon he saw many things that served to re-fuel his rage. At the fork in the Drive, where a small road went off to the back of the Hall, there had been a small board nailed to an oak-tree, and saying simply 'TRADESMEN'. Now there was a large iron plate on a stout pole, on which Anthony read:

> COMMERCIAL VEHICLES AND NON-OFFICIAL VISITORS, OTHER THAN AUTHORIZED GUESTS IN POSSESSION OF A GREEN PASS (PQ/A/243), ARE KINDLY REQUESTED TO PROCEED BY THIS ROUTE. NO STEAM-ROLLERS OR LORRIES EXCEEDING 10 (TEN) TONS.
>
> *By Order*
> *Office of Works*

'"Office of Works",' muttered Anthony, and marched on angrily.

Here was the great clump of oaks where the three boys (and Primrose) had built their Peter Pan House in the Tree-Tops, and repelled all the assaults of Captain Hook and his band. George – poor George – had always been Hook. Anthony was too young and Roderick had disliked a part which invariably ended in defeat. Till quite recently the hut and the ladders had been kept in fair repair by Simes, the venerable carpenter and gardener, safe enough, at least, for sentimental inspections. The State, it seemed, had not had the energy to destroy the House, for Anthony could dimly see the shape of it through the leafy branches. But at the bottom of the first ladder was an iron notice:

DANGER
STRUCTURE CONDEMNED

Not far on was the Lovers' Tree, a great beech, on which the children – and half the village – had carved their names. Here were Hearts and Arrows, and True Lovers' Knots: and many of the names joined there had been joined in matrimony in St

Peter's, Caraway. Now, round the tree, stood a tall ring of spiked iron railings, painted bright green. Clinging to the railings, like 'Love Locked Out', Anthony peered through, in search of his own name. Yes, there it was – a damned fine piece of carving too –

Helen Hale, the Vicar's daughter – what had become of her? he wondered.

Something was missing, he felt. Yes, that was it – there was no notice. There must be a notice. He walked round the tree and there it was:

DO NOT MUTILATE THE TREES

Below it was another notice:

WET PAINT

Anthony looked at his hands and swore. First blood to the foe.

He strode on and up through the great avenue of limes, past the Queen's Corner, and into the enormous Spanish Garden. The Spanish Garden had been built by the second Earl, who had sailed with Drake. He had populated it with statues of which the Admiral had never approved: all the other Earls had thought it right to add a few statues of their own. High old walls, whose colour was a pleasing mixture of honey and lemon and straw, kept out the wind. Camellias in many colours adorned the south wall, red roses decked the lawns in summer-time, and fat carp and goldfish swam for ever round the water-lily stems in the central pool. There was also a huge sun-dial, of which the style, or gnomon, was made of clipped yew, throwing a long shadow onto a clock-face of small round flower-beds. The Admiral had taken pride in this and supervised himself the clipping of the yew with an immense protractor, so that the angle should be always right. He could not bear the innumerable statues of ancient Greeks and Romans and Biblical characters, some small, some large, but all improperly dressed. Some had noses chipped, and some had broken arms; he did not mind that: they were all offensively well-preserved elsewhere. They were not content, it seemed, these Greeks and Romans, with single figures, or what was worse, pairs: they could not make a vase, a cistern or a drinking-trough without putting round it an insanitary huddle of naked men and women; and what the devil they were up to, making war or love, nobody could tell. The Admiral did not care to interfere with his ancient heritage and had the Statues solicitously wrapped up with sacking in the winter and punctually unveiled in the spring. The modern imitations, in plaster of Paris, were put away for the winter in the Armoury Room, and some were exiled there for ever.

Anthony looked now for the friend of his youth, the orange-coloured copy of *Susanna Resenting the Elders*, by Carlo Filipini. She was not to be seen. The Admiral's work, no doubt. But surely dear old Leda – ? The Admiral had always jibbed at Leda and the Swan. But they were too famous, it seemed, and too beautiful, they said, and too heavy, being worked in marble, to carry very far. So he had them tucked away round the corner in one of the wide alcoves, where they could not be seen by anyone passing along the stone walk. But the children had found them and stared at the couple many a time, wondering what was going on. The Admiral, when asked, said it was a hunting scene, and warned them to avoid swans, which could break a man's leg. Anthony peeped into the dusky alcove now. There was the great vase in the centre, and the ferns in the high wall at the back, and the carved shields on the wall – all as before. But now Leda and the Swan were draped with some damp and dismal sacking. The Civil Service, no doubt. Anthony removed it angrily and flung it on the floor.

Anthony strode on across the lawn, across the little stream and up the steps to the wide gravelled terrace before the Hall. He stood and looked at the ancient place, stately in the twilight, with a pang. He was the heir; it was his home: and perhaps he would never live in it again. The arms over the portcullis, with the hambone, and the lions *repugnant,* and the three ships-of-the-line, were the arms on his cigarette-case – and indeed on his best pair of braces. He walked on to the drawbridge and looked down at the old moat, dug, they said, by the fifth Earl when surrounded by the Ironsides. At least the Civil Servants had not removed the water-lilies, though now they were all shut up. But, Gosh, what was this? Another notice.

PLEASE DO NOT THROW
CIGARETTES, FRUIT,
PAPERS OR BOTTLES
INTO
THE MOAT

For four hundred years, Anthony reflected, nobody had thought of throwing things into the moat. Francis Bacon had slept at the Hall, Isaac Newton, Admiral Beatty and nearly all the wives of Henry VIII. Charles I had taken refuge there. But there was no record that any of them had been desirous to throw cigarettes, papers, fruit or bottles into the moat. He wondered what wild orgy among the Civil Servants had made this notice necessary. And why that odd list of objects? Was it permissible to throw old boots, newspapers or cigars?

He crossed the small courtyard, where the wistaria still climbed up to the mullioned windows. He had not taken two steps into the hall when a very tall broad man handed him a form.

The huge man said 'Good-evening, Sir. Your name, please?' And then – 'Lord Anthony!'

'Fantom!' said Anthony, and at once put his finger to his lips.

'It only shows' he thought, 'how the best-planned operation may fall down on some damned detail.' Fantom, the butler, also an old sailor, still in service! This was something the wise Admiral had said nothing about. Perhaps he didn't know. It was like having somebody in Troy who recognized the Trojan Horse.

'Well, milord, this is a treat. Give us a shake of your starboard fore lift.' Anthony shook the great hand: but he took out a pencil and hastily wrote STANLEY BASS in the first square of the form. Patches of green paint appeared in the other squares.

'Damn. Have you any turpentine?'

'Certainly, milord,' said Fantom.

'*Mister Bass,*' whispered Anthony, violently shaking his head.

'Very well, Sir.'

'My friend, Lord Anchor, I am sorry to say, has had a motor smash and broken a leg.'

'I am sorry to hear that, Sir,' said Fantom gravely. 'He was always the Flying Dutchman on the roads. If you will wait a moment, Sir, I will fetch the turpentine, and give you another form.'

It had never been possible to surprise old Fantom. In the old days, when it was fashionable for statesmen to have some distinction of appearance, Fantom would have qualified for Prime Minister in any Cabinet. He had the brow of Gladstone and the bearing (though not the beard) of John Bright. You could imagine him ticking off Metternich or giving good advice to Queen Victoria on a bad day. He was also a man of enormous strength, a head taller than Anthony, and broad in proportion. At Fleet Sports he had always been the anchor of some Tug o' War Team, and only one team had ever pulled him over the line. In speech he did his best to live up to his appearance: but he was apt to relapse into the language of the Fleet. He returned very soon with turpentine and a cloth.

'Your room, Sir,' he said, referring to a list, 'is Number 17 – the old Night Nursery.'

'The Night Nursery?' said Anthony, grinning.

'Yes, Sir,' said Fantom, without a smile. 'If you will follow me – ?'

'Don't bother, Fantom,' Anthony began, but Fantom bent upon him a glance of reproach and wonder than which no glance could have said more clearly 'Don't be a damned fool'.

Anthony followed, muttering startled 'Goshes!' from time to time as he perceived the rude finger-prints of the State on his home. They might have been much worse, he admitted. The interloping State had done its best to preserve the spirit and beauty of the place, which four centuries and seventeen earls had made a sort of private museum. At every turn, in every corner, was some lovely thing that caught the eye and soothed the soul and invited humble thought for the masters and craftsmen of the past: a painting, a Chinese vase, a small graceful figure in wood or ivory, the model of a full-rigged ship, acres of books in decorative bindings, a harpsichord that would never play again, an ancient elegant sofa in a corner where nobody would ever sit, a panel carved with staggering elaboration in a dark passage where few could see it. All was clean and neat and ship-shape, he confessed, especially above decks, nothing to complain of on the soft red carpets in the corridors. There were almost as many flowers as his mother had loved to see – bright beacons of daffodils at a turn of a corridor, flowering shrubs in enormous china vessels.

For the most part, the old furniture and pictures, the tapestries, the weapons on the walls, remained. But some of the ground-floor rooms had been stripped for action; and here the old carpets and rugs had given way to coco-nut matting. In the Great Hall Ely's picture of Drake, the Holbein, the Gainsborough, and other famous paintings looked down disdainfully still: but in the Long Hall only one tall suit of armour stood in its corner, and here some of the pictures had made way for notice-boards. In the drawing-room were schoolroom chairs and desks and even two small 'forms'. Upstairs each bedroom had a number now, instead of the old names, 'Brocade', 'Ramillies', 'Frobisher' or 'Pepys': and at the corners of the corridors were the inevitable notices: TO SENIOR STAFF, PRINCIPAL, CANDIDATES WING.

Anthony felt strongly again the sensations of a householder surveying the traces of a burglar, but grateful and surprised that more had not been taken.

The Night Nursery seemed much the same, though now there was one bed only. But Anthony noticed with dismay, as Fantom put his bag down, that the old servant was in some sort of uniform. A Crown badge was on his breast.

'Good God, Fantom – you're not a Civil Servant?'

'Something like it, Sir.'

'You look like a warder.'

'The young people here, Sir, are very like prisoners.'

'Well, you look pretty fit on it.'

'Hit me here, Sir?'

Anthony put a hand on the spacious abdomen. It was like an iron plate.

'Jolly good. Well, old friend, the question is, are you a collaborator – or will you join the Resistance?'

'Sir?'

'You'd like to see the family back, wouldn't you, Fantom?'

'If the family can afford it, Sir.'

'Oh, hang that. The first thing is, these vipers must be ejected. The details have still to be worked out: but that's the object of the operation.'

'Yes, Sir?'

'Will you stand by, Fantom?'

A small cloud of doubt passed over the sagacious face.

'You'll remember, Sir, that I have to live? I'm well paid now – and, begging your pardon, regular.'

'This is horrible,' thought Anthony. 'This explains how the Communists got hold of the Balkans.' But he said:

'Don't worry. I won't get you into the Captain's report. Now tell me about this blot, Mr Maple. Is he a blot?'

'The Doctor's not my favourite member of the Staff, Sir.'

'The Doctor? What sort of doctor is he?'

'Couldn't say, Sir. These days there's as many kinds of Doctors as Dagoes. All I know, he's one of the mind-sweepers. Syko-something.'

'What does he look like?'

'Fathom of pump water, Sir, with yellow fittings. Everything's yellow about his rig, Sir, hair, Sir, moustache and side-lights.'

'Side-lights?'

'Very big spectacles with amber rims. Pale, Sir, anaemic like. The nose is narrer-gutted and the moustache, I should say, was meant to camouflage the mouth. But he don't grow easy, you can see that by the head. The moustache must have been a disappointment, Sir, and the mouth's as long as Selsey Bill.'

'Two notes seem to stand out in your excellent description – yellow and thin.'

'Yes, Sir. That's the general silhouette. The hull is narrer-gutted too. I've seen it under the shower.' A small cloud passed over Fantom's face as he recalled the spectacle. 'As scraggy, Sir, as an Old Age Pension. You can count the bones. The feet should *not* be seen in the nude. The big toes – '

'Stop, Fantom, stop! You're making me sick.'

'You asked for a description, Sir. And now, with reference to general demeanour and bearing,' Fantom continued, as relentless as a Cabinet Minister moving the Second Reading of a Bill, 'you'd think, Sir, wouldn't you, that Nature having made him what he is, she'd have popped in a tot of humanity and loving kindness, by way of make-weight. But no, Sir. This perisher couldn't be more content with himself if he was Vincent How' (he named the latest idol of the film-world) 'and an Admiral of the Fleet as well.'

'That would be what they call the inferiority complex, I fancy.'

'Concerning that, Sir, I couldn't say. But I have noticed, Sir, that the Doctor is always chawing the fat in the mess. Every inch a sea-lawyer. Jaw, Sir? He'd jaw the anchor through the hawse-hole. And I've noticed, Sir, it's very seldom he don't have the last word – I don't say he has the best of it, but he wears them down, they can't stand any more. A proper Jaw Me Down. A mess-deck menace. And he's got the hide of a battleship, you can't upset him.' Fantom paused for breath.

'Not if you're on equal terms, that is, Sir. With his inferiors, I'd say – well, Sir, you've heard of a Snarly Yow. You can't please him. If it ain't half-laughs it's Pusser's Grins. Dirty too, about the ship. We don't mind a gentleman smoking in his bath, but if he's going to knock his pipe out in it he might at least run the water off, not to speak of leaving the soap in it. I'm sorry to have to add, Sir, that he tips like a Dutchman and only once a year.'

'As a word-picture of a blot, Fantom, that could hardly be bettered. To shorten the discussion now, I wonder if you would agree that he is a blot?'

'I wouldn't say about blots, Sir, but I think my Union would support me, Sir, if I said he was a King's Hard Bargain.'

'Have you a Union now?'

'Yes, Sir. The Amalgamated Society of Hatters, Boiler-makers and Kindred Trades.'

'Good gracious! Well, you'd better go below now. Stand by – and watch for my signals.'

'Aye, aye, Sir. Supper is at nine tonight, Sir.'

'By the way, Sir, one of the candidates is a Mr Lennox-Edwardes who has been through the course before. He will be able to advise you about the routine.'

'Thank-you, Fantom. Dismiss.'

When Fantom had gone Anthony burrowed in Stanley Bass's bag and extracted his electric torch. It had a small press-button, excellent for signalling. He looked towards the Lodge by the Lake and sent a succession of A's. Presently a steady light showed on the Admiral's mast. He signalled slowly:

NIGHT NURSERY I SAY YOU NEVER TOLD ME ABOUT FANTOM AR[1]

There was a pause, and then the Admiral flashed:

IMI WA ABOUT[2]

Anthony sent very slowly: F A N T O M

R[3] said the Admiral, then: MY GOD I FORGOT ALL ABOUT HIM SORRY THE DOCTOR IS DRUNK AR

GOOD SHOW, said Anthony. GOOD NIGHT AR

But now from the lake there came a succession of A's at frantic speed, as if the sender was desperately afraid of losing touch. Anthony gave him a long T, and over the lake and the moonlit woods there came the message:

TELL THEM THEY ARE A LOT OF DUSTARDS AR

'Dustards?' muttered Anthony, and signalled IMI WA OF. Slowly, majestically, came the one word: BASTARDS AR

R said Anthony. The conference was over.

Poor Mr Bass, in his painful bed, saw some flashing far away, which reminded him of morse. He was rusty, as he had said, and read a few letters only: but he wondered what it was about.

1 End of message.

2 Repeat word after 'about'.

3 Read.

CHAPTER V

It was an uneasy meal. The Skilled Staff were at one long table, the Intake, as every batch of candidates was called, at another. There were twenty-one of each, as many shepherds as sheep. Each candidate had been provided with a numbered list of candidates and two labels: and Anthony had Mr Bass's '9' pinned to his breast and back. The talk, at first, was not lively. Only two of the candidates (Numbers 13 and 18) had met before, and these at the moment thought it best to keep quiet about their acquaintance, one being a gentleman and the other a lady. All spent most of the meal trying to identify their companions, with furtive references to their lists. Furtive, because, at first, it was felt that open detective-work might be bad form. 'May I have the pepper?' said one to another, glanced swiftly at the other's label and buried his eyes in his soup. Only when the soup had gone did he think fit to flash a look at his list.

'The Feast of the Down-cast Eyes,' thought Anthony. He identified first Number 15, Captain C. Lennox-Edwardes. 'A Pongo,' muttered Anthony to his secret soul, using an expression in deplorably common use among Naval Officers to describe the members of His Majesty's Army – deplorably, and indeed, inexplicably, for the only meaning of 'Pongo' to be found in the best dictionaries is 'a large anthropoid African ape: variously identified with the Chimpanzee, and the Gorilla'. Anthony felt at once, making far too rapid an appreciation, that he did not like Number 15, and this was not only because he sat next to a fair-haired young lady in a green coat-and-skirt whom Anthony had already summed up favourably as 'a saucy frigate'. Number 15 had a considerable moustache, harsh eyes, and a sulky, contemptuous expression: his spacious ears stuck out, as if set to catch secrets; and Anthony thought uncharitably that if his target was the Diplomatic Service it was no wonder that he had failed at the first attempt. Number 15, he felt, on a sea voyage, would always be complaining to the purser, and complaining in a loud voice. Now he was talking in a low voice, having learned his lesson, perhaps, at the first course. But he was the only one who was talking busily. He was explaining 'the ropes' to Number 8, whose pretty merry face was turned up to his, and Number 9 was quite sure that he did not like Number 15. The name of Number 8, he noted, was Miss P Meridew. It was not recorded in the official list, but P stood for Peach.

Among the many good reasons for unease was the particular anxiety about table behaviour. How terrible at this first encounter to upset a glass or use the wrong knife! No doubt this huge fatherly butler and the stern-faced maid who waited upon them would make their reports when all was over. Poor Number 18 was the first casualty. Number 18 was another of the four young women, a mouse, a wisp of a girl, with a pale face, gentle expression and spectacles. She was almost opposite to him, but his roving eye was so little attracted that he had not even pursued her name. The only thought she provoked was: '*Not* the Diplomatic, I think.' But he was wrong. Lavinia Gable, through the noble pinching and scraping of her parents, had gone to Oxford University and got a first-class degree in Languages. She did aim at the Diplomatic Service, and saw herself, so unaccountable is the course of ambition, charming ambassadors and controlling the destinies of nations at Washington or Paris. Now, unhappily, she had chosen melon instead of soup; innocently she had chosen ginger instead of sugar: and suddenly she did what school-boys call 'the nose-trick'. Her small head seemed to explode and she was convulsed with something between a loud snort and a sneeze. Number 4, who sat next to her, a heavily-built man and the oldest of the party, jumped and knocked over his glass of innocuous ale. All the young eyes were turned for an instant on the unfortunates and chivalrously turned away. Poor Number 18, blushing unbecomingly, was sure that the eyes of the staff, behind her, were concentrated on her person. How, after this, would she ever have a chance to charm an ambassador? All her dear parents' saving and scraping, all her own long labours, had been blown to nothing by a puff of ginger. Tears filled Lavinia's eyes, some from the ginger, but most from sheer chagrin.

Anthony nobly, but clumsily, came to her rescue. 'Just what I always do!' he said loudly. 'I've seen an Admiral do the same – with Royalty aboard. The only rule is – Negative Ginger.' Then, staring at the poor girl's label: 'Number 18, I see,' and referring to his list, 'Miss Gable, I believe? I'm 9 – Stanley Bass.'

Nobody had dared so frank an introduction, so all eyes were now upon Anthony. But Lavinia was still persuaded that the attention of the world was on her, and stared in sorrow at the remains of her melon. Number 4, Mr Samuel Ould, was so angry about his beer that when Lavinia apologized he merely grunted. It was a bad beginning. Years later, when Numbers 4 and 18 were respected members of the staff of the British Embassy at Washington, Number 4 always referred to Number 18 as 'Nose-trick' Gable. Such is life.

The young man on his left (Number 11 – Adrian Holt) was pale and scholarly, with spectacles and a high voice, drawling a little. He had recently taken a First in Greats at Oxford University and seldom forgot it. He now pronounced an apt Latin quotation, which was not understood by Anthony and did not serve to comfort Lavinia or Mr Ould.

But the melancholy episode had somehow made things easier for those not concerned in it. Small, silly things could happen, after all, in this austere, alarming place. Captain Cosmo

Lennox-Edwardes was explaining 'the ropes' to a wider group now, in a louder voice. Something about 'two lists'. At the end of the course, Anthony gathered, each candidate had to make two lists of his competitors – one in the order in which he considered them suitable for appointment, and the other in the order in which he would like them as weekend companions.

'But that's diabolical!' said Anthony rather loudly, down and across the table.

'Yes, that's the end!' cooed fair Miss Meridew, with eyes of sympathy and more on Anthony.

Mr Lennox-Edwardes looked at Anthony as cows look at a dog.

'On the contrary,' he said, rather loudly too – and there happened to be a lull in the conversation at the Staff Table, 'it's extremely good. It's a test of your judgement, you see.'

'Oh?' said Anthony mildly. 'Oh, yes, I see.' An answer far from mild was in his mind: but he had suddenly remembered that he was representing poor Stanley Bass, and must not give him a bad start with the Staff.

Miss Meridew, he feared, was disappointed in him. But, at least, he had discovered one thing. The inflated Pongo was on the enemy's side. That gentleman was now holding forth with renewed zest, and Anthony returned to his bully beef (the meal, after the melon, had sadly fallen away).

At the far end of the long table, past the confident Pongo and his audience, he now with noticeable excitement met the two large dark and lustrous eyes of Number 10. Various unaccustomed adjectives moved through the young mariner's mind – 'sleek', 'luscious', 'velvet', 'sheeny', 'magnetic'. She was dressed in black. 'What they call exquisitely tailor-made – I suppose?' he thought. Her hair was black. She had an oval face, a spacious mouth, and a slightly turned-up nose. The figure, he decided, for she sat very straight, was fine.

'This' thought Anthony, 'is more like the Diplomatic.' And the next thought was 'This must be the Decoy.' As they stared, there was no doubt that the corners of her mouth went up in the hint of a smile: and Anthony, at the risk of ruining Stanley Bass in his first evening, smiled back. He looked away with a sensation of pleasing alarm, and, glancing at his list, read 'Miss J Daly.' What was the 'J' for, he wondered? Jacaranda, surely, or Juniper, or Jasmine. Anthony looked round the high old Dining Hall and wondered what the Admiral would have thought of the miscellaneous party there. In each corner stood on a pedestal a knight-at-arms, or rather his uniform, polished, gleaming, incredible. On two of the walls were hung vast tapestries, the size of a golf green. On the third was a fireplace, fit for the roasting of an ox, and, above that, great swords and weapons which surely no mortal could ever have carried, much less employed in battle. The fourth wall was all of mellow timber, elaborately carved like the screen of a cathedral, and up against the ceiling was the small Musicians' Gallery, where the queer old instruments of many centuries still hung. Up there, before his voice broke, he had sung, with select choir-boys from the village, many a time, Stanford's Grace before Meat or carols at Christmas. What glittering and gracious parties he remembered there, the Admiral booming at one end of the long oak table, his mother quietly in control at the other end, sweet-faced still with dignity and calm, drawing out the shy young man at her side, poking the fires of conversation in the difficult centre of the table, wondering whether she had arranged the party rightly, summing up strange guests the Admiral had wished upon her, watching the service and the handing of the wine, flattering the statesman, making the novelist talk about himself, hoping the Admiral was not going too far, feeding the dogs, ringing the bell, but seeming as idle as a captain on his bridge. Prime Ministers, poets, Admirals, musicians, Masters of Fox-hounds, editors, farmers – all had been glad to come to that table, to honour the ancient place, and be kind to the youthful heir. And now...

But the Intake, at least, was as young as a gun-room and as 'democratic' as a pub. Oxford and Cambridge had no monopoly here. He liked the look of Number 20, a robust and comfortable young lady from Glasgow. She wore a shapeless oyster-pink satin blouse with pearl buttons, which, with her jolly smile, would have done well behind any saloon bar. Number 16, another pleasant face, from Belfast University, might well have been an agricultural worker. There were other young men, old looking for their age, who had attended no University except the fighting Forces.

Number 13, the shy young man on his left, was gazing at the tapestry on the opposite wall. 'I can't make out what's happening,' he said. 'Can you?' His first remark.

'Oh, that?' said Anthony. 'Well, you see – ' and, forgetting Stanley Bass, he was about to explain the picture. But a stir at the Staff Table saved him from this indiscretion. Dinner was over, and the Intake moved into the Great Hall to hear the Principal's opening address.

CHAPTER VI

Ladies and Gentlemen, Welcome to Hambone Hall…'

'Thank-you very much,' muttered Anthony Anchor. But he liked the speaker at once, not knowing that he was approving of a Pongo. Sir Gilbert Ray was not, as Anthony supposed, a Civil Servant, for top Civil Servants, like other things, were 'in short supply'. He had enlisted in one war, and become a colonel in the next. He had been a Borough Councillor and a JP, he had served at the War Office and on two Royal Commissions, and he knew the ways of Whitehall. Sir Gilbert was one of that large reservoir of men of character and capacity in which Whitehall can always fish for – and find – the right men for the oddest job. He was tall and upright with carroty hair which was fading and thinning. Only the small moustache retained the original colour which had got him the name of 'Ginger' at school. He had a big nose and a pleasing smile, pleasing because it came as a surprise from a long and rather solemn face. Now he smiled upon the apprehensive young people, and they liked him.

'The first thing is – don't be alarmed. This is not the Spanish Inquisition. Nobody will eat you. We want you to be a happy family. You young people represent the cream of your generation, and it is from among you that we hope to fill the highest posts in the Civil and Foreign Services in years to come. All we want here is to help you to show us what you've got. Because of the war, in which most of you were busy, one way or the other, the old form of examination, a lot of written papers, wouldn't be fair. Some of you have been in the services, some in Government Departments.'

Anthony, by a happy accident, no doubt, was sitting next to Miss Meridew, near the knight-at-arms, in the south-east corner of the Great Hall. At these words, he noticed, she nodded her golden head: their eyes met and she whispered:

'Economic Warfare. *Too* insanitary.'

Anthony thought this a queer epithet for the Ministry of Economic Warfare.

'Then I was a Wren. Boat's Crew. Super.'

Somebody said 'S'sh!'

'…no University career or record. The Tests you will undergo here are designed to show us your quality by methods which are fair to all, whatever their experience. Some of them may seem strange to you: but I can assure you that they have been scientifically designed and tested, and have given good results. When you leave us you will have an opportunity to tell us what you think of it all. Most of our visitors say that they have enjoyed their stay.'

He smiled again, and Mr Lennox-Edwardes gave a grunt of approval. Anthony thought this a sycophantic act, but the rest felt better.

'You will be divided into three Groups of seven – A, B and C. You will find your groups on the notice-board…'

A small brown hand pinched Anthony's knee. 'We're A, Stanley,' said Miss Meridew.

Anthony stared at her in wonder. 'How d'you know me?' She had bright blue eyes, he observed.

'We have a mutual bosom,' she whispered.

'Bosom?'

'Bosom friend. Meriel.'

'The devil we have!' he thought. But he was very content to find himself in the same Group as this lively, decorative girl. His eyes wandered to starboard, to a chair by the fireplace; and he wondered if Number 10, the luscious Jacaranda, was in A Group too.

'Beast,' Miss Meridew hissed in his ear. 'Yes, she is.'

'This young lady' he thought, 'should have a high post in the Intelligence.' But somebody said 'S'sh!' The Principal was saying:

'To each Group will be attached three members of the Staff – a Chairman, a Psychologist, and an Observer…'

Anthony whispered to the omniscient Number 8: 'Who's our psychologist?'

'A man called Maple.'

Anthony's eyes gleamed fiercely.

'He's a squid.'

'A what?'

'A squid. Pure poison.'

'Oh, goody!'

'S'sh!'

Sir Gilbert was explaining the functions of the 'Group Team'. The Observer would concern himself mainly with the candidate's intellectual quality, the Psychologist with the candidate's personal history and background. The Chairman, it seemed, covered the whole human outfit. All three would write reports.

At the word 'psychologist' the temperature of the room seemed to fall, and anxiety returned to many eyes. Sir Gilbert had seen this before, and he said, with that comforting smile again:

'One thing more… Outside the official sessions you will be perfectly free. Do what you like. Whatever you may have heard or read, it is *not* part of the duties of the Directing Staff to concern themselves with social behaviour at all hours of the day. In other words, we are not a nest of snoopers.' He smiled again. This time it was Miss Peach Meridew who whispered: 'Sez *you*?'

'That, I think, is all for the present. You will all, please, before 9.30 tomorrow, fill up one of the 'Interest Forms' which my Deputy, Mr Rackstraw, will hand to you. This is not a Test. But it is a great help to the Staff when we come to the Interviews – and, I think, to you. Thank-you. Good-night.'

'Good-night, Sir,' said Mr Lennox-Edwardes loudly, to Anthony's intense disgust.

The candidates rose and crowded round Mr Rackstraw. This was a Civil Servant of long experience. He had a pale round face, large brown eyes, and enormous brown spectacles. His expression was gentle, almost compassionate, as if he had seen so much of mankind in so many Departments that he had lost all hope for the race: and this was roughly correct. In Whitehall he was known as 'SD' Rackstraw, for it was he who had first written on a minute:

'This proposal opens a serious door.'

'Stay here,' said Miss Meridew, 'I'll get you one,' and she slipped into the scrum.

'This is very gratifying,' thought Anthony. 'A self-appointed First Lieutenant already. A Wren too. Might be useful.'

The ex-Wren returned with two large foolscap sheets, covered with stencilled questions and small rhomboidal open spaces.

'Here you are,' she said. 'They say it's perfectly septic. Shall we do it now – or would you like to go to the Bar?'

'Is there a Bar?'

'Through there.'

'The bleak prospect brightens,' said Anthony, rising at once.

She led him to a small room off the drawing-room.

'Good God!' muttered Anthony. 'Sacrilege!' For it was the Admiral's old study. The great desk, the old chairs, had gone. There was the inevitable notice-board: and in the far corner hung, largely printed, the one word TOILETS. At two of the three small tables candidates were studying the Interest Forms with the aid of an anaemic beer; and Miss Meridew secured the third table. She asked for gin: and, to his surprise, they got it.

'Well – down the hatch!' said Anthony, raising his glass. 'You seem to know your way about here, Miss Meridew.'

'Moo told me a lot.'

'Moo? Oh, yes, of course.'

But he thought: 'Moo? Who the Hell is Moo?'

A distant bell rang faintly at the back of his mind: but that was all.

'How are your knots and splices?' he said.

'Knots? Pretty good. But how does that arise?'

'Can you make a bowline?'

'Certainly.'

'Reef knot? Clove hitch?'

'Of course.'

'Rolling hitch?'

'Not so hot.'

'Eye-splice?'

'Nebulous.'

'Never mind. Get some string, and mug up your knots.'

'What, if I may coin a phrase, would all this be in aid of? Is there a knot-examination here?'

'You never know,' said Anthony darkly.

'I wish I knew what you were thinking about.'

Anthony was silent. He did not know himself. But in his mind was a distant vision of a superb adventure in which the body of Heriot Maple was present and a knowledge of knots was important.

Miss Meridew sipped her gin, and broke the silence.

'By the way, I *may* call you Stanley?'

'Certainly.'

'My name's Peach. Moo said to give you a big kiss.'

'Bless her. We must go into that.' 'Moo?' he thought. 'This Moo again.' And he had no clue to Moo. He said, cleverly, he thought: 'Was Moo a Wren too?'

'Moo Maynard?' Miss Meridew exclaimed. 'But of course she was! You *know* she was! Only she was an officer, with a tiddly hat. I thought you were bosoms?'

Moo – Meriel – Maynard. A faint light shone at the end of the tunnel. Stanley Bass's friend! Of course! He had put a foot wrong, perilously wrong.

'Miss Maynard?' he said. 'Naturally. But I know so many Moos. You muddled me. Sorry.'

Miss Meridew looked at him queerly, but said only:

'My fault, Stanley.'

Anthony thought: 'I am not so clever, not clever at all. I have been here for two hours only, and already I am knee-deep in the soup. But courage! Proceed!'

He said: 'Well, we must have that kiss, Miss Meridew.'

'Peach!'

'Peach. Pardon. And now let us study this alarming tripe.'

In silence they examined their Interest Forms for more than a minute.

'But this is inhuman!' said Anthony, at last.

'Septic,' said Peach, 'I think, was an under-statement. Toxic is the word.'

It was, indeed, a formidable document. The candidate was asked to say, among other things, how he had spent his free moments during the last six months, and how he would have liked to spend them if he had had the opportunity: what books he had read, English or foreign (in the last four years), what music he enjoyed (if any), what he listened to on the wireless, and what theatres he visited. He had to write down at least three propositions he would be 'prepared to defend in debate', three subjects on which he would give a short talk, and two humorous topics upon which he would say a few words. And the spaces reserved for the answers to these enormous questions were about the size of Olympic postage stamps.

'I don't know where to begin,' said Anthony. 'How long have we got for this?'

'Tonight. Or three-quarters of an hour in the morning.'

'I could not, in the dawn, remember any books that I have read.'

'I can't remember many I have read tonight,' said Peach. 'Let's do it now – and compare notes.'

'Aye, aye, Miss.'

'Have you any pencils?'

'One. All yours.'

'What about you?'

'I've got my Biro.'

'Rather dangerous. You can't rub out.'

'Never mind. Here we go.'

Anthony began on the Leisure question. It should be easy enough for Peach, he thought, to enumerate her own simple pleasures. But he had to imagine the activities, the books, the pet subjects, of Stanley Bass. How on earth had Stanley spent his leisure hours in the last six months, if not in the bed or the bar? There was not much evidence that he had ever read a book.

'Does the *New Yorker* count as a book?'

'No,' said Peach. 'Quiet, please.' She was frowning anxiously and sucking her pencil.

'Pity to frown,' he said, 'with a forehead like that. It looks like sparrows' feet on snow.'

'Pipe down. What books have I read?'

'*War and Peace. Decline and Fall of Roman Empire*. Homer – '

'How about "foreign"?'

'Homer was an alien.'

'Oh, goody!'

Anthony at last wrote in the tiny space:

> *Spent most of spare time visiting sick friend in hospital and washing up at home. Should have preferred visit museums, see Roman Wall and construct sun-dials.*

'How does that look?' he said.

'Magical. But you have to be careful. All this, they say, may be brought up in evidence against you.'

'How?'

'At the Interview. They'll say, How do you construct a sun-dial? Then you'll be sunk.'

'Not at all. I *can* construct a sun-dial.'

'Goody. I grovel.'

Other candidates had come in, and a loud voice boomed from the little Bar where Number 15 was explaining the ropes to an awed group of four.

'Hark!' said Anthony, 'the Pongo's come aboard!'

'Does he revolt you?'

'Just a little, yes.'

'He's practically the last thing, I *think,* but I haven't decided yet.'

'There are two forms of tests,' the Captain boomed, 'the psychological, and the analogous...'

'He'd do well at a Fair,' said Anthony.

'Or the House of Commons.'

'Or an auction of fish. Now, what are my books?' After much thought he decided that in the last four years Stanley Bass had read:

Shakespeare's Plays, Manual of Seamanship, most of Dickens, The World Crisis, Admiralty Navigation Manual Vol. 1, Alice in W.

Any foreign book, he thought, would be going too far.

'But why "analogous"?' said one of the disciples at the Bar. 'Because they give you things to do which are more or less like the things you have to do in the Service. That's what the "groups" are for. You have to take the chair at committees, you have to...'

'What have *you* read?' said Anthony, and peered at the infantile scrawl.

'What you said: *War and Peace*, Homer, *Decline and Fall of the RE*, *No Orchids for Miss Blandish* and all Peter Cheyney.'

'I should rub out *No Orchids* if I were you.'

'Would you? Got any rubber?'

'No.'

'Deadlock,' said the girl. 'I could write something over it, perhaps. What do you suggest?'

'*The Idylls of the King*. It's the same number of words.'

'So it is. And the laughable thing is that I did read bits of them. There!'

'But what will you do if they ask you snooty questions about Homer?'

'I shall cry. *Very*, very quietly.'

Miss Meridew gurgled. She had a glorious, golden little gurgle, Anthony thought, as if tiny bells were attached to the bubbles in a glass of champagne.

'Then,' proclaimed the Pongo, 'there's a thing called the "Island Story". There's an imaginary island – it's like some real island, of course – in the Empire. They get the group together and give you a problem to discuss – like – like – like – what would you say and do if they wanted to land a thousand DP's on you? You take it in turns to be chairman. And all the time the Staff are taking notes.'

'But how appalling!'

Many gasps and groans of apprehension greeted this information. A deep feminine voice said slowly: 'I don't think I shall get very many marks at that.'

The voice was velvety and languid. If Peach's voice was bubbly, this was vintage port. It had, he thought, the faintest touch of a foreign accent.

'That *must* be Jacaranda,' Anthony thought. He looked up – and it was.

The lovely Number 10 was leaning against the Bar. She was so tall that she could almost sit on it; almost as tall as Anthony himself.

As if drawn by his gaze, she turned her large and lustrous eyes upon him: and once again the young man felt electric imps galloping up all his veins to his unprotected heart.

'Eyes front, Stanley,' said Miss Meridew sharply.

'I love you dearly, Peach,' he murmured, returning his eyes to the Form. 'But candour compels me to admit that Number 10's eyes, when fully loaded, would sink a stouter ship than me. They make me feel like a strawberry ice melting swiftly in the sun – about the middle of the Indian Ocean. They make me feel – '

'Stop it,' said Peach.

'And now that I have heard her voice,' the sailor continued, 'a voice like a bell – '

'Big Ben, perhaps?'

'A voice like a deep flute, a voice like a viola, a voice like the queen of the nightingales, a voice like Melba on a low note, a voice like – like the clink of ice against glass in a tropical garden under the moon – '

'Stop it, will you?'

'And the odd thing is' said Anthony thoughtfully, 'that I seem to remember it.'

'What proposition am I prepared to defend?'

'That mariners prefer brunettes. – Look out!'

Captain Lennox-Edwardes had brushed aside the feeble fears of his companions: 'It'll come quite easy, you'll see.' Now, with his retinue, he bore down, still booming, upon the table in the corner. And as upon the battlefield where the shells whistle over as numerous as birds, and fierce explosions everywhere confuse the mind of man, suddenly the soldier hears the savage particular sound of the high-velocity projectile which says 'I am coming. This is for *you*': so did young Anchor perceive without eyes the approach of Number 15, and he hissed ''Ware Pongo!'

The Captain looked down upon them, and, glancing at his list, said: 'Miss Meridew? Bass? Then this is the whole of A Group. Miss Daly, Ould (4), Holt (11), Tom Crawley (13). I'm Lennox-Edwardes. Call me Cosmo,' he added graciously.

'I couldn't,' said Peach.

'Oh, come. There's no ceremony here.'

'But I don't like the name.'

Anthony, gurgling in his secret soul, examined Number 13, Mr Crawley, the only one of the group he had not identified. He was young and handsome, but seemed as shy as a swallow. His eyes darted everywhere, seeking for someone who was not looking at him.

'Oh, well, can't please everyone,' was the Captain's polite reply to Miss Meridew's rude left-hook. 'I've been through all this before, you know. Failed last time – I don't know why. But I'm out to help anyone I can.'

'But if you help us,' said Anthony mildly, 'you may fail again.'

'Yes, I know, we're all against all, of course. But I'd like our *group* to be good, as a *group*, I mean, a good group-spirit and all that.'

'This man' thought Anthony, 'should go backwards and forwards through the Mediterranean as permanent secretary to the Games Committee of a cruising liner. After two trips he'd be organizing the Captain.'

Anthony himself was beginning to suffer shyness: for whenever he glanced at Number 10, those enormous eyes were engulfing him, and he felt like a man in a dream about to fall down a well.

'This Form, for example,' the Captain was saying: 'There's nothing in it – at least, there's no competition about it. I thought I might give you all a few hints. Care to come along? One can't do it in the Bar, very well.'

'We've done pretty well in the Bar,' said Peach, displaying her sheet of squiggles.

'I *couldn't* do it,' said Anthony, 'unless the Demon Alcohol was driving me on.'

'Oh? As bad as that, is it, Bass? Well, we'll be cutting along.'

'One thing?' said Anthony.

'Yes, Bass?'

'How about A Group's Staff Team, Orderly Room, Goat-Herds or what-not? What are they like?'

'Oh, first-rate. Chairman – Egerton, Observer – Chinlip, Psychologist – Maple. All first-rate. You'll like 'em.'

'Including Maple?'

'Oh, yes. Absolutely first-rate. Not everybody's meat perhaps. Too clever. But first-rate. Quite first-rate. Well, good-night,' said the Captain, driving his prisoners through the door before him. '*Good*-night, Miss Meridew. And, if you can't call me Cosmo, call me Mervyn. My other name.' The smile was, at least, intended to be charming: and Number 8 melted.

'Good-night, Mervyn,' she said, with an angel's smile.

' 'Night, Bass.'

'Good-night, Mervyn. Call me Anthony.'

The door closed. The allies were left alone, except for the Irish girl behind the little bar.

'Peach,' said Anthony, 'we have *not* made a good beginning. You were noticeably rude.'

'That doesn't matter. The frightful thing is that he was polite.'

'The brute!'

'Anyhow, we finished well. I did call him Mervyn.'

'You did. So did I. That was heroic. "Cosmo Mervyn". Can you beat it?' He brooded awhile. 'I did not *quite* like the way he said "As bad as that, Bass?" '

'No, that was fairly odious. Worse still, I have an inkling that he has ambitions about my body.'

'I shouldn't be surprised. Nor, indeed, could I blame him.'

'That's the first nice thing you've said. By the way,' she continued sweetly, 'why did you say "Call me Anthony"?'

'Did I say that?'

'You did.'

'Just a joke. I thought he might dislike the name of Stanley. I do myself.'

'I like it,' cooed Miss Meridew, looking for his eyes.

But Anthony kept his eyes on 'Propositions you would be willing to defend'. 'It is not so easy' he was thinking, 'to lead a double life as I thought it was after a rum or two with the Admiral.'

'Of course,' said Peach, satisfied, it seemed, 'it's easy to see what our Mervyn is after.'

'You?'

'Me, perchance. But, far more than that, this "mutual ranking" racket.'

'What's that?'

'He told you at dinner. At the end we all have to write down a list of each other – two lists, rather – '

'Oh yes, I remember.'

'Well, you see what I mean? Our Mervyn is marketing himself as a good mixer – '

'A loyal pupil – '

'A friend to the young and helpless – '

'A co-operative bastard and universal Yes-Man. He will' said Anthony, 'be Number 21 on *all* my lists.'

'He will be pretty low on mine,' said Peach demurely, 'but not as low as that.'

'Why not?' said Anthony, meeting her eyes.

'My Number 21' said Peach, with a stare, but a dimple or two, 'will be Number 10 – I could – *garotte* her!' she added savagely.

'Do, my dear,' said Anthony coolly, 'if you think it will help. And now,' giving an imitation of Mr Winston Churchill no worse than most, 'to the task, to the toil! Let us concentrate upon these barbarous interrogations!'

They concentrated.

After long thought, Anthony put down as his defensible propositions, in a tiny script:

> *(1) That there should be One Time (preferably Greenwich Mean Time) all over the world (2) That Women should receive Double Pay for Equal Work (3) That Whisky is good for Polyneuritis.*

'I wonder' he thought, 'how dear old Stanley would deal with those.'

For the three subjects on which Stanley Bass was willing to talk he wrote:

> *Stars*
> *Sticklebacks*

There he halted. So far, he thought, all was well. He knew many stars, and much about them. He had kept, with brother George, an aquarium in boyhood, and remembered vividly the bravery and beauty of the little British father stickleback – nesting, mating, breeding and defending his young. He wanted to add 'Women', but he was still thinking nobly of Stanley Bass's interests, though Women, he thought, perhaps, was Stanley's principal subject. (Looking back, he was not quite happy about the Whisky–Polyneuritis proposition, though he was sure of his facts. But there it was, in ink, unrubbable out, so to speak: and nothing could be done about it.) At last, thinking of Stanley still, he added:

Ceylon

The 'two humorous topics' led him astray again. He wrote impulsively:

> TUC
> TPQ

and regretted it at once.

At this point he peeped over the pleasantly scented shoulder of his neighbour. He was a little surprised to see, in her 'Three Subjects' square:

Men *Women* LOVE

Well, that was her affair. His own Form was nearly full. He crossed a 't' or two, wrote 'Shakespeare' in the Theatre square, 'Music' under 'The Wireless', and 'Avoid it' under the Cinema. 'Well done, Bass,' he thought. Then he wrote his name, dutifully, in block capitals, at the top. After that he said, very loudly, *'Damn!'*

'What's the matter?' Peach Meridew peered, in turn, over his shoulder, which to her was pleasantly-scented too, with tobacco and tweed – and man. Her keen eyes caught at once the fatal entry:

Name and Christian names in full (Block capitals please): ANCHOR. ANTHONY BLAKE

A happy smile surged over the small, sweet face.

'So you're *not* Stanley Bass?' she whispered. 'Darling, I somehow *knew* you were spurious.'

'I'm awfully sorry,' said Anthony, stricken, less by the fact of discovery than by his sense of inefficiency. 'Who am I' he thought, 'to tackle a job like this? I couldn't deceive the blind!'

'But I'm delighted!' she cried.

'Why?'

'Because now I don't have to worry about Moo.'

'Moo?' This deplorable, nebulous 'Moo' again!

'I thought that Moo had prior rights,' she said. 'But now – '

Anthony had two thoughts in his mind:

(A) This damned girl is far more attractive than I thought.

(B) I must be far more attractive than I ever thought. These two thoughts, together, are nearly always fatal.

All he said was, rather stupidly: *'Now?'*

She said: 'I suppose you couldn't tell me, very approximately, what it's all, rather roughly, about?' He did. He told her everything. Here and there she gave her golden giggle. At the end she clapped her little hands and said:

'It's wonderful. It's excellent. It's practically super!'

Anthony was as much relieved by this reception as a theatrical manager who has had a good Press after a bad First Night.

'Dear Wren,' he said, with feeling, 'then you'll stand by the Navy?'

'I will,' she said, 'on one condition.'

'What?'

'That you close your eyes whenever you meet Number 10.'

'But then I shall run blindly into her bosom – which, by the way, looks pretty good.'

'Beast!'

'Besides, we're in the same Group. How can I?'

'I think I shall ask for a transfer,' said Miss Meridew.

'No, no, Comrade! We must stick together.' He was so earnest, and clutched her hand so tightly, that Peach was mollified. She said:

'Aye, aye, Sir. But what are the plans?'

'There's not the tiniest tadpole of a plan. But there are two objectives.'

'Yes?'

'One, to discomfit and disperse the said Heriot Maple. Two, to expel this pestilent gang from the House of Caraway. And Three (I forgot this), to acquire cash enough for the Admiral to dwell at home with dignity and comfort.'

Peach nodded her head, and thought for half a minute, the sparrows' feet in the snow again. Then she said:

'Two, of course, is the fundamental fellow. But that might well be combined with One. For Two, it seems to me, you want the *most* obscene scandal, the *hugest* headlines, questions in Parliament and all that. If Two could be combined with One, two dirty birds might be slain with a single stone. Follow?'

'Yes. I thought I loved you for your brains. Now I know.'

'Thank you, Sir. Do we know anything evil about the said Maple?'

'Only what I told you. For all I know he may be the next thing to a Bishop.'

Peach shook her head, and the golden curls stirred like young beech leaves about her tiny ears. Anthony enjoyed this.

'Not very likely,' she said. 'A trick-cyclist is fairly sure to have some murky secrets. Besides, I've seen him.'

'I haven't.'

'I met him in the passage just before dinner. It was *exactly* like looking into the eyes of a slug. Or possibly toad.'

'As bad as that?'

'Pond-life, purely. Well,' she said, 'I'll do a snoop or two. What about your Form? You can't send that one in.' She looked about. 'Oh, goody!'

She darted across to the Bar, Anthony observing two silken legs of classic shape, and came back with a form.

'Wonder-girl,' he said, and attacked his task again, in pencil. This time he omitted the whisky proposition, and wrote instead: 'That full employment is a bad thing.'

Suddenly the door was flung open and Captain Lennox-Edwardes entered like a bison charging. He surveyed the room, leaned over the Bar and examined the floor, looked under the tables and into the fireplace, and emptied the waste-paper basket onto the floor.

'I say, Bass,' he said at last, 'you haven't seen my Form, have you?'

'Form?' said Anthony blankly.

'Not a sign,' said Peach.

'Most extraordinary. I must have left it here. I know I had it. They've none at the Office, and Rackstraw's gone to bed. Damn!'

He marched out, leaving the contents of the basket on the floor.

'Good-night, Mervyn,' Peach called sweetly, but her salute was marred by the slamming of the door.

'I've decided,' she said. 'He *is* the last thing. Utterly.'

'Evolution completed,' said Anthony, having successfully set down: 'BASS. STANLEY.'

'Finished? Let's look.'

They exchanged Forms and read in silence, but for an occasional 'Goody!' and a golden giggle or two.

Anthony read Peach's confessions with surprise and some dismay. A girl so evidently bright, and even brainy, should surely do better than this.

'Look here,' he said at last, 'this won't do at all.'

'What's the worry?' she said.

'Well, for one thing, "Peter Cheyney" won't get you into the Foreign Office.'

'Why not? I bet they all read him.'

'That's hardly the point. Then I can't give *full* marks for your "Humorous Topics" – SEX and ST A L.'

'Well, *is* there anything funnier? Especially sex. It shows, at least, that a girl doesn't take them too seriously.'

'Something in that,' he admitted. 'But how do you defend your three Talk-subjects: "Men – Women – Love"?'

'That's the whole world, isn't it?' Peach said simply.

'And what about your third proposition: "That all young couples should have a trial trip"?'

'I don't think they want you to be stuffy. They want to see if you've got an electric mind. Like me.'

'Yes, but – I bet they'll never pass you after this.' She slipped a hand under his arm, and put her chin on his shoulder. Her hair tickled his cheek pleasingly.

'Darling Anthony – '

' "Stanley", please.'

'Darling Stanley, but I hate the name – I'll let you into my guilty secret. I don't *want* to pass. I should rage if I did.'

'Don't *want* – ? Then why the Wellington are you here?'

She lifted her chin. 'It's Daddy. He's a Civil already – a regular. He's in Town Planning, of all the swamps! Poor sweet, it's *eternal* toil for him. He's desiccated and drear, brings home work every night, and writes minutes in the loo. But he loves it. And he aches for me to be a Civil too. I hadn't the heart to say I wouldn't go *in*: but I shall perish miserably if I get *through*. Whitehall, I trust, is not my way of life. See?'

'What do you want to do?'

'Do? Well, for one thing, I want to be a bride, and have six boys almost at once.'

'Six?'

'About six. And two of them twins. But, before that, I'd like to inspect the planet a bit. Air-hostess perhaps: or one of those liner-ladies – most of them were Wrens. When I've been flung out of this lot with shame and scourges I shall have a look round. Poor Daddy. But there it is.

'Meanwhile, Sir,' she continued with a bow, 'I am your devoted servant. And you see what a miraculous arrangement it is? You have to be a good boy because of Mr Bass. But the badder I am the better.'

'Steady on! There's to be no scandal about *you*. Nor indeed about me,' he added, remembering the Admiral.

'Not about the two of us?'

'Certainly not.'

'A pity,' she said softly, with downcast eyes. 'That would be a beautifully simple Plan.'

All was quiet. The bar-girl had gone.

'I suppose' he said, 'it's about time we were turning in?'

'Yes.'

'There's one thing.'

'Yes?'

'What about that kiss from – what the Hell was her name? – Moo Somebody?'

'Moo Maynard. But that was for Mr Bass. You're *not* Mr Bass.'

'I certainly am. Look at that Form!'

'Yes, I see. Well, if you're Mr Bass you may have a kiss from Moo.'

'I'd rather it came from you.'

'No, no. There must be no scandal about *us*.'

'Damn you.'

'Oh, Mr Bass!'

They kissed. It was gentle but exciting; and reasonably long. The lips of Peach were not like the rich red downs and valleys of Jacaranda: but they were fresh, and soft, and efficient.

'One more,' he commanded.

'No, no. Moo's very refined – I kiss much better,' she added.

'Let's try.'

'No, this is Moo. And Moo's rather a prig.' She held her hands protectively before her face.

'Well,' he said, raising his glass, 'here's to the Grand Alliance. Skaal!' With due solemnity they finished their second gin.

The Great Hall was silent and empty. All the other visitors, it seemed, were seeking strength through sleep. They parted at the first landing, Peach with a pretty curtsy and a naughty grin. Anthony walked on up the stairs well pleased with himself. He had enjoyed his intimate evening with the charming girl. He had acquired a Wren and clever ally: and in reserve was the faithful Fantom.

The passages at Hambone Hall had curves and twists and sudden sharp turns like an old English road. Walking without sound on the soft red carpet, he came round a corner and beheld two young people locked in a close embrace beside a fire extinguisher. On the back of the man he read 13. It was Mr T Crawley, the shy boy. Over his shoulder Anthony could see now the frightened eyes of Number 18, Lavinia Gable, the spectacled mouse who had done the nose-trick.

The lovers sprang apart like ballet-dancers, trembling with alarm; Lavinia blushing like a gas-stove. The young man stammered: 'I'm sorry. You won't – you won't – say anything?'

'Not a word,' said Anthony. 'I like it.'

'As a m-matter of fact we're – we're engaged.'

'I should hope so,' said Anthony with a squeak. 'I congratulate you.'

To put them at their ease, he kissed Lavinia himself, and marched away.

'What Stanley Bass is missing!' he thought.

But Anthony's evening was not yet over. The second door from his own was ajar. Though a perfect gentleman, he was unable to avoid letting his eyes wander to starboard through the opening. The room had been his brother George's after all, and a professional sailor cannot suddenly cast off the habits of the weather eye. He saw a dark female figure standing, with her back to him, before a dressing-table mirror. More important, in the mirror he saw the face of Jacaranda, and her eyes like two large water-lilies in a lake. He could not suppose that she was watching for him, but certainly she saw him at once, and, without turning her head, she inclined it inwards – to be exact, South by West – in an unmistakable invitation.

'Personal Qualities!' thought Anthony. 'What a test! Am I to embrace three girls on the first night?'

But the electric imps were charging about in his blood-channels again. He went in and quietly closed the door.

'Jacaranda,' he said softly, 'are you the Decoy?' That was the end of the question. The tall, beautiful creature strode swiftly over and enveloped him – 'embraced' would be too weak a word. He was lost in a sea of prehensile arms and scented flesh and elastic underwear.

'Stanley Bass! Stanley Bass!' the deep voice crowed, on a note of triumph. 'You beast – you devil! At last I have got you! Take that!' She kissed him with a violence that knocked his head back. Her luxuriant lips closed over his like a large pink jelly-fish contracting and expanding. So she held him till he was near to asphyxiation. He thought 'How right Peach was about sex being funny!' Then he thought: 'This must be like drowning.' But as he went down for the third time she let him go. Not for long.

'And *this*' she said, 'is for my poor sister.' Savagely, most painfully, she bit his upper lip.

Anthony hated this. All sense of fun departed from him: and all the electric imps were still. He pushed her angrily away. She stood panting under the light, her head a little lowered, like a bull at bay, her superb bosom heaving. She should have been both alluring and alarming. But suddenly Anthony laughed.

'You laugh? Why do you laugh? My sister does not laugh!'

He had laughed – how fatal! – at her appearance. She had dropped her wrap. She was sheathed in one of those elastic – or was it rubber? – suits of armour so much displayed in the advertisement pages of weekly journals and even on the Underground Railways. He could understand that these tight envelopes might preserve and fortify the female figure. But he had often wondered – and debated with brother officers – why they should be regarded as things of beauty, any more than the pants of men. Evidently they were, or they would not be so much displayed. By themselves, no doubt, it could be said that they did not conceal or muffle any of the curves so dear to man. There was a good view of the fine arms and shoulders of Jacaranda, a gentle honeybrown in hue from last year's sun. Some of the thighs of Jacaranda were pleasantly visible. But over the thighs, from the bottom of the suit of armour to the tops of the stockings, were four absurd pink elastic suspenders, ending in ugly metal clips. At the other end of the stockings (so sheer as to be almost invisible) were black high-heeled shoes.

The whole effect, Anthony thought, was not alluring but ludicrous. He had seen ladies with little on before, but never in the rubber rig. So he laughed. And probably the lady had ambushed him in this queer rig, fondly believing that it was irresistible. But it made him laugh. Respectable folk, moreover, would think it dangerous, probably fatal, for a young man to be alone with a lady in nothing but her underwear. So it may have been, in other climes and generations. But, he thought, to attempt Jacaranda's virtue, a man would require the equipment of a burglar. So he had laughed.

He did not laugh again. He said:

'What is all this about your sister?'

She laughed now, a bitter, husky laugh.

'Ah, Stanley Bass, you humbug, you hypocrite, you cruel man!' Then, suddenly, 'You know she had twins?'

'Lord!' thought the Lieutenant. 'What has old Stanley been up to now?'

'I certainly do not.'

'But she wrote to you! You never answered.'

'S'sh!' he said. 'Your voice is beautiful but penetrating.'

'I will *not* be sh'shed! The world shall know.' But she dropped her voice, none the less.

'I got no letter,' he whispered.

'And you have forgotten, I suppose, the Café Topolski and a certain meeting in the snow?'

'In the snow?'

He gaped. But old things were stirring in his mind. Snow. One of the Gdynia convoys, carrying supplies to the Poles. A night ashore. A British consul, or somebody, with a Polish wife and two attractive furry daughters. Stanley Bass had had a big success with one of them, and much ragging in the Wardroom.

'Yes,' she said, 'two beautiful boys.'

'How are they?' he said, having nothing to say.

She shrugged the tawny shoulders. 'They are at the Centre of Child Culture. They will be well, of course.'

'Then what is she complaining about?'

She flared up again.

'Because you have forgotten her! Because you do not write!'

'S'sh. I have not forgotten her,' he whispered earnestly. 'I will write if you tell me where.'

She opened a drawer. 'Do you remember her name?'

'Not very well,' he said.

'My God!'

'S'sh!'

'Then look at *that*!' She thrust a letter before his face and with a crimson finger-nail pointed to the end:

If you see my inhuman Stanley Bass bite him.

OLGA

'Olga,' he murmured, 'of course. Dear Olga. Where is she now?'

'At Wimbledon.'

'Good Lord!'

'There is the address.' She turned the letter over.

'I'll go and see her. May I keep this letter?' Stanley Bass, he thought, should see this letter soon.

'You may keep the letter. But you will not go to see her. I *know* you, Stanley Bass!'

'S'sh!'

'Oh, I am so glad!' she muttered. 'When I saw your name I could not believe it. Poor Olga. But *I* will punish you. *I* will make you sorry.'

'How?' he asked.

'I will make you love me. I will make you mad about me.' With a swift movement she bent and cast off the clips at the top of the stockings, so that the suspenders dangled free, more funny, Anthony thought, than before.

'Hey!' he said warningly.

'But if you touch me, I shall scream.'

There was a sharp tearing sound. She had pulled the zip fastening on the port side.

'Then' she said, with rising force, 'you will not pass the examination.'

'S'sh! I believe you *are* the Decoy.'

She crossed her arms and put her thumbs under the shoulder-straps. Then she paused:

'The Decoy?'

'You were sent in here by the Government to corrupt the candidates.'

'Fool! I was sent here by the good God to ruin *you*, Stanley Bass. You shall see me in my beauty. You shall go mad. But if you touch me – '

'S'sh!'

The shoulder-straps began to come down. Anthony stepped towards the door and said lightly: 'Well, good-night. It's been jolly.'

But she was too quick. Few modern panthers could have sprung so swiftly to the door. She turned the key, and took it out. He grabbed at the key. She put it in her mouth. It was not a large one but it made one cheek bulge a little.

'No wonder' he thought, 'old Stanley has lost touch with the family.'

He said: 'Well now, at least, you can't talk.'

She grunted at him, and slowly removed the suit of armour. With her hands on her hips, she circled slowly like a mannequin at a dress parade, casting now and then a glance of unfeigned admiration into the glass, or, over her shoulder, of mocking provocation.

'Your stockings are slipping down,' he said.

She made an angry, muffled, sound, lay down on the bed and gracefully moved a brown beckoning arm.

'Do you go to bed in shoes?' he inquired, and politely began to remove them.

She shook a threatening finger at him, and made sounds which might have meant: 'Don't touch me – I shall scream.'

He sat on the edge of the bed beside the naked beauty. With one finger he prodded thoughtfully the flesh here and there, as agricultural men prod cattle in the market. At every prod the beauty gave an angry grunt, and waved the threatening finger.

'Have no fear,' Anthony whispered. 'Were I a cannibal king I should be highly excited. For I am sure that you would eat well.' Another prod – another grunt. 'But as a chap, an ordinary chap – with fairly fleshly appetites, I must confess – you do not excite me at all. You see, for one thing, you are like a piebald mare.'

The beauty heaved, and pinched his thigh.

'These sunkissed knees,' he continued quietly, 'these honey-coloured arms are, without doubt, beautiful and, when the rest of the body is covered, alluring. Unhappily, you have not taken the precaution to expose the entire form to the sun. The result is a mess. You look like a shapely lobster which has been boiled at the extremities only. So, if you'll pardon the opinion of a layman, it was a great mistake to take your clothes off even that repulsive rubber arrangement you wear.'

She took the key out of her mouth, hissed 'Petty bourgeois *beast!*' and put it back again.

'I say,' he said, solicitous, 'that key must be rather a bore. Let me relieve you?'

But she shook her head, savagely.

Anthony again cast a critical eye over the form. He said reflectively: 'Of course, I'm not one of those who *ever* think that the naked female form is a good thing to see. It should always be partly covered, like a bottle. A nude bottle, as you know, is most uncomely. But put a pretty label round its middle, and it's nice.'

Suddenly, he smiled upon her, a friendly, happy smile.

'I think' he continued, 'these artists are to blame. The sculptors, especially. If they did women as they really are there would be practically no Love at all.'

She took the key out, and said: 'One more word, and I scream!' The key went back.

'Not with that key in your mouth,' he said. 'Turn over.' He gave her a little push, and she turned over obediently.

'This' he said at last, 'is, I think, a less repellent aspect of the form. The behind is not bad – and looks good eating. I could use a steak or two of that. But there is a red spot on the left cheek, and against the sand-coloured legs and the tawny lower vertebrae the general effect is anaemic, slug-like and ridiculous.'

The body shook with fury, and tried to move, but he held it down.

'The figure is worthy,' he continued smoothly, 'but of course, the trouble is, you've not got a good skin. With a skin like this you should wear a mass of clothes nearly all the time. Waft about in silken draperies, undulate in clinging wraps, or even risk beach-wear: but the nude – oh *never*! It's better, of course, where it's been in the sun, but the unsunned area is deplorably stippled, if that's the word, and unfriendly to the touch. You know, of course, that your rubber arrangement has left hideous weals and red bits all *over* the form. And I don't suppose you can see it, but there's another spot here, just under the port shoulder-blade. Oh, and here's another, lower down. You should take some salts. And if I may make a suggestion – '

The body heaved and struggled and there was a strangled sound from the pillow. Jacaranda was trying to scream. Then there was an alarming coughing, and Anthony thought 'If she swallows the key, is it murder?' But she turned on her side, and out came the key. The tigress lay panting and subdued.

Anthony daintily wiped the wet key on his handkerchief and stepped to the door.

'Good-night, Jacaranda,' he whispered sweetly.

She said not a word. But her glaring eyes were like the interior of Etna on the day before an eruption.

All this goes to show, perhaps, what a mistake it is to bite the most virile and affectionate young man in the upper lip violently.

It was not too late, Anthony thought, and he got to work with his torch. The Admiral's light showed at last over the trees, and he signalled:

ROLE OF IMPERSONATOR NO SINECURE AAA HAVE KISSED THREE WOMEN ALREADY AAA BUT LIGHTS BURNING BRIGHTLY AND ALL'S WELL AR

The Admiral made him repeat 'impersonator' and then replied:

STEADY AYE STEADY AR

Anthony went to bed.

CHAPTER VII

'Good-morning, Peach.'

'Good-morning, Number Nine. Names, I gather,' she said, 'are not the done thing.'

'Sorry, Number Eight. Good-morning.'

'What have you done to your mouth?'

'Hit a door in the dark,' said Anthony, feeling his swollen lip.

'Whose door?' said the young girl innocently: and she looked so innocent that he thought it better to make no reply.

The Interest Forms had been completed and collected. They had laboured for an hour at – according to Peach – a 'perfectly obstruse' General Knowledge Paper. And now the candidates were gathered in the drawing-room for the first of the psychological tests. Only Number Fifteen knew exactly what was to come: and there was a buzz of apprehensive chatter. At their desks, or forms, with the foolscap sheets before them, the cheap pens and inkpots, they felt very much at school again.

'I'm glad' said Peach, 'we're on the same form. And, as it's our numbers, there can't be any talk.'

'Anyhow, there's a chaperon on the way, I fancy.'

At the door he could see the lofty Jacaranda, with those huge eyes upon him, and a tiny smile. She moved through the crowd towards him, and he feared the worst.

'That elongated pest!' said Peach.

'I've been talking to Fantom, who's the human encyclopaedia. He told me a murky secret about the Maple.'

'What?' said Anthony eagerly.

'Well, it seems he's *quite* bosoms with the female trick-cyclist – Miss Slice.'

'Good Lord!'

'Gospel. It seems quite *anything* might happen. Look out!'

Like a great black swan descending on the waters, Jacaranda came to rest in the empty chair on Anthony's right.

'Good-morning, Number Ten,' he said, and from nervousness, indeed, from terror, the voice squeaked high. 'D'you know each other? Number Eight – Number Ten.'

The ladies looked at each other as two cobras might meet and greet on the first day after the winter sleep.

'Good-morning, Number Eight.'

'Good-morning, Number Ten.'

But Jacaranda, to the young man, was like a well-fed, happy cat.

'You have hurt yourself?' she purred solicitously.

'A door,' he said shortly.

'Lucky door,' she cooed huskily, but loud enough for Peach to hear: and Peach kicked his ankle.

'What is all this "Jacaranda"?' the velvet voice inquired.

'I thought it suited you. What is your name?'

'My name' she whispered loudly, 'is Number Ten. But Jacaranda is nice. "Jac-a-*rand*-a." She savoured the word like an old man palating his port.

Peach kicked his ankle again and said:

'Stand by! The enemy!'

Anthony looked upon Dr Heriot Maple at last. He knew him at once from the vivid words of Peach and Fantom: but he thought that even they had not done justice to the subject.

'You were right,' he whispered.

'The last thing?'

'Further than that. It's worse than Fantom said. He's got amber eyelashes.'

'I know. It's ghastly.'

'This is a Jee-had.'

'A what?'

'A Holy War.'

'Oh, goody!'

'S'sh!' said Jacaranda.

'S'sh! yourself,' said Peach.

Dr Maple, it seemed, could not bear to let his eyes rest on the youthful folk before him. As he announced the conditions of the test he peered over their heads at a point high up the opposite wall.

'Even the *voice'* Peach whispered, 'is *exactly* like a slug's.'

A succession of single words were to be exhibited. In fifteen seconds – no more – each candidate was to write down the thought which the exhibited word suggested.

There were tremors everywhere. Anthony thought: 'Remember, you are Stanley Bass. Do your best for the old firm.'

A young woman member of the staff held up a bit of white cardboard on which was printed large in black the word:

S T E E P

Anthony thought for a moment, and wrote:

Steep Climb Aspiration Summit

He sat back. 'Good,' he thought, 'that *must* be good.' And the time was not yet up. Everybody else was frowning and busy.

He glanced, feeling a little guilty, over Peach's shoulder. Peach had written in her childish hand:

Steep
Hill
Down

Avalanche
Bottom

Well, he thought, that's one way of looking at it.

He glanced to the right. Jacaranda had written:

Steep Stairs Bed

'STOP!' cried the assistant loudly.

Still staring at her words, Jacaranda, too audibly, cooed:

'Have you any india-rubber?'

'Not allowed,' Peach whispered.

Jacaranda shook her head.

The next word was:

MOTHER

'Now then, Bass!' thought Anthony.

Fifteen seconds seemed a very short time. There was no time for second thoughts – even if you had any india-rubber. He wrote at last:

Mother Holy Purest Relationship

'Well done, Bass,' he thought: and peered to port and starboard again. Peach had written:

Mother
Babies
Smack
Bottom

Jacaranda had written:

Mother Baby Bed

But she had scratched out 'Bed'.

'STOP!'

Anthony glanced at his companions with a faint sense of unease: but both were waiting intently for the next word. It was:

BAYONET

'Ha!' thought Anthony, remembering his brother. 'I know this one!' Jacaranda moaned. 'But what is it *for*?' 'God knows!' he whispered. He had to sympathize. What on earth was the sound psychological reaction of any young girl to 'Bayonet'?

He wrote:

Bayonet Up Guards and at 'em! Kill! Victory!

'Well done, Bass!' he thought again.

But there arose a horrid after-thought. His words, no doubt, would have been just the thing for an aspirant to a commission in His Majesty's armed forces. But – a future ambassador? Should he, perhaps, have written something like:

Bayonet Force Avoid Tactful negotiation?

Jacaranda had written, simply:

Bayonet Wounded Bed

Peach had written:

Bayonet
Russians
Puncture
Bottoms

A sort of dizziness swept over the sailor: and when he came out of it the next word was up. It was:

CLASS

Anthony wrote:

Class Quality Aim High

'Bass, old boy,' he thought, 'you're *in*!'

Fearful, now, of what he might see, he peeped to right and left. Jacaranda had written:

Class First Sleeper Bed

But she was still staring at her work, as if uncertain of its worth. Peach was sitting up already, as well satisfied as he was. She had written quickly:

Class
Bottom
Bottom (of)

'Hey!' he whispered, as the crowd cry 'Hey!' to a polo-player who looks like doing the wrong thing. 'What is all this?'

Miss Peach Meridew gave him a shining smile and a golden giggle: 'That' she said, pointing, 'is where I want to be. Didn't I tell you?'

'I know,' he said. 'But don't overdo it!'

'STOP!'

The 'STOP!' technique, the tyranny of time, was beginning to afflict the nerves of many: and it was to rule their lives for three or four days.

Peach continued to 'overdo it'. There were thirty words and she never failed. The next was:

B L A C K

'What the Hell?' he thought. But he wrote, fairly soon:

Black Empire Develop Liberate

Jacaranda wrote:

Black Pyjamas White Bed

She sighed, and stared at what she had done.

'But this is terrible,' she whispered to herself. Peach wrote:

Black
Bottom

'What on earth – ?'

'It's a dance.'

'Yes. But you weren't born!'

'Mummy told me. S'sh.'

Peach evidently was enjoying herself and there was nothing he could do for her. Though he cared little what examinations were passed by Jacaranda, he was fascinated by her performance, and almost sorry for her. Jacaranda, he was sure, was not having fun with the examiners. She was lost, she was concentrated, she was doing her best. She gazed at the Words as a devout worshipper gazes at the altar. She wrote her own with her eyes half-closed, as if in a trance. The last word was:

S H E L L

He watched her write:

Shell Fish Oyster Bed

She opened her eyes wide and made a low moan.

Anthony, only just in time, wrote:

Shell Oil Navy Sea-power

Peach wrote:

Shell
Sea
Bottom

and giggled musically.

The papers were collected. As the young woman approached, Jacaranda crumpled up her reactions and threw them on the floor. But 'Excuse me', said the young woman, and she picked them up, with a reproving glance.

There was a brief interval. Peach said:

'It seems there's some tremendous snooper from London coming down tonight.'

'Haven't they enough?'

'Yes, but all sorts of miscellaneous top-noises come from time to time, Fantom says. This one's an MP.'

'Ho, ho!' said Anthony. 'Cue for Scandal, perhaps.'

'Oh, goody! Have you got a Plan?'

'A germ. I must see old Fantom again.'

'Can I be in it?'

'Would you scream in a Secret Passage?'

'With you?'

'M'm.'

'Not very much.'

'How about mice? Up the little legs?'

'Mice have no terrors for me, Mr Bass.'

'Very well. Stand by before dinner.'

During the interval Jacaranda sat quite still. Occasionally she threw a wicked glance at the chattering couple beside her; but for the most part she stared ahead, grimly.

Next, the future rulers of the race were given a 'projection' exercise – a task in which each candidate, it was hoped, would throw or 'project' some indication of his own personality. Dr Maple, in his high and haughty voice, explained the drill. Six pictures, in turn, would be thrown on a screen. They would be allowed to look at each picture for half a minute and then – in 2 1/2 minutes – they would be asked to write 'a very short story or plot' suggested by the picture. All had to be done in six not very generous spaces on Form TPQ A/21 C12389 Q4598763 PROJECTION EXERCISE (2).

'Six!' said Anthony, dismayed.

'It's gruesome,' whispered Peach. 'If I do *one* – !'

The first picture looked like a 'still' shot extracted from an old French film. A man with a great black beard and a straw hat sat beside a café table. A newspaper lay on his knees, a long glass was on the table. A waiter, standing near, was regarding his customer with quizzical eyes.

The twenty-one victims stared at this uninspiring scene in silence.

'I want to do my best by Bass,' Anthony whispered, 'but to me it suggests hardly anything but gin.'

'The glass is *full*,' Peach whispered.

'Ah! An idea.' He began to write – slowly:

> Many years ago Boris took the pledge. An occasional visit to a café, where he sips his lemonade, is his only indulgence.

('How do you spell trick-cyclist?' whispered Peach.

'P-s-y-c-h-i-a-t-r-i-s-t. But for God's sake don't bring them in!'

'I have.')

> Today [Anthony continued] he read in the paper that his beloved wife had been killed in a railway smash. The temptation is great to drown his sorrows in drink. The waiter tempts him. 'Pourquoi pas, Monsieur?' he says. After all, he has nothing left to live for now. It would be so easy to slip into the old ways. The hot fangs of the Demon Alcohol

'STOP!' yelled the young woman.

'Damn! And we were doing fine. That was your fault,' he whispered, 'now they'll never know.'

'What?'

'Never mind.' He looked over her shoulder, and read:

> This is a psychiatrist who has gone to seed through brooding *messily* over other people's perfectly good psychs, the beard is unkempt and the washing is *elementary*, he sits for days at the café thinking about *Psex*, and drinks the *most* glutinous teetotal liq

But there the guillotine had fallen. A confident writer, in good form, might get down 100 words in 2½ minutes: but these poor slaves were far from confident.

Jacaranda had written simply:

It is a false beard. The gentleman is a Russian agent bravely working in London. He is waiting for a beautiful dark lady who will bring him the English secrets soon. Then they will go to bed.

Anthony read this and looked at her with awe.

It was an exhausting exercise, Anthony thought. The second picture showed a steamer in dock; the third a foreign locomotive puffing at a station; the fourth an empty church; the fifth a large policeman on point duty. These were well chosen for Jacaranda, and she did not work a bed into any of them, except the foreign locomotive, which reminded her of *Anna Karenina*. Then she gave up.

But Peach managed to bring her 'trick-cyclist' into all of them. In the steamer and the train he was fleeing from the *uncountable* victims whose lives he had ruined. The church was empty because he had taken refuge there and all the congregation had gone out, *quite* revolted. And the policeman was just going to arrest him for *obscene* meditation.

Anthony laboured nobly for Bass, keeping always to the line of faithful and strenuous effort: but he did not think he had done very well.

For the sixth story, as Dr Maple had announced, the screen was left blank, and candidates had to imagine their own picture as well.

'Do you think' said Anthony, 'it would be cheating to go on with my Number One?'

'Why not?' said Peach. 'I'm going on with my trick-cyclist.'

The reasoning, he thought, was not conclusive: but he accepted it.

He wrote:

(The Scene is as in Picture Number One – but with a difference.) Continued from 'Demon Alcohol'.

> ...are close behind him. Will he surrender? It is a near thing. He turns to the waiter. The order is on his lips. But something stays him: perhaps the sly triumphant smirk of the waiter, perhaps some memory of his mother, his wife, of the dead child, Irene. The battle is won. He stands up, squares his shoulders, and with a new light on the old face he

'STOP!'

'Just in time,' said Anthony. 'It was making me cry.'

'Oh, goody! Let's look!' They exchanged stories. Peach had brought the Saga of the Psychiatrist to a tremendous climax:

> We now see the trick-cyclist in *Hell*, he sits all day in *full* evening-dress under a *cruel* light in the middle of the cell, all round him are a swarm of *tormenting* civil servants and psychmongers who *quite* never stop asking him insanitary and half-witted *questions*, like what do you think of when you think of *mother*, they shout suddenly BLOOD or STOMACH, Answer quick, and he has to make a *sage* remark without a *single* moment's thought, nearly always there are *bells* ringing, and of course

Anthony shook his head sadly.

'Don't you like it? Yours is Bliss. It's *practically* Dickens – I *must* see the first chapter.'

But Jacaranda, who had been watching the two intimate and busy heads morosely, now tossed her Short Story Number Six in front of Peach.

'What do you think of *that*?' the sleek voice said.

Anthony and Peach read the story together. As he read, there crept about the complicated body of the man, first, an icy rivulet of dread, as surprising as the Humboldt Current crawling up the warm west coasts of South America, and then a hot disturbing stream of shame: and as, when the Labrador Polar Current encounters the Gulf Stream, dense fog is formed over the Newfoundland Banks, darkness and confusion commanded his mind.

He read, incredulous, alarmed, and angry:

> The little bedroom is cosy and warm. The innocent student combs her hair before the mirror, thinking of the examinations tomorrow. But in the passage a Wolf is prowling. The door of Number Seventeen opens slowly, and in comes the seducer. Horror overwhelms the girl. Long ago this rough sailor has ruined her sister. Now he comes to ~~compleat~~ compleet his deadly work. She tries to scream but a savage hand is on her soft throat. He throws her onto the bed. All is over. But before all is over the desperate virgin has bitten him. The wound, like hers, will remain for ever. Never again will he force his *filthy* embraces without a

The 'STOP' girl had mercifully cut the narrative short.

'Jolly!' said Peach, and threw the story back. She slid a queer sidelong glance at Anthony: but she said no more.

'Well, what about a beer?' said the officer brightly, though he felt no brighter than the man in the dock on the fifth day of a murder trial. He had no desire to drink with Jacaranda, much less to buy her refreshment; but he thought it best to ignore her outrageous behaviour.

There was a general exodus to the small Bar, where the candidates compared notes about their word-associations and picture-stories. Most were indignant and bewildered: they thought that they had been made fools of, and could not understand why. Only two seemed calm and content. Number Eleven, Adrian Holt, the superior youth with the First in Greats, said:

'The oldest technique in the world. Read your Petronius.' No one could imagine what he meant: and no one tried very hard. Cosmo, loyal to the régime as ever, thought the whole thing was 'jolly good fun'. He went round asking people what they had put down for Mother, and telling them where they were wrong.

(Fortunately, he did not ask Peach or Jacaranda.) He remarked that many of the same words had been used at the last attempt. Number Eleven thought it unfair and foolish that any words should be used twice; and scored his first good mark in the popularity race.

'You might have warned us,' said Peach reproachfully. Cosmo said that Anthony's response to Mother was 'Not bad. The sort of thing I said my first time.'

'What did *you* say?'

'Oh,' said Cosmo, 'I put "*Mother Pre-natal advice and treatment Clinics Query grants-in-aid*". That' he said, with quiet satisfaction, 'is the sort of thing they want, I fancy.'

'How utterly pompous!' Peach remarked, and got a black look.

Number Eleven said he had written *'Mother Parliaments Westminster Macaulay'*.

The brilliant pair filled everyone else with gloom. Someone began to question Cosmo about the 'matrix' exercise, where you had to do queer problems about queer geometrical designs. Fantom came in, looking like an enormous Mr Gladstone among a crowd of undergraduates, and handed Anthony an envelope to which a receipt was attached. He opened it and read:

NAVAL MESSAGE

TO: LIEUT. BASS
FROM: FLAG OFFICER IN CHARGE
REPORT ABOARD BEFORE SUNDOWN WITHOUT FAIL AAA SERIOUS LEAKAGE PRISONER RECALCITRANT AAA UP SPIRITS

ADMIRAL
1143

By hand: Yeoman of Signals

Anthony signed the receipt. 'By the way, Fantom,' he said, 'I want a word with you.' He went out and conspired with Fantom over a sherry in the pantry.

CHAPTER VIII

'What Hell life is!'

'Why, especially?'

In fact, Peach was thinking of that horrid story about the young man and the bite. Obviously, she thought, the bitch-in-black was mad. Obviously, her crazy tale could have nothing to do with Anth – with Stanley Bass, who was not, she was sure, that kind of man. But he had got a wounded lip: and he had looked uncomfortable when he read the story. Well, but, of course, she thought, any nice man would. It was worrying: but she was not going to talk about it.

She said: 'All this unutterable stuff today. It's worse than I expected.'

'I know,' said Anthony. 'I feel like something under a microscope.'

The day's inquisition was over. They had done a baffling exercise with diagrams, in which they had to distinguish quickly the similarities and differences in one set and another. They had had the preliminary meeting of Group A, the 'get-to-know-each-other' meeting, at which there was a general discussion on Equal Pay for Women. They had read the Island Story – about the imaginary British island for whose many problems they would have to find solutions later. They had done one of the Intelligence Tests which kept cropping up. These were on printed forms, and very trying. Word-sequences, rhyming synonyms, and other horrors. And now, in the pink and golden evening, they were hurrying down to the Lodge by the Lake, Anthony striding along and Peach tripping beside him.

'I feel' said Peach, 'as it must feel when they take out all your insides, scrub them with saline, and put them back again.'

'Do they do that?'

'Of course. A nurse told me. And I resent it. I hate these swampy little men poking about in my own little psych.'

'Fantom calls it mind-sweeping. It's more like a stomach-pump.'

'It's *exactly* like a stomach-pump. And the ghastly thing is, you can't tell *what* they may not bring up.'

'You should have seen some of Number Ten's reactions.'

'Do you ever open a girl's bag and poke about in it, Number Nine?'

'No.'

'Well, don't. Some men do. The entire sex hates it. And that's how I feel about – I say, how simply spiffing all this is!' ("Spiffing" came back in 1953.)

Anthony had halted at the entrance to the Spanish Garden. In silence they looked back to the Hall, splendid and mellow above the terrace. The last of the sun lay on the grey roof and upper stories: the portcullis and drawbridge were in shadow. Beyond was the orchard, a mist of blossom in the dusk.

Anthony gazed at his old home, with the sunlight dying on it. His chin went out: his mouth was stern and angry. Peach, who had a more delicate sense of fitness than her miscellaneous prattle suggested, was quiet for a little. Then she said, in a small voice: 'I'm sorry,' and touched his hand. 'It must be *enraging*.'

He pressed the small strong hand, and turned. 'It is fairly bloody.' He strode off, like a camel in a hurry, past the statues, and the daffodils among the rocks, Peach's shoes pattering on the old stones beside him.

'All this,' she said, 'in the hands of those miasmal specimens!'

'We'll get 'em out,' said the young lord grimly.

'I say! What indecent stone-work!'

'That? That's nothing. Come and look at this.'

He led her, impulsively, into Leda's alcove, which was just ahead. There was little light left in the damp enclosure: but the white Swan and his companion were a brilliant island in the dusk.

'Oh, goody!' Peach remarked at last.

'That' he said, 'is not the sort of thing you should have said.'

'If you expected me to be shocked,' she said, 'you shouldn't have shown me.'

'You have something there,' he said: and they marched along, out of the Garden and into the Park.

'That, I suppose,' he reflected, 'was rather a bad action. The truth is, I feel I've known this girl for ages. And we only met last night. Extraordinary.'

'Do you know who they were?' he asked.

'I know the girl, but I never can place the Swan.'

'Zeus.'

She gurgled.

'I was just wondering what I'd have said if they'd put up SWAN this morning.'

'I can guess.'

'What would you?'

He thought. 'I should have said: "Swan – Belongs to King – Grace – Dignity" or something.'

'Fake!'

'This, I suppose,' he thought, 'is the Modern Girl, innocent but uninhibited.'

'I say! I dare say you're proud of your stride: but I'm practically *running.*'

He slowed down, and they talked more 'shop', as everybody did, all the time, at the Hall.

'I don't think the Group exercises may be quite so odious. But I don't like Number Eleven. If he mentions Plato again I shall scream.'

'Number Fifteen was quite unendurable.'

'You mustn't have a row with Cosmo. I don't think you ought to have said that about Pongoes.'

'I know. It slipped out.'

'What I can't *stand*' said Peach, 'is knowing that those three owls are sitting there behind us taking elaborate *notes* about everything we say.'

'Are they?'

'I looked round now and then because I was too sure that the Maple was *devouring* the little body with his gelatinous eyes. And every time he was.'

'I expect he'd read your word-associations.'

'I wouldn't mind if they didn't all look so smug and soapy – as if they knew everything and we were a lot of certifiable voles. I wonder how *they'd* like to answer some of those ferrety questions.'

'And I wonder how they'd behave in a jam.'

'Such as?'

'We'll see,' said Anthony darkly.

'Oh, goody! Is this the Plan?'

'We'll see.'

That Friday morning, after two fried eggs and crinkly bacon, Stanley Bass felt better. Primrose, blushing a little, had washed most of him, which he found enjoyable. The doctor had called, subdued and queer, but satisfied with his condition. The Admiral had paid him a hearty visit and commended his gallant behaviour in action.

'Anything you want, my boy, you've only to tell the steward, or pass the word to the officer of the watch.'

'There's just one thing, Sir,' said the casualty. 'Why does this doctor keep calling me "my lord"?'

'Round the bend,' said the Admiral, without hesitation, 'not very far, they say, but just enough to notice. He's got a thing about lords, as the young folk say. But don't pay any attention. He's a first-class officer, by all accounts. Well, I must do my rounds.'

Anthony, it seemed, had gone away on a weekend the moment he returned home. This seemed odd: but so was Anthony.

Stanley, always reluctant to read, did easy bits of *The Times* cross-word puzzle, and then gave it up. He thought he would write some letters, and, when Primrose came in with hot coffee, he asked if he could have his coat, in which was his diary, with the addresses of his friends.

Primrose stared at him, blushed rosily, and went out without a word.

'I *am* in a madhouse,' he thought. 'Or is it me?' He felt the top of his head again. Yes, there was a small indentation which he did not remember to have felt before. Probably he had hit the windscreen after all. A bone was pressing on the brain. A tumour…? Was it imagination – or did his head ache a little?

Primrose did not return for ten minutes. She said, gazing at the floor: 'I'm very sorry, Mr Bass. Your suit can't be found.'

'But it must be somewhere,' he said politely. No one could be cross with this tender little mouse.

'It isn't. Not anywhere.'

'What an extraordinary thing!'

'Potter took them downstairs to clean' (what *shocking* lies, thought Primrose) 'and now – they're not there.'

'Good Lord! Burglars, perhaps?'

'That's it,' said Primrose, brightening. 'It must have been the burglar.'

'*Was* there a burglar?'

'I don't know. I – I'll go and see.' She burst into tears and fled from the room.

Stanley Bass put his finger in the hole again. Yes, there was no doubt now – his head was aching.

Lady Primrose, when she had stopped crying and powdered her nose, walked up and down her room in great agitation, with her little hands clenched.

Then she went to see the Admiral, who was in the Chart Room, preparing the preliminaries for his noon observation.

'Father,' she said, 'it's no good. I *must* tell him the truth.'

'I was afraid of this,' said the Admiral kindly. 'I knew it was the weak point in the whole Plan. Very well, my dear, if you feel that way. But mind, no nonsense. No signals. No traffic with the enemy. We can't put Anthony in hazard.'

'But, Father, we can't stop Mr Bass from speaking to the doctor.'

'I can deal with the doctor.' – 'Or can I?' He reflected. The doctor, he thought, was not likely to be ready for a second hangover such as he must be suffering this morning. He might be difficult. 'I tell you what. Anthony must come down and reason with the lad – explain the whole Evolution. I think he deserves it.'

'Why don't *you*, Father?'

'If I do it, I shall simply tell him he's under close arrest and must obey orders. That might upset a wounded man. No, I'll make a signal to Anthony. Carry on, my dear.'

Primrose confessed with such sweet contrition that she almost moved the sick man to tears. His first feeling was one of relief.

'D'you know, Lady Primrose, I really thought I was going round the bend.'

'Round the bend?'

'Potty. Demented.'

'Oh, Mr Bass! I am sorry.'

'Never mind. That's over now.' Impulsively, he held out an enormous hand. 'I say – may I call you Primrose?'

Primrose blushed, but said: 'Yes, Mr Bass.'

'My name's Stanley.'

'Am I forgiven – Stanley?' She put her tiny hand in his, a hand so small and warm, it was like holding a young bird.

'Of course you are.'

He looked with warmth into her gentle eyes. Few men can have their backs washed by a young lady without some emotional result. Primrose was very different from the usual run of Stanley Bass's young ladies: but she might, he thought, be a wholesome change. The robust, rampageous ones, to whom he was so often drawn, were always a trouble in the end. They made scenes, like that tempestuous Pole. This tender little bird aroused the mother in him; he felt he would like to keep her under his coat, build her a nest, and protect her from the cruel elements.

But at the back of his mind was boiling up the enormity of Anthony's offence. 'But, Primrose,' he said suddenly, severely, 'I shall *never* forgive your brother! Never!'

What might not Anthony be up to? All that foolish talk in the train came back to him. That had been crazy enough. But if he was perpetrating the same sort of mischief in the name of Stanley Bass – !

Notepaper, *please*, my dear? I must write at once!'

'Who to?'

'To the what-name – the Principal.'

'Oh, Stanley, *no!*'

'But, Primrose, don't you *see* – the thing must stop! Anthony will ruin me.'

'He won't, I'm sure.'

'You don't *know* what potty ideas are in his head. He may be arrested.'

'But Stanley – Stanley *darling* – '

'Did you say "darling"?'

'I did,' she whispered, with downcast eyes.

'Wonderful girl!' he said as tenderly as the deep voice could.

'He's coming down to see you – this evening. He'll explain everything.'

'Honest?'

'Honest. Will you wait till then?'

'For you, dear Primrose, yes.'

They kissed. Primrose could not have said how it happened, but they did.

'This' thought the young man, 'is the quickest thing in the history of Bass.'

And one of the best. After the numerous rough embraces he had known, her kiss was like dew falling on a lawn, like Scotch mist caressing a mountain. And – unique experience – she wore no lipstick.

'Darling!' they whispered, in joint delight and wonder. 'All the same,' said Stanley, 'I shall give Anthony *Hell!*'

'I think I *may* be going to faint,' said Primrose, and went out, holding her heart.

All the afternoon Stanley brooded on his wrongs: and the more he thought of them, the more Hell he determined to give to his old companion.

When Anthony and Peach were ushered in by Primrose, he lay with (he hoped) a set, stern face. He would not, he had decided, turn his head towards the door. He would lie still, look at the window, and suffer, angrily.

But he had not foreseen a visit from a luminous, golden girl. Nor had he thought that even Anthony would wear so breezy an air, and so little sense of guilt and shame.

'Well, well, *well*!' that gentleman bubbled at the door. 'How's the old casualty? How's the comfortable sufferer? Look, Stanley, I've brought a Ray of Hope! Miss Meridew.'

The casualty slowly turned his head and gave the golden girl a wintry grin.

'How d'you do? Will you sit down? Sit down, Anchor.' They sat down. The sufferer's angry eyes returned to the window. Primrose stood by the door.

'Anchor?' said Anthony. 'What is all this, companion of a thousand bottles?'

'You know, I suppose?' said Bass portentously.

'Know what, King Lear?'

'You know – that I know?' A pause – a sigh. 'Dear Primrose told me.'

'Dear Primrose!' Anthony thought. 'What *is* this?' He looked at his sister: but his sister looked at the floor.

'Of course I know, dear hero! And now you're in the Evolution, too. I've come to report. I'm delighted!'

'Anchor,' said the patient heavily, 'we are not amused.'

'Not?'

'No. Repeat – No.'

'Dear, dear.'

'We remember, we suppose,' said Anthony after a pause, 'our talk in the train?'

'We do. I'm sorry about your troubles, Anchor: but, think what you like, I'm far more troubled about my career.'

'Your *career*!' said Anthony, with indignation. 'Here have I been slaving away, *Bass*, for your blasted career, *Bass*, for *days*. And all I get is disgusting umbrage!'

'Really, Mr Bass,' said Miss Meridew sweetly, 'Anthony – may I call you Anthony?' (He nodded vigorously.) – 'has been doing wonders for you. I've seen his *work*. You may not be sent to the Foreign Office – ' Stanley nodded grimly. 'But I'm *too* sure they'll make you Archbishop of *Canterbury*. That is just the *kind* of effect that Anthony, I *think*, has made.'

Anthony looked with glowing warmth and gratitude at his defender. The little speech had sounded so sincere and compelling that his sense of rectitude was stronger than ever.

But Bass said, 'Thank-you, Miss – Miss – '

'Meridew,' said Anthony. 'And – believe it or not – the other name is Peach. "*Dear*" Peach,' he added.

'Thank-you, Miss Meridew. I'm sure that Anchor has done his best for me. Well, fairly sure. But I prefer to pass my examinations under, my own steam, so to speak. I – '

'But – '

'My mind is made up. Either, Anchor, you make a clean breast of it to the authorities – or I write to them myself.'

'But, dear old comrade, have you no feeling at all for the *Evolution?*'

'None,' said Stanley. 'To be quite frank, Anchor, I don't think much of it.'

Anthony now looked almost as cloudy and cross as Stanley.

'Prim, dear,' he said, 'at this point it would be convenient if you took Peach below and gave her a rum-punch or something of that sort. Do you mind?'

The girls, without a word, departed.

Anthony stood up and marched about, like a statesman preparing to dictate a great oration.

'*So*, Bass,' he said, at last, 'you would like me to tell the world that you, *Bass*, are lying sick in bed at the Lodge by the Lake?'

'Quite quietly – yes.'

'In that case, Bass, you will no doubt be prepared to receive visits from any *Polish* friends in the neighbourhood.'

'*Polish?*' said Stanley blankly. But Anthony thought that the face became less firm.

'Jacaranda, for example?'

'Jacaranda? Never heard of her.'

'Quite likely. I forgot. But you'll have heard of Olga?'

'Olga? Yes, I knew an Olga once. But Olga who?'

How many times had both these officers seen the proud blue sky of the night give way to the creeping pallor of dawn! So paled, thought Anthony, the face of his old companion-in-arms.

'Olga,' he said. 'Damn it, I forget the name. No, I don't. *Daly*! Olga Daly.'

'Olga Daly,' Stanley whispered. And now the sky was pale indeed. 'Yes, I knew a girl called that. Why not?'

'Where, would you say, is Olga Daly now?'

'Gdynia – I *hope*,' he added.

'Well, Olga is at Wimbledon.'

'Wimbledon? Good God!'

As a man throws the last trump upon the vital trick, did Anthony throw Olga's letter onto the bed. Then he lit a cigarette and mercifully turned away.

'That's her,' said Stanley Bass, at last, a stern fellow no more.

'You know she had twins?'

'Why?'

'My dear old chap – '

'Anthony, you don't think – ? I swear – there was never anything but a chaste hug in the snow – '

'In the snow?'

'Under a tree. I can see the tree. And she wore about four layers of fur. Anthony, you must believe me!'

Anthony surveyed his twittering friend severely.

'Twins is what *I* heard. Two beautiful boys. Didn't she write to you?'

'Time and again. But not a word about twins – or anything.'

'I must and do accept the word of a brother officer,' said Anthony kindly. 'But, you see, there is worse to come.'

'Worse?'

'Your Olga may be far away in Wimbledon. But her sister is up at the Hall.'

'Gosh! Not a candidate?'

'A candidate. And her sister, as you may know, is a cross between a tiger and a female snake. Do you see this degrading trauma on your old friend's face?'

'I noticed something.'

'That, Stanley Bass, was intended for Stanley Bass, the father of Olga's twins.'

'Gosh!'

'You see now, Stanley, why *I* am entitled to be wounded? It is nothing to me if you go about wronging the Poles and littering Europe with your uncounted young – though sister Prim might take a different view – '

'Anthony!'

The orator, with dignity, held up his hand. 'Order, please. I am willing, for the general good, and yours, to be chewed and lacerated by a raving harpy with the jaws of a bull-dozer. But when, on top of all this, you propose to ruin the entire Evolution for the sake of your wretched career, I must say I find it fairly discouraging.'

'Yes, I see that,' said Stanley humbly.

'Of course,' said Anthony ruminatively, 'I'm entirely in your hands. If you would *like* me to tell them up at the Hall that you are here on a sick-bed, I will. But Jacaranda, I warn you – '

Why Jacaranda?'

'I forget. What *is* her horrible name?'

'I can't remember.'

'Then don't interrupt. Jacaranda will be down here like a rocket with fangs flashing and flails flying. Tied to your bed, you will have no defences, and I should hardly be surprised if you lost the other leg. Jacaranda, I may say, does believe in the twins.'

'For God's sake! Anthony, you wouldn't do that?'

Stanley was white and trembling.

'It's up to you, old boy. If you'll agree to lie quiet and not put the Evolution out of gear I'll say no word to the human jaguar.'

'And not a word to your sister?'

'My dear fellow, Prim shall *never* know about the twins.'

'But I tell you – '

'Is it a bet?'

'I'll do anything – anything, Anthony.' Stanley Bass lay beaten. Not a gun was firing.

'Well, then, everything is perfectly splendid. I say, would a tot of rum go down?'

'Make it a double,' said the stricken sailor.

'Aye, aye, Sir – and I'll send Prim too.'

'Eating out of both hands,' Anthony told the little party below.

'Well done, my boy.'

The Admiral had been vastly entertained by Peach's vivacious account of the inquisitions: and was more than ever convinced that such beastly proceedings were a desecration of his ancient home that could not be allowed to go on.

'Could we have an Appreciation of the Situation?'

'No time now, Sir. Night Operations tonight. Fall in, Number Eight.'

They marched back swiftly, Peach at the trot.

CHAPTER IX

"Where does this go?' Peach whispered.

'The stairs go up to the Armoury Room – and down to the Cellars. This is the room where Charles I was hidden.'

'Oo!' Peach looked about the small and dusty space with awe.

'There's your peep-hole. There's your torch. Don't be alarmed. And stand by at *Loch Lomond*. 'Bye.' He kissed her quickly and was gone.

Back in the Great Hall, Anthony surveyed the scene with satisfaction. It was twenty minutes to eight. Everyone was making ready for dinner, the Hall was empty and the economical Fantom had switched off all the lights but those that lit up the two pictures under the gallery. A sweet-smelling wood-fire blazed in the enormous grate and threw dancing gleams and long leaping shadows into every corner. They danced in the polished breast-plate of the suit-of-mail that stood in the corner, and played across the sofa below it; a long sofa without back or sides.

From her peep-hole on the south side Peach could see, to her left, the stone staircase that led up to the Staff and Guest Rooms, and much of the gallery, now dark, that overlooked the Hall.

In the north-west corner was the console of the organ, the pride and joy of the 16th Earl, who had been no mean musician, and one of the best private organs in the country. The pipes of the organ were concealed under the stairs, and when a shutter in the Hall was opened and the swell panels were in use the boom and vibration of the music went up to the roof and the knight-in-armour clattered on his stand.

The Admiral, to his great regret, had no more music in him than a mouse: but he had encouraged his sons to play, and Anthony had been the best of them. He could play the piano very pleasantly, had a light touch, could read pieces of reasonable speed, knew a few by heart, and many by ear. But he had little harmony and anything could happen in the bass. On the piano a light left hand, a firm right, and a liberal use of the pedals can cover a multitude of sins in the bass. But the organ picks out every error and proclaims it to the world in agonizing squeaks or sonorous booms.

He sat down now, turned on the light, and pressed a button. A muffled rumbling began in the bowels of the instrument, as the electric blower came into action. He pulled out a few stops on each key-board, not forgetting the Tremolo and Vox Humana, his favourites, on the Choir. He began to play *Annie Laurie*, very softly, on the Choir keyboard. He always began softly and, in the interests of the community, it was always his resolve to continue softly. But soon the sense of the power at his command would be too much for him. Like a youth with a powerful car, he must show the world what the great instrument could do. Out would come the coupling stops, down would go his right foot, out would go his knees to the swells, and thunder rolled to the roof. Very fine and thrilling if the chords were right: but, if they were not, an outrage to humanity.

But now the sweet old air came trembling and hovering from under the stairs, rich but reedy, like a shepherd's pipe blown by a gentle giant; and the firelight wavered about the walls: and Peach thought that it was beautiful. Now and then the musician would stretch out a long leg and touch a pedal. But he had never been quite sure which pedal was which, and there was generally a deep boom, like a distant gun, in the wrong key, which made Peach jump in her secret room.

Doctor Maple, too, thought the sound was pleasing as he came out onto the gallery, on the north side, where Peach could see him. Few candidates had been able to play the organ, and he looked down to see who it was. Oh, yes, Number Nine, one of his own Group. It annoyed him a little that this mere sailor (the Staff knew all about the records of the candidates) was able to do this thing, when he, the much more gifted Maple, could not. But he stood and listened. He had arranged to take sherry with Miss Slice, the female psychologist, who loved him, he sometimes thought; and he was before his time.

Then Anthony came to the second half of the verse, and the itch for Power, the appetite for Noise, prevailed.

'Gave me her promise TRUE.'

He pushed out his right knee, and depressed his right foot, and with his left hand pulled out a coupling stop. A red light shone. Now he had all three key-boards in harness together: all the artillery at his command was in action, trumpet and clarinet, viola, 'cello and all – except the pedals. But he was out of practice, and his fingers slipped, and on the top-note he played a chord so wrong, so thunderously, deafeningly wrong, with shrill discordant shrieks at the top and deep shattering errors at the bottom, that Mr Maple gripped the rail in terror and Peach in the cell felt like screaming. Anthony himself heard the horror of what he had done, and took his fingers from the fatal keys at once. He passed abruptly to Handel's *Largo*, not quite so loud but loud enough: for this was his principal 'piece' and he was confident of every note, bass and all.

Doctor Maple thought he would go down and ask the young musician to restrain himself. But suddenly a log fell from the high pile on the hearth, and scattered sparks and rosy light. He stopped and stared down into the Hall. Was he mad? Was he dreaming? If not, he had seen a naked woman lying on the long scarlet sofa. She lay on her back, her pale skin bright in the half-dark. The figure was slender, short, but beautifully shaped. She seemed to have one arm across her head and eyes: but a scarf lay over her neck and face, and it was hard to see. The other hand lay across her belly, modestly protecting her middle, as if she had died defending her virtue. There was another flash of rose from the fire, in which Doctor Maple clearly saw her shapely breasts, like dawn (or sunset) on the Himalayas. He could also see her navel. Now he was sure.

Men of other professions might have thought: 'What shall I do?' Doctor Maple's first thought was: 'I must note my sensations.' He did try to note his sensations, and found them pleasant on the whole, but not so easy to catalogue and clarify as they should have been to a man of his training and experience. Then, to do him justice, he thought, 'I must do something.' The beauty, after all, might be dead or dying. But then he saw a figure approaching the head of the stairs on the west side of the gallery. He was not very keen to be the first discoverer of a dead body, and he drew back into the shadows. Mr Nathaniel ('Serious Door') Rackstraw was in a contented mood. He had had a nice hot bath, and cut his toe-nails at last. He looked forward to a fairly good dinner (the thick soup was always good) and a glass of port. Young folk would be about him. He was fond of music. Anthony was coming to the end of the first verse of Handel's *Largo* (he always gave himself an encore for this), and the swells and couplers were in action. In the *Largo* he could even, now and then, put a confident foot on a pedal, and was thrilled to hear the response, the profound and pompous boom of a distant heavy gun. The noble old tune, rolling like thunder round the noble old building, gave Mr Rackstraw a fine sense of the solidity of the English Thing (after all, Handel was practically an Englishman), of a continuous irresistible march, of an impregnable and beauteous castle, in the midst of which toiled, ever tireless and ever indispensable, the British Civil Service. Filled with fine and comfortable thoughts, he almost floated down the stairs. On the bottom step, in full view of Miss Meridew and Doctor Maple, he stopped dead, as stops the rabbit when it sees the snake (they say). He saw what Doctor Maple had seen: but the range was much shorter, and he had no doubts – except upon the question – dead or alive? His first thought was not the same as Doctor Maple's. His sensations were tumultuous and horrid, but he did not bother, for once, to make a list or memorandum. He thought: 'What shall I do?' He had read many detective stories (he read little else, these days): and he knew very well how perilous was the position of the man who found the body – what questions, what suspicions! Apart from that, nothing in his long and honourable career of public service had equipped him to deal with such a situation – a naked lady, dead – or, worse, perhaps, alive – on a sofa in the Hall at a Government institution. Scared and wary, he looked round the Hall, at the door on the left, at the passage on the right, as a cat looks for dangerous dogs before it darts across the road. Then he turned, passed swiftly up the stairs, and scuttled back to his room.

High on the right side of the console was a mirror, designed to give the organist a helpful view of the choir and clergy, or the bride, coming up the nave. It may be that Anthony saw the Civil Servant depart. At all events, as he mounted the stairs, the last triumphant bars of the *Largo* made the knight-in-armour clatter like a milk-cart: and the picture of Lord Shaftesbury crashed to the floor.

The noise was deafening. But Doctor Maple's professional interests were commanding him: and he hardly heard it. 'Extraordinary,' he whispered, as he watched the exit of the ruler of men. He felt a hand upon his arm: and there was Miss Elinor Slice, in a severe grey coat and skirt of inferior cut.

'What's up?' she said. 'And who is making that Hellish noise?'

'Look!' he said. She looked down, stopping her ears with two slim fingers.

'Gracious! But we must – '

He restrained her. 'Wait! Rackstraw has funked it.'

'But why not – ?'

'Someone else may come,' he hissed into her ear. 'This is field-work. Note your sensations.'

While waiting for the next development he noted his own sensations. One of them was disturbing. He tried to project Miss Slice into the costume and posture of the lady on the sofa below: and he found that the picture did not excite him.

Anthony was playing the Russian National Anthem, the grand old Anthem of the wicked Czars.

Miss Slice, too, was noting her sensations. She noted that she was unprofessionally piqued by the interest (though, no doubt, professional) of Doctor Maple in the scene below. She was thirty-two, a little plump, but by no means repellent. She wore no spectacles, had a good complexion, and keen green eyes which darted everywhere like a suspicious bird's. Peach called her 'The Hen': but this was unfair.

Suddenly, he gripped her arm, which she liked. Through the door under their gallery Number Fifteen ('Call me Cosmo') had entered the Hall. He sauntered in with a cigarette, the Monarch of the Glen, and threw an indignant glance at the back of Number Nine. Then he strolled ahead, and at once the sterling qualities of the man of action were displayed. Mr Rackstraw would have been ashamed. Number Fifteen had read detective stories too. Nothing must be touched, he knew, nothing disturbed. He observed the scarf drawn tight round the neck and feared the worst. Down on one knee, as far off as possible, he delicately touched the body with one finger. It was cold, deadly cold. He threw a shrewd strategic glance round the Hall – the killer might be lurking still. He strode up to the suit-of-mail and looked behind, then back to the telephone, which was in the south-west corner, on the other side of the passage to the drawing-room. He jiggled violently and yelled at Anthony 'Stop that noise!'

Anthony, blissfully unaware, swelled up into a noble but deafening din.

'POLICE!' cried Number Fifteen into the telephone. 'Will you stop that NOISE?'

'Time we went, I think,' said Maple, and Peach saw the two psychologists slip away through the dim-lit arch of the corridor opposite.

'Police? Hold on! – WILL YOU STOP THAT BLOODY NOISE?'

Anthony pushed his right knee out, and laid his left foot crosswise over about five pedals. There was a noise like thunder, like a broadside, like houses falling down, and on top of that, the shrieking of clarinets, the blast of many trumpets, the shrill of a thousand flutes.

'God damn it!' shouted Number Fifteen, beside himself 'Hold on!'

He dropped the receiver and strode masterfully down the long passage to the drawing-room.

Anthony looked over his shoulder, looked round the room, and did a singular thing. He stopped playing the Russian National Anthem and, with scarcely a moment's pause, began the *Bonnie Banks of Loch Lomond.*

The huge and stately Fantom came in from the long passage, in which was the swing-door into the servants' quarters. He switched on all the lights and saw the Thing. With eloquent movements of his arms he expressed his horror and dismay. But he acted quickly. Tenderly he picked up the body and carried it, staggering a little, into the passage. He had not far to go. Before he reached the swing-door he turned left through a door which was no door, a panel conveniently opened for him by Miss Peach Meridew.

'Well done, Fantom. She must be heavy.'

'Thank-you, Miss. She is. The torch, if you please?' Panting, he let the feet of *Susanna Resenting the Elders* descend to the floor and rested her against the wall. Then the white sheet decently covered her again.

'Now, Miss, if you will follow me, you can go through the Armoury Room and down by the other stairs.'

Anthony made a tempestuous end to *Loch Lomond,* and paused to press a few stops back and select a softer combination. *The Pilgrim's Chorus*, a favourite piece of the 16th Earl's, was on the music-stand, and he began that, quietly but not very well.

Number Fifteen came back with urgent strides from his successful call. He was pleased with his promptitude and resource, but he thought he must find the Principal and make a report. At the entrance to the Hall he pulled up on his haunches, like a horse refusing a fence, and stared at the empty sofa. Then he marched over to the maddening ass at the organ.

'Once for all, will you stop that bloody awful noise?'

'Why, Pongo? Don't you like music?'

But he did stop – and just as well, for he had nearly got to the Venusberg music, which would have been too much for him. He swung round and sat astride the music-stool with a happy smile.

'Where is she?' hissed the soldier.

'Who?'

'The body!'

'The body?'

'Didn't you see anyone?'

'Not a soul.'

When Peach tripped in at the north end in her dark green, full-skirted dress, with a wide golden belt round her small waist, she heard, with some dismay, a voice say: 'My dear old Pongo, you must be round the bend.'

Number Fifteen was ranging round the Hall like a hound who has lost the scent, peering behind tapestries and curtains, under the sofa and inside the suit-of-mail. He stopped dead and said savagely:

'Less of this "Pongo", please, Number Nine.'

'The less the better, I agree. I apologize. But honestly, you can't have seen a body.'

'I tell you – I *did* see a body!'

By a happy chance, the Principal and Sir William Blant, MP, met at the top of the stairs and came slowly down together. Sir William had been the able and popular General Secretary of the Amalgamated Association of Nail-Hammerers and Kindred Trades. The word 'kindred' had been stretched rather far. To the original humble but useful body of nail-hammerers Sir William, in his fighting days, had added, one by one, the Metropolitan Ferrymen, the Stagedoorkeepers' Association, the Parliamentary Cleaners, the Lockmen's Deputies and Assistants, the Casual Carpenters, the Orchestra Messengers and Call-boys, the Laundry-workers' Tea-fetchers, the Newsvendors' Boy-helps, the Alarm-Clock Winders, the Municipal Rodent Officers' Bagholders, the Organ-blowers' Deputies, the Cathedral Tenors, the Dog-Totalisator Girl Operators' Association, the Caddies' Union, the Transferred Footballers, the Continuity Girls, the Park (Unestablished) Overseers and the Organized Ball-boys. The discreet but forcible leadership of this diverse but valuable regiment of workmen had made him a power in the land. Few could put so sure and sensitive a finger on the important pulses of Home Affairs. So they had made him a Parliamentary Secretary to the Foreign Office. He was honest, patriotic, bluff, respectable and genial: and everybody liked him.

Hambone Hall had sent so many young men and women to the Foreign Office – and kept so many out of it – that his Chief had desired him to go and see the famous place in action. He was already favourably impressed by the Principal and the atmosphere: and he hoped that the dinner would be as good.

'Always nice to hear the organ,' he said, as they descended. 'Nearly blew me out of me bath.'

'Yes, in good hands' said the Principal cautiously, 'it's a warming instrument.'

They halted half-way down at the arch in the wall, and surveyed the gracious scene – the tapestries, the pictures, the comfortable crimson fire, the dark discreet panelling, the delicate light.

'You didn't always' said the Minister, impressed again, 'have quarters like this, I believe?'

'No – in the old days – before my time, of course – it was just a small house – Nissen huts and so on.'

'All this' he said, with an eloquent gesture, as the stately descent continued, 'helps the work, I think. Brings out the best in them.' *'Sit mens sana'* he thought cleverly, *'in mensa sana.'* But he did not try that on the Minister.

The Minister said 'That's right': and then they were in the Hall.

They saw two young men staring savagely at each other in the gracious surroundings. One of them was saying hotly: 'I *did* see a body!'

'A *body*, Number Fifteen?' laughed the Principal. Some jolly, juvenile joke, no doubt.

Number Fifteen rushed at him and began to explain. But he had got out no more than a few stuttering words when Fantom came in, majestic.

'Pardon me, Sir Gilbert. A police officer.'

The police officer was not far behind.

' 'Evening, Sir. A fatality, I believe?'

Then there were many questions – many explanations.

'The fat' whispered Peach, 'is *practically* in the *fire*.'

CHAPTER X

A light mist steals over the summer sea, and up the gleaming river, and soon the laughing mariners are alert and anxious. The mist will pass, maybe, and they might see the sun again: but now the rigging and the decks are damp, the watch is doubled, men talk in low tones and the ship wails doleful warnings: for, though the crawling cloud is pale and tenuous, who knows what devils and dangers it may mask? So did a sudden mist of unease confine and trouble the company of Hambone Hall that night, and hearts that had beat high and confident were low. There was little talk at the evening meal; the Minister said hardly anything: and the Principal afterwards confessed that dinner had been Hell.

All this may be nothing to the dense and blinding fog, father of dread, that is to follow: but at present it is uncomfortable enough.

The easy – but uneasy – official explanation was that the excited Number Fifteen was perhaps a little mad, or perhaps a little tipsy ('I suppose it *is* wise' the Minister had said, 'to let them have a bar?'), and had not seen a body at all. Or else it was some kind of practical joke. There had been no body when the cool Mr Bass came in to play the organ: and, badly though he played, a girl could hardly have been done to death quite close to him without his attention being drawn to the affair. Nor had anybody seen the alleged lady except the excitable soldier. The Principal inclined strongly to the 'practical joke' theory. With the Minister there, that seemed the best way out. Even that was far from comforting to his inner mind: but he seemed to take the thing so lightly that the police accepted his lead, and, after a perfunctory search of the ground floor and the grounds, departed.

The candidates, who were herded into dinner during the rumpus, did not know about the official view, and did not know what to think themselves. Anthony and Peach, when they came in to dinner, had nothing to tell them. Cosmo Lennox-Edwardes, when he came, later, was almost speechless with bewilderment and rage. 'Am I *mad*? Do I *look* mad? Am I *drunk*? Do I *look* drunk?' The sad thing was that in his just anger he did look a bit of both. Whatever had happened, they thought, it would be put down to the candidates: and they looked at each other queerly, wondering who could do – or had done – what.

But the mist was thickest, perhaps, about the souls of Mr Rackstraw, Doctor Maple, and Miss Elinor Slice.

After dinner, Anthony and Peach had a council of war in their old corner (it seemed 'old' already, after twenty-four hours) in the Bar.

'The course is clear,' said the sailor. 'The crew are in good heart. But where exactly are we?'

'Away up!' said his eager ally.

'Well, it worked, certainly,' said Anthony modestly. 'Better than I expected.'

'It was magical. But what *luck*! Suppose anyone had seen Fantom! The psychies nearly did.'

'That was provided for. If anyone had seen him, the story was that he took her to his own room, put her down and went for help – and she disappeared meanwhile.'

'H'm. Not so very hot.'

'Not quite so hot, I admit. We did have a little luck. Now have another drink, and tell me all you saw again.'

She did.

'Of course,' said Anthony, at last, 'the odious thing is that I have a sort of weak-minded sympathy with the Pongo. While you were powdering your nose I had a quick word with Fantom in the pantry. And it seems that the high line is that nobody believes a word the Pongo says.'

'It is a bit hard. At dinner he was *practically* demented.'

'The *cardinal* thing is that you are quite sure that Rackstraw, Maple and – what-name – '

'Slice. Elinor Slice.'

' – saw everything?'

'*Too* sure.'

'And did nothing?'

'Not a thing.'

'And they, it seems, have said nothing. Otherwise our beloved Pongo would be believed?'

'Absolutely.'

'Well, then,' said Anthony slowly, 'that gives me an idea – I *think*.'

'Oh, goody! A Plan?'

'Tomorrow we have a Group Meeting about that squalid island, don't we?'

'Yes.'

'Well, I must be Chairman – part of the time.'

'Anything you say, Chief.'

'Give me a kiss.'

'How did you hurt your lip?'

'Can't tell you – yet.'

'All right. No kiss.'

'Snake!'

'Seducer!'

'Let's go to bed.'

'*Do* tell me. *Please!*'

'Well, it wasn't a door.'

'I *knew* it wasn't,' she wailed faintly – and began to cry.

So he told her all.

'I shall chew her into a thousand pieces,' she said.

Not long after breakfast on Saturday, Doctor Maple sought out the Principal. 'Something rather queer here, Sir. I'd like your advice.' He laid before Sir Gilbert the Word-Associations of Number Eight, and her Short Plots or Stories.

Sir Gilbert was still worried about the Episode of the Disappearing Body: but it was a fine Spring morning, and his sense of humour was undefeated. At the end of the Saga of the Psychologist he smiled.

'You don't take that too seriously, do you? I should say, a lively soul with a strong sense of fun. Of course, I'm no psychologist. But don't you think she's pulling your leg – *our* legs, I should say? I should have a private word with her. You'll soon know.'

The notion that anyone could pull a psychologist's leg was repugnant to Heriot Maple: but he was uneasily aware that the Principal did not think much of his craft.

But Jacaranda's reactions made the Principal laugh loudly.

'You don't think that's funny?' said the psychologist, flushing.

'I suppose I shouldn't, really. Yes, I expect you have something there. Yet this girl's papers are capable enough – I've read them.

'That' said the Doctor, 'is why I suspect a fixation.'

The Principal gazed out of the mullioned window at the last of the daffodils, across the moat, a shimmering cloth of gold on the lush grass of the orchard. Privately, he considered that all psychologists had a fixation – whatever that was.

'This' he said with a sigh, 'seems to be the Humorists' Intake. Look at last night.'

'Do you think that was a joke?'

'What else is one to think?'

'You're quite sure it wasn't a real woman?'

'If so, where is she? It's a pity nobody saw her except that bull of Bashan Number Fifteen.'

'Yes,' said Doctor Maple, wondering if he should say more.

'Of course,' he went on slowly, 'if these tests of ours mean anything it might have been – Number Ten – or even Number Eight.'

'Good Lord! What a horrible idea!' The Principal was shocked. 'I couldn't believe that.'

'Many things happen in this world' said the psychologist darkly, 'that ordinary people would not believe.'

'Yes, I know. Still – ' ('What a mind!' he thought.) 'Well, if you think that, keep an eye on them, by all means – Number Ten, at least. I can't believe that little fair girl – she looks like a daffodil.'

'The daffodil' said the Doctor, 'has a sex-life too.'

'What a mind!' thought the Principal, as the learned man departed.

'A' Group gathered for their first discussion on the Island Story in the Great Hall. They sat in a semi-circle of comfortable chairs in front of the fire-place, with notepads on their knees. Behind them sat the three members of the staff team, Mr Egerton, the Group Chairman, a mild and fatherly Civil Servant, Mr Chinlip, a retired schoolmaster, acute and angular, and Doctor Maple. These would make notes throughout the proceedings of the things said and the form shown by the candidates in the arena. From time to time other members of the staff might wander in and watch the young rulers at work. Today they were warned that Sir William Blant might be looking in: but they were to take no notice of him.

The first thing was to choose a chairman. As there was a new chairman every fifteen minutes the practical importance of the choice was not high. But it was of subtle interest to the invigilators. The candidates had had an opportunity to weigh each others' 'personal qualities'. Whom would they choose for their first chairman? The strong and 'thrusting' type, eager to take command, knew that he must not seem to be too keen. But to seem too shy or reluctant would lose marks the other way.

This time the matter was soon settled. Anthony said: 'I should like to propose Number Fifteen, who has, I think, the respect – and sympathy – of us all.'

A murmur of approval ran round the Group, almost a Parliamentary 'Hear-hear', for most felt that Number Fifteen had been hardly used. The Observer, though faintly disapproving of the demonstration, noted a good mark for Number Nine at once. He had correctly interpreted the sense of the meeting. Number Fifteen was astonished and moved by this tribute from the truculent sailor. The sullen face melted and he threw a grateful glance. 'Oh, really – ' he said, with a modest 'show of reluctance' (he had read about the Speaker's election). But Number Four said firmly 'Agreed': and Cosmo took the chair in front of the fire-place.

(Number Four got a good mark too. A man of affairs. Knew how to cut the cackle, and get on with the business. Moreover, he might well have thought himself to be the obvious choice, but gave no sign of it. He was the most mature of the party, had served in the Ministry of Supply, was married and had two children.)

The imaginary Island of Nobona was about the size of Ireland: but it suffered almost all the troubles and problems that a single British island can contain. About half the population were coloured, mainly Bulus, and about half of them were illiterate and poor: but they had thrown up many clever politicians with strong 'nationalistic' notions. Four or five religions raged: three languages, besides the English, were spoken. The capital of the island was continually destroyed by hurricanes, tidal waves, or savage fires, causing impossible housing problems which the Groups were asked to solve. Every kind of pest attacked the banana and sugar plantations. The natives were lazy – at least, they were lazy on the white men's land, though they laboured busily on their own small plots during their too protracted weekends. Agriculture was nearly always in a bad way. Nobona Fever was nearly always fatal. Now and then there was an earthquake, and the capital was destroyed again. In the old days, the white planters, who had founded the island's fortune, had ruled the roost in the Assembly, mainly nominated. But democracy had reared its ugly head: the Assembly was now mainly elected, and the whites were being squeezed out. As a result (they said) three years earlier the island had gone bankrupt. Whitehall had, reluctantly, taken charge, and Nobona was temporarily governed by seven Commissioners appointed from London. Prosperity had come again: but that only made the natives restless, and they wanted their Assembly back. In the north of the island there were believed to be vast resources of *piturium*, essential for the new bomb; but all five religions forbade the faithful to work underground among the evil spirits. Cambia, the great Dominion not far away, would like to work the minerals, and there was talk of her absorbing the difficult island. But everyone in Cambia hated the sight of black men, especially the Bulus. Whitehall was heartily sick of the place (the local money was dollars) and eager to give it away; but it had great strategical importance in time of war – and then there was the *piturium* (perhaps).

As if all this was not enough, the Skilled Staff at Hambone Hall loved to invent new and quite unnecessary problems for the afflicted island, and tossed them to the Groups for statesmanlike solutions. United Nations would propose importing 100,000 Displaced Persons from Central Europe, and the young men and women had to decide what to do with them, and where to put them. America would ask for 'Bases' or bombing-ranges. American millionaires would offer to build and endow new hospitals and libraries, with very tiresome conditions attached to the offer. Sometimes they started general strikes, mutinies, or cholera, and asked the boys and girls – or the seven 'Commissioners' – what they would do about it.

These exercises, the candidates thought, mostly, were difficult but fair, and probably – to the bosses – instructive. Each candidate was given, privately, an Individual Subject, and had an hour to think about it. Then, as chairman, he had to expound it, and, in fifteen minutes, try to get an agreed conclusion.

That morning, the subject allotted to Number Fifteen was Prohibition. The Bulus – and, less vigorously, the Casaris – were religiously opposed to the use of strong drink. All the natives were excitable and quick with the knife: and all the native leaders were troubled by the number of stabbings, murders, assaults, and rapes which followed a visit to the tavern, especially in the jungle villages, where there were no police. All the five faiths, for once, had united and were pressing for total prohibition of the import, sale, manufacture or consumption of spirituous liquor. The white population were naturally indignant, for they did not see why their simple pleasures should be taken away because of the bad habits of the Bulus (and indeed the Casaris). The Government were worried too, for the revenue from this base indulgence was enormous, and, if it came to an end, the island might well be 'in the red' again.

'Well,' said Number Fifteen, having expounded, 'what do we think, Ladies and Gentlemen?'

(He got a good mark for not starting with what he thought himself. Normally, that was just what Number Fifteen would have done: but this morning Number Fifteen was a subdued and different man.)

Number Four came in at once, as he generally did, with some shrewd common sense:

'The first question is – *can* you have Prohibition?'

Most of the Group looked blankly at him, each thinking: 'I ought to say something – but *what*?' It was nerve-wracking to think of those watchful eyes and busy pencils behind them.

But Adrian Holt (Number Eleven) drawled easily: *'Naturam expellas furca, tamen usque recurret* – you mean?'

'I couldn't say,' said Number Four, who had no Latin. 'I mean, those natives can brew an alcoholic drink out of anything – a bark, a vegetable, a banana, I dare say. Cut off the good stuff, and they may take to worse. That's always the way.'

Anthony, when the perilous topic appeared, had thought: 'Anthony Anchor, beware! Stanley Bass, hold back! Something statesmanlike and spurious is required.'

But suddenly he put in:

'As the poet Herbert said:

'There's alcohol in plant and tree.
It must be Nature's plan
That there should be in fair degree
Some alcohol in Man.'

Peach giggled, softly and nervously: but the Observer wrote quickly '9. Acute but flippant.'

Number Four came back for a good mark: 'Mind you – I'm not saying "No control". The question is – what?'

'In vino severitas,' said Number Eleven: but only the Observer knew what he meant.

Doctor Maple was not paying much attention to all this. He was sitting behind the right side of the Group, and was looking across at Miss Meridew's profile and the swell of her breasts under the pale-blue jersey. How fresh and sweet, he thought. And the impossible notion that she could have been the girl in the Hall he found exciting. But his expression was still disdainful and lofty.

Peach, as she confessed afterwards, was 'petrified', and, for once, could not say a word.

Jacaranda spoke, with surprising sense, Anthony thought:

'If the black men do not want to drink, all right,' she said. 'But make arrangements for the white men.'

'What do you suggest, exactly, Number Ten?' said Cosmo politely.

'In Bombay there is Prohibition,' she said, 'I have been there. But the white men have permits – on medical grounds – so much a month.'

'But,' said Number Four, 'don't they have to be certified as "Licensed Addicts"?'

Peach gurgled, and Anthony snorted.

'That is correct, I think.'

'Not very complimentary to the ruling race, is it?' said Number Eleven. 'Or to God's gift of wine?'

'It's disgusting,' Anthony burst out, 'it's insulting!' and regretted it at once. He was itching to add 'Prohibition is *always* wrong.' So were others: but nobody dared.

The Observer scribbled: '9. Impulsive.'

'Unhappily,' said Number Four coolly, 'we are not discussing good wine at the Athenaeum, but raw spirit in the jungle. But I think there is something in what Number Ten says. The individual permit – they have it in parts of Canada too – '

Number Four was scoring heavily.

'But on what basis?' asked the chairman. 'Medical – or what?'

'Human rights,' drawled Number Eleven. '*Jus bibendi*.'

'Supply,' said Number Four, 'a rationed or controlled supply. Every man has his card – and so many bottles a month.'

'But suppose' came the husky voice of Jacaranda, 'a black man asks for a bottle – or a card?'

There was a short silence.

Anthony had an inspiration.

'I suppose' he said, 'he would have to bring a permit from his head-man: and if all the head-men were against it, he wouldn't get it.'

'Good,' said Cosmo.

'Hurray!' thought Anthony. 'I've scored a mark for Bass!'

He was right. '9. Artful compromise,' the Observer wrote.

But Number Four said heavily 'H'm. I think I see a few loopholes there.'

He got a good mark too.

Number Fifteen thought it time for him to come into action.

'I think we're getting somewhere,' he said. 'Of course, all this implies State control of the traffic, doesn't it? State purchase – State liquor stores. State shops. What do we think about that?'

They chattered on; and all scored marks except the tongue-tied Peach, and the young man Crawley, who was silent too. By the end of the fifteen minutes they had almost reached an agreed system of State control under which the whites could get all they wanted and the blacks very little. But Number Ten disliked the idea of State purchase and supply: and Number Four was still worrying about the lethal liquids the Bulus would concoct from wayside plants and old boots when Mr Egerton cried 'STOP!'

'That girl is strangely silent,' thought Doctor Maple. 'Can it be conscience?'

It was for the out-going chairman to nominate his successor. Number Fifteen could hardly do anything but nominate Number Nine – and he did.

'Cunning old coot!' thought Peach.

Anthony took the chair. He was now the only member of the Group who could see the invigilators, though, even to him, they were supposed to be like gods, invisible. He noticed at once that Doctor Maple was, as Peach had prettily put it, 'devouring the little body with his gelatinous eyes'.

At that moment in walked Mr ('Serious Door') Rackstraw, escorting Sir William Blant. They sat down quietly behind the Group, who dutifully ignored them, and between Mr Egerton and the Doctor.

'Well, Ladies and Gentlemen,' said Anthony, 'the question before us now is simple enough – but difficult. An American firm of mining engineers have asked the Government of the island – that is, *us* – for a twenty years' concession to survey and work the resources of *piturium* believed to exist in the north-west corner of the island. Now, having regard to the known interest of our great and beloved neighbour, Cambia, in these deposits, we must evidently approach this question with the utmost care and caution. It is of great import to the future of the island. But I hope you will not misunderstand me when I say that in my opinion – it can wait.'

The other chairman, Mr Egerton, sat up. The Observer's pencil hovered like a hawk over his pad. The young man had begun admirably: but what was this?

'There is' continued Anthony smoothly, 'a question affecting the members of this Group – this Group, not this Government – which, I think, deserves our prior attention.'

What was *this*? 'Number Nine,' said Mr Egerton, nicely, 'we never like to interrupt: but any personal complaint should be discussed privately with myself – or the Principal.'

Anthony gave him so charming a smile that Peach's heart fluttered like a bird in her breast.

'It's not *that* kind of personal question, Mr Egerton,' he said. 'Nothing to do with me. But it does affect a person – a member of our Group.' (Mr Egerton began to whisper to Sir William Blant.) 'And, though I know that on these occasions the Staff are' – another sweet smile – 'only spiritually present, as it were, I hope that, perhaps, on *this* occasion, the Staff may be willing to assist us.'

All this, of course, was hopelessly irregular, but Sir William whispered profoundly – everybody could hear him – 'Let him have his head,' and Mr Egerton said no more.

Sir William thought that this might be interesting. He had seen already Groups B and C at their normal business, and had had enough of it. This, he thought, sounded like someone raising a point of privilege, or making a personal explanation, before the debate of the day, in the House. You didn't know what to expect, and it might be fun.

The field clear, Number Nine charged ahead:

'Last night, in this very room, our late chairman, Number Fifteen saw – shall I say – a "certain phenomenon" – rather a disturbing phenomenon. It was seen by no other person – at least, no other person *confessed* to seeing it.'

He glanced at poor Mr Rackstraw – who dropped his eyes at once: and at Doctor Maple – who still stared disdainfully at him through the lower half of his glasses.

As for the rest, Anthony had never enjoyed such an audience. Nobody stirred. A million pins could have dropped, and no one would have noticed that metallic cataract. None of the invigilators made a note.

'Before I go on,' said Number Nine, 'it would perhaps be courteous – and convenient – if the Group turned their chairs and faced our respected Staff officers – and visitors.'

The Group, wondering but obedient, turned their chairs. A queer feeling filled the invigilators. This was all wrong. Instead of surveying loftily the backs of their defenceless victims, they were faced by seven keen young searching pairs of eyes. What *was* all this?

The relentless young chairman continued:

'May I begin with myself? I came into the Hall a little before twenty minutes to eight, to play – or *try* to play – ' (a disarming, modest, smile) ' – the organ. I certainly saw no – er – phenomenon – on that red sofa there.' He looked, and everyone looked, at the empty scarlet sofa. 'But, of course, the lights were low. I might have missed it. At about – about when was it, Number Fifteen?'

'About seven minutes to, I should say.'

'At about 19.53 Number Fifteen came in and saw the phenomenon. He has no doubt about it: and from his conduct in the chair just now – if we had no other reason – all, I am sure, would agree that he has his wits well about him.'

Number Fifteen made a slight bow of acknowledgement. Anthony glanced round the invigilators' ring, as if to challenge a contradiction. Sir William wore a faint smile, as if he was enjoying himself. The others did not.

'Now, it is true that when Number Fifteen came to me at the organ, just before 20.00 – or eight p.m. – there was no phenomenon on that sofa. That, however, by no means proves that it was never there. Engrossed in my musical efforts as I was – and making, I confess, a good deal of noise – I might – well, all sorts of things might have happened behind my back, unwitting, so to speak.'

He paused, to let the thing sink in.

'But because the phenomenon had gone, and had been seen by no one else, the word of Number Fifteen, I understand, has, at the highest levels, been doubted. Doubts have been cast, I believe, not only upon his credibility, but even upon his sobriety. Alternatively, I understand, it is thought that the – er – phenomenon may have been a somewhat unseemly practical joke. If that theory was correct, it could only have been the work of some candidate or candidates. You will understand now, Mr Egerton, perhaps, what I meant when I said that this, though a personal matter, was not a personal matter in the ordinary personal sense, if you see what I mean?' 'That,' he thought, 'was not a very good sentence.' But Mr Egerton nodded, almost benignly: and he went on, encouraged: 'It is a matter that affects not only Number Fifteen, but the whole body of candidates: and, as such, we are upset.'

Again, the grammar, he thought, had gone wrong somewhere. But the Group, by now, were so much moved by their chairman's honest eloquence that a low murmur of approval and indignation went round the ring. This unprecedented sound was like the rumble of distant tumbrils in the ears of the invigilators – or some of them. But Sir William was delighted. He saw himself telling this strange tale in the Smoking Room of the House of Commons.

'Now,' said Anthony, 'information has come my way that, *in fact* – ' he was pleased with that. In his early youth he had often been taken to the Law Courts by his Uncle, the King's Counsel: and had heard famous cross-examiners in action. That emphatic 'in fact' had stuck in his memory, two little words that, often, added nothing to the sentence but made it quite clear that the other fellow was a liar.

'...that, *in fact*, the phenomenon was seen by *others*, – I mean, besides Number Fifteen. And this' he said mildly, leaning forward, 'is where, perhaps, some of the Staff may be able to help us.'

Mr Rackstraw still stared at his knees. Doctor Maple still stared haughtily at Anthony: but 'the general effect', in Fantom's words, Anthony thought, was more yellow than before.

'Can you remember, Number Fifteen, what tune I was playing when you first saw the – phenomenon?'

'I know the tune – but I don't know its name,' said Number Fifteen. 'It was something like this. He hummed atrociously. 'DA – da – da – Da – da – da – DA – de-da-DA – DA...'

'Thank-you,' said Anthony, 'the old Russian National Anthem. Of course, the candidates, in the Candidates' Wing, could not hear much, I expect. But the Staff's quarters are immediately over the organ. I wonder whether any of the Staff heard me?'

'You blew me out of me bath,' said Sir William genially. Everybody laughed, and the tension was eased, at last.

'I wonder, Mr Rackstraw,' said Anthony gently, 'if you heard me playing – if I may call it that?'

Mr Rackstraw raised his eyes at last.

'Of course,' he said frankly.

'Any particular tune?'

Mr Rackstraw did not mind now. Truth was of the essence of him, and he had failed in truth, and he was ashamed of himself. Now he felt like a man who must have an operation – 'let's get it over'.

'Yes,' he said, 'I remember you were playing Handel's *Largo*.'

'Would that' said Anthony simply, 'be when you saw the body?'

'Yes,' said Mr Rackstraw.

Number Fifteen gave a gasp. Everybody looked at Mr Rackstraw. Sir William and Mr Egerton swivelled round in their chairs to look at him. Mr Rackstraw lowered his eyes no more, but met with a slight brave smile the young prosecutor's eyes. Nobody said a word.

'Thank-you, Sir,' said Anthony, at last. He was sorry for Mr Rackstraw. He thought 'I'm a toad. This is like hitting a baby.' But then he thought of the Admiral – and 'the bastards' – and Hambone Hall. He must not weaken. And there was larger game ahead.

'I wonder' he said sweetly, 'whether Doctor Maple heard me playing?'

'Heard you?' said the psychologist, with a harsh laugh. 'I agree with Sir William. You could have been heard at Land's End!'

This was the second laugh of the Group Discussion: but it was not a very hearty laugh.

'Any particular tune?' said Anthony mildly.

'Well, I heard several. The one I remember most – because you made such a hash of it – was *Annie Laurie*.'

'Annie Laurie?' said Anthony, reflecting. 'That's very interesting. That was the first tune I played – at about 19.40 – Where were you, may I ask, Doctor Maple, when you heard me playing *Annie Laurie*?'

'In my bedroom,' said the psychologist impatiently. He was getting rather tired of this impudent boy, and he could not think why Egerton did not put his foot down. Also, he had an idea that the delectable Number Eight was laughing at him. Anyhow, he was not going to be such a damned fool as Rackstraw.

Another fragment from the Bar stirred in Anthony's memory.

'I put it to you, Sir,' he said, rather stern now, 'that when you heard me playing *Annie Laurie* you were standing in the gallery, looking down at this Hall!'

'Nonsense!' But the witness was not quite so confident. What the Hell did this boy know – and how?

'And *that'* said the insufferable youth, 'was when you saw the body – about *ten* minutes before it was seen by Number Fifteen?'

This was too much. And, by God, now the young people were taking *notes* – about him – about the Staff! He turned to his chairman.

'Really, Mr Egerton, I cannot sit here and be bullied by one of our candidates.'

Mr Egerton, secretly, and strongly, agreed with him: but, after Rackstraw's surrender, he did not know what to think. And Sir William was still enjoying himself.

'It's all a little irregular, I agree, Doctor Maple. But why not think of it as a novel form of "exercise"? After all, it's a simple question: Did you see a – a – body, – or not?'

'Certainly not. I don't know what it's all about. I came down just before dinner and found the rumpus going. I remember' he said, with an ingratiating smile, 'seeing this young lady – Number Eight – talking to Number Nine as I came down the stairs. Is that correct?'

'Certainly,' said Peach, with a glance like a cobra's.

'Well, Number Nine,' said Mr Egerton, 'there you are. All this has been a most interesting diversion from our usual routine, and I congratulate you. But now, perhaps, we had better get back to business. Will you – ?'

'Certainly, Mr Egerton,' said Anthony, polite, but firm. 'But, I wonder if it would be possible to secure the attendance of Miss Slice. I should like to ask her a single question – or two questions.'

Mr Egerton was inclined to demur. But, he thought, we must show Sir William how reasonable we are. And he said, 'Very well, Number Nine. But two questions only.'

The Observer was sent to find Miss Slice.

'While we are waiting,' said Anthony kindly, 'shall we return to Nobona? I don't want to influence anyone unduly, but in view of the considerations mentioned already I do not *myself* think that we ought to grant this concession to the American firm till we have had more talk with dear old Cambia. I propose, therefore, that we politely put the Yanks off for another six months. Is that agreed?'

The Group, bewildered, but loyal, murmured 'Agreed!': and Number Nine got full marks from Sir William, at least.

Miss Slice came in.

'Thank-you so much, Miss Slice,' said Mr Egerton. 'This is somewhat unusual: but, as part of our exercise this morning, I have promised Number Nine that you will answer, as frankly as you can, a question – or two – that he would like to put to you. If, of course, the questions are of too intimate a character, we shall not expect you to reply.' Gay laughter, as intended: but not so gay as all that.

'Certainly, Mr Egerton,' said Miss Slice.

Anthony stood up. 'Miss Slice,' he said sternly, 'may I ask you exactly where you were when you heard me murdering *Annie Laurie* last night – and who you were with?'

'Certainly,' said Miss Slice, 'I was with Doctor Maple – in the gallery – up there.'

'And that was when you saw the body?'

'Yes.'

'Thank-you, Miss Slice.' Anthony sat down.

But Number Fifteen sprang to his feet, anger all over him.

'Mr Egerton, Sir, may I ask why none of this was said last *night?*'

'Order, order!' said Anthony, in mild, but dignified, rebuke. 'Number Fifteen, it is not for us to make such comments. Our only task was to establish the facts. I nominate as the next chairman Number Four. Thank-you, Ladies and Gentlemen.'

But Mr Egerton said: 'I think perhaps that the Group had better now adjourn. Thank-you.'

Sir William said, as they passed out: 'Keep an eye on that Number Nine. He's got his head screwed on where it should be.'

Number Fifteen came up and hotly grasped Anthony's hand, and worked his arm like a village pump.

'I never thought' said Peach, 'that I should see *you* two embracing madly. Did you *see* the Maple's face?'

CHAPTER XI

At the interview with the Principal, Mr Rackstraw offered his resignation. Sir Gilbert would not accept it. His deputy's weakness, he said, had been such as might have afflicted any man in similar circumstances, himself included. 'But why didn't you *tell* me?'

'I was so *ashamed* of myself And then – the Intake – I thought it would be so injurious from the standpoint of prestige.'

That was the sort of sentence Mr Rackstraw liked.

'You haven't done much good to our prestige, as it is,' said the Principal glumly. 'I don't know what sort of report Sir William is going to make about us.'

'I cannot too keenly express my regret.'

'Well, well, forget it, Rackstraw,' said the Principal, kindly. 'Of course, we're still no nearer to knowing what happened last night. You're sure that what you saw was a – female body?'

'I have never seen a female body,' said Mr Rackstraw. 'But certainly I should have said so. And, you'll remember, I didn't take a very good look.'

'Well, well.'

Doctor Maple, whatever he felt inside, did not seem to be ashamed of himself. He was unabashed and brazen.

'Principal, it was all part of a plan. There's something fishy going on, and I'm trying to get to the bottom of it.'

'Yes, but need you have lied? Not only did you lie in public, I gather, letting us all down. You – er – deceived even me. Only this morning – '

'I don't think I lied to you, Principal,' said the Doctor hotly.

'Well, you didn't tell me the truth, did you?'

'You were not very sympathetic, if I may say so, this morning. I'm a little sensitive, perhaps, but – '

'I'm sorry, I'm sure.'

'As for the Intake, I didn't want any of them to know. Deliberately.'

'Know what?'

'How much I had seen.'

'I don't follow. It might have been a murder. It was your duty to say what you saw.'

'It wasn't a murder.'

'How do you know?' The Principal did not think so either, but he was becoming a little impatient.

So was the Doctor. 'My dear Principal, I don't *know*. But I must remind you that I am a psychologist. Sometimes it's a help.'

'Of course, of course,' said the Principal, pacific. He knew that the last thing he must do was to question the superhuman powers of the 'psychies'. 'But what do you mean by "fishy"? What do you suspect – and whom?'

'That damned Number Nine, for one. I'll be even with that young man!'

The face looked uglier than usual, and the Principal was shocked.

'Vindictiveness won't get us anywhere,' he said. 'From all accounts he handled the matter very well. Anyhow, he was playing the organ. Why not Number Fifteen?'

'Perhaps. I'm going to do a little detective work, if I may.'

'Very well. But keep in touch. I don't want to be in the dark again. – How's Number Ten?'

'She did quite well on the Island. I was surprised.'

'There you are, you see. Your old Words. I never did think much of them.'

Doctor Maple departed with a slight snort.

The Principal wondered whether he should send for Miss Slice, who had also seen the body and done nothing about it. He decided not to bother. She would say that she was working with Maple. They were pretty 'thick', he believed.

He sighed. It was rather odd, he thought. Here were his staff, working like beavers to test the personal qualities of twenty-one young men and women. Here was he, worrying about the personal qualities of his staff.

He looked out at the daffodils. 'Quite naked,' he thought. Good Lord, that Maple man was putting ideas into his head!

Saturday was a full working-day. On Saturday evening any candidate could go off, if he pleased, till Sunday evening, and about half of the 'Intake' did.

Saturday afternoon was severe, it was thought, for a Saturday afternoon. They had another discussion on the Island ('Would you suggest importing labour to work the *piturium* deposits – and if so, how? from where? etc.'); a discussion on a General Topic, tossed into the Group without notice; and some of them did their Short Talks. It was a glorious warm Spring day, and they fretted like schoolboys 'kept in' during a cricket match.

But there was a startling change in the atmosphere (and all three Groups had the same experience). The candidates seemed, somehow, to be liberated. They were no longer afraid of their lofty inquisitors, now shown to be human and fallible. They even laughed openly at each other's little jokes, a thing that was rare in any Intake, partly from jealousy, partly from doubts about the propriety of laughter. The Staff, on the other hand, were subdued and gentle. Mr Egerton had always been polite; in giving his instructions now he was almost apologetic. Even the 'STOP' girl cried 'STOP!' in a milder tone, with a little upward interrogating lilt, as if she wanted to say 'I'm awfully sorry. If you'd really rather go on still, please do.' Doctor Maple came in for a few moments only, glared savagely at Anthony and went out again.

'We've got 'em on the run,' said Number Nine jubilantly, in the interval after the Island exercise. 'The morale of the Staff can practically be written off.'

'With one exception,' Peach said.

'The Maple?'

'Yes. Did you see him come in?'

'I did. He had a malignant gleam. He looked at me like a fanatical rattle-snake. That beast is by no means broken. In fact, I expect a counter-attack. Are you going home tonight?'

'No.'

'Nor am I. I have arranged for a gala Spring night, with the first nightingales and a Full Moon. Stand by for Night Operations.'

'Aye, aye, Sir.'

'And, who knows? a bit of love?'

'Oh, goody.'

The subject for General Discussion tossed shyly to the Group by Mr Egerton was 'Public Service and Private Life', an old favourite. 'On the highest intellectual level, please, Ladies and Gentlemen' – 'though that we shall have, I know,' he added – as no Chairman had ever added before.

Here Number Eleven began to score heavily: for marks went to the man of high academic quality who could prance about happily in the field of general concepts. The more practical and earthy fellow did not do so well.

Adrian Holt said that ideally any public servant should have no private life, for any private entanglements or interests must hamper his efforts for the public good. Plato, he thought, would have approved of the celibacy of statesmen. There was a significant connection between the private lives of the Emperors and the Decline and Fall of the Roman Empire. The Papacy was the perfect imperium. There were many modern examples.

Number Four said that statesmen so aloof from life as that would tend to make inhuman laws. The best ruler was one who was intimately acquainted with every corner of life. No bachelors should be allowed in Parliament.

Anthony said that Nelson had had a good deal of private life but had done pretty well. He got no marks at all.

Jacaranda said: 'But if there is no private life the world will come to an end.'

Number Eleven said flatly: 'I did not say everyone. I said the statesmen.'

'But how does the young man who falls in love know that he will be a statesman?'

'He should be dedicated to his calling at an early age, like the priesthood.'

Number Fifteen said: 'But even statesmen have to have mothers.'

Number Four grumbled: 'I don't like this exclusive priesthood idea. You'll get something like the House of Lords.'

'Not a bad model. The best of them *are* dedicated to public life from boyhood.'

'But they all have large families,' said Peach, daring an utterance at last.

'STOP!'

Peach blushed and looked delightful. Anthony applauded with a pat on her knee.

'Intellectual level low,' wrote the Observer.

'Number 11–5 marks. Number 13 still dumb.'

(Number Thirteen, the handsome Crawley, had not yet opened his mouth at any meeting.)

Nor did the Group (excepting Number Eleven) think they had done very well. But now, somehow, they did not mind so much.

The change in atmosphere and 'morale' was well illustrated by Anthony's 'Short Talk'. In his Interest Form, it may be remembered, he had indicated three topics on which he would be willing to talk – Stars, Sticklebacks, and Ceylon. Now the

'STOP' girl handed him a slip of paper on which was written 'PUBLIC HEALTH'. Some error in staff-work, no doubt; but he made no complaint. The mood of victory was strong in him: and, as he confessed later, he 'forgot about Bass'. He was given twenty-minutes' notice, and he took an old newspaper cutting from his note-case and studied it. Not only had he to prepare a speech, but to decide and declare what sort of audience he was supposed to be addressing.

This exercise was the most odious of all to most of the candidates, few of whom had ever made a speech of more than a sentence or two to an audience of more than one. Each was glad that the lot had fallen on the lively Number Nine: but they felt a sympathetic tremor when he rose.

He stood up, long, lean, stooping a little, pulling at his Navy tie, as anxious speakers do. He had never addressed anyone except the Lower Deck.

'Ladies and Gentlemen, my subject is "The Public Health". You are the Chancellor of the Exchequer and his advisers at the Treasury. I am Lord Arrowroot, President of the British Medical Association.'

Peach suppressed a gurgle with difficulty.

'I approach you today, Sir, on the subject of the high tax on whisky, which, in the opinion of my profession, is inimical to the nation's health. For very many years the medicinal qualities of this liquid have been recognized by doctors. The "hot toddy at bed-time" for the common cold or chill may be a layman's prescription: but it has the support of the profession.'

He paused for a reconnaissance. The faces of the Chairman and the Observer were blank, but not hostile. Faint smiles were beginning to flicker on the faces of the Group, excepting Jacaranda, who had no sense of humour, and Number Four, who disapproved of flippancy.

'These opinions' the speaker continued, 'have been strongly fortified by some recent experiments in the United States, reported in the *Journal of Nutrition*. The report is headed "Polyneuropathy delayed by Alcohol".'

He was not quite sure how to pronounce 'polyneuropathy': but he put an accent on the second 'o' and hoped for the best.

'The old theory, as, of course, you are aware, Mr Chancellor, was that a deficiency of vitamin B (B1) was present in the diets of alcoholic, polyneuritic patients. The assumption was that the metabolism of alcohol increased the need for thiamine – '

('What, I wonder, is "thiamine"?' he thought. 'But what matter?')

'And, there being no evidence to the contrary, alcohol was indicated as a more or less specific factor in producing the polyneuropathy noted in alcoholic patients. In other words, Sir, if you intook alcohol, you needed vitamin B, and if you did not intake vitamin B you suffered from polyneuropathy.'

He was pleased with 'intook': and Peach grinned happily.

'That was the theory. But certain scientists were not ready to accept it without evidence: so they carried out a series of experiments upon some unfortunate *rats*.'

His voice squeaked on 'rats', and three of the Group laughed, a thing unheard of in a Short Talk. The Observer whispered to the Chairman. Mr Egerton shrugged. The whole point of these tests was to assess a candidate's ease and fluency of expression: and, as to that, Number Nine was doing well. There was no rule against laughter, though it was unusual. Number Nine, himself, had a perfectly straight face. The choice of subject was another matter. But Mr Egerton himself was fond of a drop of Scotch, and could rarely afford one. He listened attentively.

'They shut up twelve pairs of rats in twelve cages, and fed them all on diet Number 461. That, I should explain perhaps – may I refer to my notes, Sir?'

Mr Egerton nodded. It was not usual: but this was not a usual Talk.

'That consists of "Leached and alcohol extracted casein 18 per cent; sucrose 73 per cent; cottonseed oil 3 per cent; cod liver oil 2 per cent; Osborne and Mendel salt mixture, 4 per cent – and a daily supplement of riboflavin, calcium pantothenate, pyridoxine, nicotinic acid and choline". Also, for the first forty-two days they added four milligrammes of thiamine – that is, vitamin B1 – to the daily vitamin supplement. They then cut off vitamin B1 entirely, and recorded the number of days from that day to the onset of complete neuropathy. – Is that clear?'

The Group goggled. Peach gurgled. The Observer thought he would call the bluff.

'Complete neuropathy?' he gently inquired. 'Could you, perhaps, develop that?'

'Thank God' thought Anthony, 'that was explained!' He glanced at his cutting, and continued:

'In complete neuropathy, Sir, the rat is *spastic*, and has an ataxic tonic convulsive seizure when dropped on its back from a height of three to five inches.'

'Thank-you,' said the Observer humbly.

'The first experiment was directed to the effect of whisky with isocaloric intake. One rat in each pair drank whisky *ad libitum*, and the other water *ad libitum*. The whisky, by the way, was a 100 proof commercial brand diluted with an equal volume of water. And, by the way, because of the calories supplied by the whisky the average intake of diet Number 461 for the rats receiving whisky was about 79 per cent of the amount of the rats getting water. In other words, Sir, the teetotal rats had to eat much more.'

At this, Number Fifteen gave a loud guffaw, and Peach gurgled freely.

'Now, Sir,' said Anthony, still with a straight and solemn face, 'may I direct your attention to the result of this experiment?

'In every case,' he said slowly, wagging a school-masterish finger at his audience, 'in every one of the twelve pairs of rats polyneuropathy first occurred *in the rat that drank water*.

'In the rat that drank water,' he said portentously: and now he seemed so solemn that nobody laughed. Mr Egerton was enthralled.

'There is more. The rat that had nearly all water suffered polyneuropathy first – in twenty days. The rat that had five parts whisky and one part water survived for fifty-five days. Of course, Sir, they all died in the end, because they were getting no vitamin B1. It is not suggested that whisky is a substitute for that.

'Now, Sir, may I pass to the second experiment – "The effect of whisky with equal food intake". Here, in eleven of the twelve pairs polyneuropathy first occurred in the rat drinking water. (The twelfth pair, I should explain, Sir, was discarded because one of the rats died from some other and irrelevant cause.) All the experiments had the same result.

'Finally, the rats were given a good feed of vitamin B1 as well as water – or whisky. And this showed that, as long as they had vitamin B1, it did not matter whether they drank water or whisky. None of the rats, Sir, on water or whisky, that received 15 milligrammes of thiamine chloride daily *showed any signs of polyneuropathy*.

'The grand total, Sir, is given as follows: "In paired feeding experiments, with a thiamine-deficient diet, fifty-four rats on water *without exception* developed neuropathy before the paired litter mates on alcohol or whisky."

'The report, Sir, concludes: "It is clear, from the results of the above experiments, that under these conditions alcohol and whisky *caused a delay in the onset of polyneuropathy*. No definite explanation of the mechanism of this delay is evident. But it is obvious that the ingestion of alcohol increases the thiamine requirement." '

Anthony put his cutting away, as a statesman tosses his notes aside before his peroration.

'Now, Mr Chancellor, to go back to the beginning, it cannot, I submit, be beneficial to the Public Health that this healing liquid, proved to be an active cause in the delay of the frightful conditions of polyneuropathy, proved to be harmless in the company of a sufficient intake of vitamin B1, should be taxed at the rate of 400 or 500 per cent of its true sale value. Sir, you and your colleagues have put this gift of the gods out of the reach of the poor and made it almost inaccessible to many of the well-to-do. Neuritis, polyneuritis, arthritis, fibrositis, and all the rheumatic enemies of the race are stalking the streets and fields of our land, and I and my colleagues, Sir, responsible, under the State, for the Nation's Health, are gravely concerned.'

The Group clapped warmly when he sat down, an event without precedent: but Mr Egerton smiled. Doctor Maple, who came in just before the end of the oration, stared as an aged Conservative peer might stare who found Karl Marx in his bed.

After tea Peach said: 'I say, the Maple wants to have a private word with me.'

'Your interview? We all have that.'

'No, this is unofficial, he said.'

'Did you feel that the fangs of passion were biting his vitals?'

'As a matter of fact, I did. He stuttered: he vibrated like a blancmange. I do believe he finds me rather a magnet.'

'But this is splendid. This is Victory!'

'It's revolting. I felt like a Christian slave.'

'It's good.'

Anthony reflected. 'I must go down to the Lodge. And you must come down with me as far as the Queen's Corner.'

'I was going to do my "mutual ranking" nonsense.'

'This is Operations.'

'Oh, goody!'

On the walk down they discussed the niceties of 'mutual ranking' – the two lists which every candidate had to make.

'Does one put oneself in these lousy lists?' said Anthony.

'Not in the weekend list, no, I suppose. But in the other, yes, I suppose. Reduce the stride, please.'

'Sorry. Then where does one put oneself?'

'I shall put myself bottom,' said Peach firmly. 'In the *most* tiny letters.'

'All very well. But where do I put Bass?'

'After your whisky speech I should put him top. I thought it was *radiant*.'

'Bless you,' he said, and gratefully pressed her arm. 'What muscles!'

'Sailing.'

'But if one puts oneself top, isn't that slightly like shooting a line?'

'If you put yourself too low, they'll say you have no self-what-is-it.'

'Tricky, isn't it? I shall put Bass about third.'

'Who top?'

'I think old Four.'

'Yes, he's practically doomed to be a Civil Servant. The grisly thing' said Peach, 'is the other list. I can't think of a single one of this lot I want to spend a weekend with. Can you?'

'I can think of one,' said Anthony, and took her hand.

'Only one?'

'Only one. And only a weekend.'

'Beast. Sure it's not two?'

'Positive.'

'Oh, goody! I've just thought of one myself.'

They walked on, hand in hand, the falling sun behind them throwing long shadows down the Spanish Garden.

Queen's Corner was at the far end of the Spanish Garden, before the avenue of limes began its stately march down to the lake. At that end of the Garden there was a glorious view over lake and valley to the far blue hills: but it faced East. Partly to keep the keen east winds from the Spanish Garden, partly because he was a little mad, the 9th Earl had created a monstrous Maze of clipped yew, a hundred yards wide, and fifty deep. It was no ordinary Maze. To give it a varied sky-line the Earl had set round it a guardian ring of giant yew-men and yew-monsters, huge figures like Buddhas with rotund yew-stomachs, armed men with spears, bears and enormous birds. Some of the monsters were inside the labyrinth, towering above the walls, and gave the visitor fits as he came round a corner.

In the time of the 11th Earl, the young Princess Clothilde (of Trier), staying at the Hall with her mother, had incautiously entered the Maze alone one winter afternoon. She lost herself. Darkness fell. It rained. She thought it unseemly for a royal person to scream, and feared her mother. Silent and distracted, she trudged up and down the dark and dripping alleys, shuddering away from the monsters. Search-parties with torches roamed the fields, and the lake. No one thought of the Maze. At last, bedraggled, almost demented, the Princess found her way out.

The 11th Earl had never been proud of the Maze: and, contrite now, he broke it up, or much of it. He kept the main battlements of yew against the invading east wind. He kept the great yew monsters and yew-men who stood majestic, like rocks of yew, in a sea of lawn. But among them he made many corners of calm. Wherever the sun and the wind might be, you could find a warm and sheltered crescent seat, protected by thick encircling walls of yew. Near the centre he built a little pavilion in marble, in the Moorish style. The floor of this was raised above the level of the walls of yew, so that it commanded the view of the valley. Here, many years later, when Queen Clothilde came to stay with him again, the 11th Earl gave a lordly supper-party, and the misadventure of her youth was laughingly recalled and forgiven. Thereafter, she spent many happy hours in one or other of the sunny crescent seats, looking over the valley, or sheltered in the heart of the Maze. She went home sadly, and, the following year, was assassinated. So the place was named after her. The 10th Earl had added electric light to the pavilion, and given a great dinner there, to celebrate the end of World War I.

'It's a fairly crazy spot,' said Anthony. Bits of the Maze remained: and, though you could hardly be lost altogether, it was easy to miss your way. You would plunge into a cool inviting walk, turn a corner, and find yourself at the end of a blind alley, where was a carved Spanish bird-bath, or a nymph in marble, alone in a dark green cell. But Anthony led the way surely through the jungle of yew, past the white stone vases, now gay with daffodils, and the green birds and beasts. They came out on the farther side, not far from the pavilion. 'Here' he said, 'is the real Queen's Corner. This was her favourite spot, they say – the Three-Cornered Hat.' Here was a three-sided island of yew, in each side a crescent seat guarded by wings of yew, and backed by a tall curved overhanging wall of yew, like a huge oyster-shell of green. Two sides had a view, and the other a glimpse of the valley, and one or other had the sun.

'On one of these commodious benches' said Anthony, 'you will have your private word with the Maple.'

'Why?'

'I shall be in the Pavilion with a square box we have at the Lodge. In the middle of this island, or what-not, there will be a microphone.'

'I say,' said Peach, 'isn't that a bit beastly?'

'The box is the box we use for recording the nightingale. He is just about due for song – especially on a night like this. That, over there, is his favourite tree.'

'Then why not put the mike over there?'

'Not enough wire. I have to plug in at the Pavilion.'

'I repeat,' said Peach, 'is there not a touch of the beastly about all this?'

'It has its unethical side, perhaps. But war, as I said before, is war. This beast is quite untamed and rampant. If we don't get a good grip somewhere he'll be off and away.'

'I see that. But I don't like it a bit.'

'Nor do I. I wish you'd known my brother George,' he said simply.

She knew that he meant that: and it moved her.

'Are you sure there's only one on your weekend list?' she said.

'Certain. Will you do it?'

'I'll try,' she said, and went back to the Hall.

Anthony came back up the hill, pushing a bicycle, with a square box on the carrier. Till after sundown he was busy at the Queen's Corner.

CHAPTER XII

It was Saturday night. Over a sherry in Fantom's pantry, Anthony considered gloomily the family finances. Even if the Evolution succeeded and the Civil Servants surrendered, how was the Admiral to keep up his estate?

Fantom said: 'I should have thought, milord, that the Admiral, with his head for figures, might get to windward of the Pools. It's the only way of turning an honest penny without it going to the perishing taxes.'

'The Football Pools? But football's over, Fantom!'

'I was thinking, milord, of the Parliament Pools. But, of course, they started while you were in China.'

'Oh, yes, I read about them. How do they work?'

'The dividends don't come up to the standard of the Football Pools, not as a rule, but some of the prizes would have bought the Hall. A cousin of mine, a barber, won £30,000 last year with Fifteen Divisions.'

'Good Lord! Fifteen Divisions?'

'Yes, milord, that's when they vote. You can bet on the number of speakers, on the number of divisions in a day, or a week, or the figures of the first Government majority, or the number of questions the perishers ask on any particular day. Then there's the Second Readings of Private Members' Bills, and the number of Members present in the Chamber at a given hour, or the number of Peers in the House of Lords, or the number of amendments accepted by the Government, and so on. Then there's the outside chances like the suspension of a

Member. I've been investing threepence in that chance for some weeks. No Member's been suspended yet – they're a gutless lot, milord: but it accumulates, you see, and one day I ought to get an old age pension. I used to go in for the Ten Bishops.'

'Ten Bishops?'

'Ten Bishops on parade together in the House of Lords, milord. As rare, I believe, milord, as a sky-pilot in a pub. Of course, a Divorce Bill might do it: but they don't come every day.'

'But, I say, don't the Parliament chaps object to all this?'

'They tried to raise a point of privilege, milord. But nothing was done, because of the educational effect, you see. They say there's more public interest in the Gas-Works than ever before.'

'Well, this is very interesting, Fantom. I'll speak to the Admiral. He might nobble ten of the Bishops.'

'It's a long chance, milord. I'd sooner see him on the Fifteen Divisions.'

It was Saturday night, Saturday night at Hambone Hall, true, but still Saturday night. Even those who were anxiously awaiting the ordeal of private 'interviews', and tricky essays in 'mutual ranking' and 'self-analysis', felt a lifting of the spirit. Besides, the Spring was singing in their bones and blood. The night was warm and lovely, a Summer night in Spring. The moon, nearly full, lit up the Spanish Garden and silvered all the statues under the northern wall. Huge shadows crept like the hands of giant clocks round trees and nymphs and ornamental urns. At dinner there had been much talk of the nightingale. The young folk were free. A few of the men walked down the drive and out through the great gate to the *Hope and Anchor* at Caraway. But those who could find a lady were drawn by silken irresistible threads to the Spanish Garden, across the stream into the moonlit walks of the wood, or down the long avenue of limes to the lake. There was enchantment in the air, strong sap in the trees, champagne in the blood; and even Sir William

Blant went out for a solitary stroll. The Principal had gone home for the night, and Sir William thought that Mr Rackstraw was a poor fish.

Peach saw Doctor Maple's amber glasses aimed at her across the Hall and nerved herself for duty. But Elinor Slice bore down upon him, and pressed his arm and said:

'Come out.' She had made a slight surrender to the Spring, and was in a rather kittenish outfit of pale blue, with a Peter Pan collar.

'Tally-ho!' said Anthony, and they went out too.

'I say, what a sterling evening.'

'First-rate,' said Anthony, and looked about him with an owner's pride and an exile's resentment.

Jacaranda saw him go with smouldering eyes, but consented to seek the nightingale with Number Fifteen. They did not like each other much. But who could walk alone in such a garden – under such a moon? Only Sir William – and Adrian Holt. Even he had thought of inviting Jacaranda, but she alarmed him: and he walked alone beside the statues, composing a Short Talk on Art and the People.

Ahead of all, most fittingly, walked Young, Secret, Frantic Love, pure, shy and miserable – Numbers 18 and 13, Lavinia Gable and the handsome boy, Tom Crawley. They walked down the south side of the Spanish Garden, in the shadows under the trellis of young green leaves. But there was a yard between them. Whenever they touched they tingled. Electric currents flowed between them, even in a crowded room. He thought there was a special scent about her, like the scent of no other human being, though in fact Lavinia carried no scent at all. She trembled when she thought of him, and the sound of his voice was like someone plucking at a stringed instrument all down her spine. But their love was holy. No dreams of the marriage-bed disturbed Lavinia – or even Tom. They had kissed but once, and then that amiable Number Nine had seen them. They were afraid of Love: they were still more afraid of their pastors and masters. Who could tell what fatal mischief would follow an indiscretion? Next time it might not be the amiable Number Nine. They had even kept their engagement a secret: for Lavinia had heard that marriage was frowned upon by the Foreign Service. So they walked slowly in the shadows, as close as angels, as far away as two ships in a convoy.

Far off on the other side Anthony and Peach marched swiftly past the statues – and Adrian Holt. 'Oh, look, the young lovers!' muttered Anthony. 'Oh, goody! Where?' 'Over there! Don't look! Thirteen and Eighteen.' 'I didn't know.' 'Never mind.' He led her on through the jungle of yew to the pavilion. The yewmen and monsters, bright silver one side, black and purple the other, threw fantastic shadows on the lawn.

'I'm *too* intimidated' said Peach, 'by all this *unnatural* vegetation.'

'S'sh!' Anthony looked warily into the shadows and then slipped up the marble steps into the pavilion.

They sat on the wooden floor, their backs against the low wall, so that they were screened from any wanderer in the jungle of yew. At Anthony's side was a square box.

'Mr Pye's 1952 model,' he whispered. 'A rather cunning piece of tape-work – thirty-five minutes a reel.' He put in a plug which connected the microphone at Queen's Corner, put a pair of ear-phones over his head, and pushed a switch. Two flat discs on the top of the box began to revolve, the cunning tape snaking from one to the other. There was a faint whirring. Soon Anthony grinned.

'I'm damned,' he whispered. 'It *is* the old nightingale!'

'Oh, goody! Let *me* – '

He picked up another pair of ear-phones and fitted them over the golden head. Together they listened to the absurd bird warbling and trilling softly – it seemed a long way away. He put his arm round her, and his hand on her breast. She liked this and made no complaint. Lavinia would have fainted: but, as someone has said, it takes all sorts to make a world. Peach's opinion still was that 'sex was fun', and not much else.

He kissed her. She gurgled. 'This is *utterly* the best view of the nightingale.'

They listened to Philomel again. The moon, nearly over the meridian now, was to their right, and lit a little of the pavilion floor. To his left, Anthony could see the tail of the Bear, and Arcturus, the orange star. Warm waves of fondness rolled over the young sailor. Peach, he thought, was dear and delicious. Another nightingale began to trill.

'That's Arcturus,' he whispered. Beauty and wonder commanded his soul.

'Is it?' she said. 'I say! this floor's a bit severe on the little bott.'

'Sorry. Sit on me.' She did.

The mournful music of the nightingales was silent: and some of the light seemed to go out of the moon. In the ear-phones a man's voice said, 'That's Arcturus.' (Peach giggled.)

'It's very bright,' said a girl's voice. 'Is it a planet?'

'No, it's a star. – Lavinia, darling?'

'Yes, Tom?'

'Thirteen and Eighteen,' Anthony whispered.

'Turn it off. We mustn't – '

But Anthony shook his head. And Peach listened still, her eyes twinkling in the moonlight.

'I've been thinking.'

'Yes, Tom? So have I.'

'How have you been doing, do you think?'

'In the exams? I think pretty well.'

Since the unfortunate affair with the melon, Lavinia's days had been surprisingly untroubled and serene. She had done the written work coolly and calmly, and had contributed a sensible sentence or two to the Group discussions.

'You think you'll get through?'

'I think I might, Tom. How have you done?'

'I don't think very well.'

'What did you write for "Mother"?'

'Mother – Children – Nursery – Electric trains.'

(Peach gurgled.)

'Oh, Tom, what's wrong with that? I think it's rather sweet.'

He did not want to tell her the truth, that he had done dismally in the Group discussions, that he had not a hope of getting through. Handsome Tom had been a fine young officer and won the Military Cross. Alone in charge of some far post in the Sudan he might be splendid. His decisions were swift, his orders clear: he could talk easily and simply to men in his command. But in a room, in a crowd of others, he was shy and silent.

'It's the Group,' he said unhappily. 'I think of things to say, but somehow I can't say them. I have tried, but always somebody else butts in.'

(Peach nodded vigorously: 'Just like me!')

'I don't think' said Lavinia, 'they're so keen on people who talk all the time.'

'I know.' And now it came out. 'But I haven't said a word. Not *one*.'

'Oh, dear.'

'Lavinia, darling?'

'Yes, Tom?'

(The soft sad voices! 'They're making me *cry*!' Peach whispered.)

'I was thinking – suppose you get through – and I don't?'

'Yes, Tom? But I'm sure you will.'

'I *know* I shan't. And suppose they send you to Brazil or somewhere – what are we going to do?'

'What will you do, Tom?'

'I shall have to go home, live with Dad, and learn to be a doctor. But it takes *years*.'

'Oh, Tom!' Lavinia sighed.

('I can't *bear* it,' whispered Peach.)

'Lavinia, darling?'

'Yes, Tom?'

'I suppose, if you do get through – and I don't – you'll have to go on with it?'

'What do you mean, Tom?'

'I mean – I might not go for a doctor. I might do something else – business, or something – and earn some money quickly. I mean – we might get married then. But, of course, if you're in Brazil – '

'Oh, Tom, I'm sorry. But I think I must go on – with all – this.'

'That means, I suppose, that you don't really love me – not as I love you.'

'Oh, Tom, you know I love you, so very much. But I must do something in the world besides – electric trains. You know – a career – for a bit.'

'I see,' said melancholy Tom. 'One can do both, of course.'

'I know. But how can *we*, Tom?'

That was true enough. If they both got through, Tom knew, things would be no better. For how could a junior man and wife insist on appointments to the same foreign station? Moreover, he would always be best in a jungle or desert – and she in a city office or embassy. Secretly, of course – he would never confess it – he had hoped that he would succeed and Lavinia fail. Then, somehow, he could have taken his bride to his place of duty. But now – now he was a failure, and all was over.

The two sad lovers stared silently across the floods of moonlight in the valley, thinking how cruel to young love was the public service.

('It's worse than nightingales,' Peach whispered. 'I *am* crying.' And she was.)

'I see now,' said Tom at last, 'I should never have asked you to marry me. It was mad. I'm sorry, Lavinia.'

'I'm not sorry, Tom. I'm very glad. But – '

'But what, darling?'

'Why don't we leave everything till we know – I mean, who gets through?'

'I know already. I know, at least, that I'm not the chap for you. You'll be in one place – I shall be in another. Darling, I think we'd better say good-bye.'

'Oh, *Tom! Now?*'

'Now, darling. Then I shan't be a worry to you any more. You'll pass. I'll go home.'

'Very well, Tom.'

'May I kiss you, Lavinia?'

'Yes, Tom.' They stood up. 'Do you love me, Tom?'

'I love you, Lavinia.'

'And I love you, Tom.'

'Good-bye, Lavinia.'

'Good-bye.'

They kissed under the moon, the kiss of cherubs, the kiss of gazelles, of lilies. But Sir William Blant, strolling out to see the view of the valley, saw the two young figures instead. He could not know, poor man, that he had seen the fond farewell embrace of the purest lovers to be found in all the surrounding counties: and, turning away, he said to himself, 'My God, what a place!'

The nightingales began to sing again.

'Get off. You're a lump.'

Peach returned to the floor and removed her ear-phones. The melancholy birds were too like the handsome Tom and his Lavinia.

'What a bitch!' she said.

'Do you think so?'

'Of course. What does it matter about her fatuous career? What will she ever be, anyway? I say, how filthy we were to listen!'

'I'm glad we did. And I wish all the blasted Inquisition had heard it too! Fancy a chap like that being turned down because he can't gabble in a Group!'

'You must help him,' she said.

'Me? How?'

'Draw him out – if we have another Group jaw. *Make* him talk. *I* know – he hasn't done his Short Talk yet. Make up a good one for him. Rehearse him in the morning.' Peach was eager.

'To make him talk,' said Anthony reflectively, 'we should have to make him tight.'

'Do that, then!'

'S'sh!'

Anthony's eyes shone like the eyes of a huntsman when the fox goes away and hounds are mute upon a perfect scent. Peach put on her ear-phones again. The nightingales were dumb.

'The Maple!'

'And the Hen!'

'You mean you love me?' said a male voice, in a lofty pitch.

'Oh, must you use these loose expressions? We're scientists, aren't we? Can't we talk in our own language?'

'Very well,' said the Doctor sulkily.

'It's just that I felt we had to assemble and clarify our reactions. That's why I brought you out.'

'Well?'

(Peach's eyes were goggling like the eyes of those elaborate fish in the aquarium at Honolulu.)

'Sometimes I feel you have a trend to the schizophrenic.'

'Yes?'

'Too true,' thought Doctor Maple grimly. 'Here am I, listening politely to this importunate female, for whom I once felt almost an affection: and all the time I am itching to be off after Number Eight, about whom – in my position – I have gone quite mad.'

'Yes?' he said. 'But aren't we all?'

'Oh, I don't mean the normal rational schizophrenic. That's to be expected, of course, in any male of the higher brain-groups. One moment he's on the Bench, the next he's in the bar.

A man who's *not* a schizophrenic on the vitalogical plane is simply a case of pituitary-deficiency.'

('Gosh!' gasped Peach, and gurgled loudly.)

'What worries me about *you'* the voice continued mercilessly, 'is that you seem to me to have a split *libido* – a duplicated id.'

(Peach lay back and rolled about on the floor.)

'That, I know, is only a clinical estimate. To clinch it, some careful field-work would be necessary. But the symptomatic factors are fairly numerous and notable. Only two weeks ago, I should have said you needed me. Our egos were a perfect blend. Our ids made rather a cosy pattern. On the psychocerebral level, of course, you needed me, you always will: and I should have said – Oh, let's face it! We're scientists – there was a *psychosomatic* urge – you needed my *body*. That, I know, can only be proved by controlled experiment: but that was my provisional diagnosis.'

('This is one way of making love,' said Anthony.)

' – You can't deny it, in the last two or three days, I'm sure – there's been a significant switch. Well, I won't say a switch: but the attitude's *ambivalent*. I had almost to use physical force to get you out here for our routine Saturday assessment. Now, I can't suppose that you've received any significant contra-stimuli from any of the current Intake – '

('Oh, no?' thought Doctor Maple, Anthony, and Peach in unison.)

' – and therefore I've wondered whether perhaps there's been some new psychotic development in my own system. I've been examining myself. I can find no trace of endocrine anomaly. The psychosexual reflexes seem to be operating normally – at all events, Heriot, in propinquity with you. Of course, our work here is bound to contain some factors of sublimation: but I compensate for that by nightly brooding exercises – '

'What do you brood about?' said the Doctor.

'You, Heriot,' said the lady simply.

(Peach put her handkerchief in her mouth, and gave a slight yelp, like an injured puppy.)

'Go on,' said the Doctor hoarsely.

'I deliberately release the dream-mechanism with you at the centre of some appropriate fantasy. This, I find, gives me considerable relief. It keeps the endocrines fully charged and offsets any tendency to over-sublimation.'

(For the first time, Anthony began to feel some sense of compassion for Doctor Maple.).

'Altogether, then,' Miss Slice surged on, 'so far as a subjective analysis can be relied on, I feel myself just the same cosy sort of cycloid I have always been, syntonic, extrovert, and fundamentally sound. There is, of course, in spite of all I've said, this small area of repression. But that could easily be corrected, Heriot,' she finished softly, 'by a little sex-therapy.'

There was a short silence. When he spoke at last, the Doctor sounded a little dazed.

'Thank-you, Elinor. Shall we run through some of the Intake now?'

Miss Slice sounded disappointed. 'You're sure, Heriot, you wouldn't like to give yourself a short analytical overhaul? It helps, you know. It helps a lot.'

'Not tonight, thank-you, Elinor.'

'Very well. Let us begin with your Group? What do you make of Number Fifteen?'

'A cycloid type, of course – short, stocky, thick-necked. And a typical hypomanic – overactive, restless, garrulous. Some signs of grandeur delusion. Ambitious, busy: but not much behind it.'

('Poor old Fifteen!' whispered Anthony.)

('Wait till they get to you!')

'I agree. Number Thirteen? I haven't heard him speak.'

'He doesn't. Clinically rather an interesting case. Typical schizoid in appearance, tall, athletic: but marked anomalies. Good Army record, but shy to the point of agoraphobia. Signs of anxiety neurosis. Sexual instinct, I should say, rudimentary. Word-Association brought nothing out at all. Possibly homosexual. Paper-work quite good. Might do well in a lonely outpost.'

'Number Four?'

'Phlegmatic cycloid. Stolid, bovine, unimaginative, but mature. Sex – nil. Third-class Civil Servant: and that's where he should stay.'

('The frightful thing is' Anthony whispered, 'that, so far, the bastard's been pretty well right.')

'Number Eleven?'

'That's the Oxford boy. Schizoid type, hyperaesthetic, with endocrine anomalies and a touch of the paranoid.'

('Gosh!' said Peach. 'What *will* they say about you?' He pinched her. 'You mouldy, underaesthetic schizoid!' she whispered sweetly.)

'Clever, brilliant now and then, but touchy, aloof and angular. Doesn't think he's properly appreciated. Practically asexual. Possibly homo. Make a first-class Civil Servant.'

('Gosh!')

'Number Nine?'

(Peach grinned wickedly, and kept her eyes on Anthony, who looked as embarrassed as the Guest of Honour at a Public Dinner, when his health is being proposed by a noted wit, and who knows what the wit will say next?)

('I'll bet you're a schizoid! Ten bob?' 'Done!')

'Number Nine?' The Doctor's face clouded. 'Rather difficult. Physically the perfect schizoid.'

('Ha, ha! Ten bob, please!')

'Tall, thin again, athletic, cool, reflective, dislikes showing emotion. On the other hand, has many marks of the syntonic cycloid and cheerful extrovert.'

('The bet' said Anthony, 'is evidently off.')

'Makes friends easily, laughs and talks. Good Navy record. Efficient, I should say; and business-like, when need be. Queer mixture. I can't quite place him.'

('The bet is off,' said Peach. Anthony bowed, and looked a little pleased with himself. After all, he had baffled the High Priest.)

'Sex?' Miss Slice inquired.

'Oh, masses of it. Super-charged,' said the Doctor viciously. (Peach spluttered happily, and Anthony smacked her.)

'He does his best' said the Doctor, 'to suppress it. Not a trace in his Words. But there it is.'

('You're blushing,' whispered Peach.)

('Damn you!' said the Viscount Anchor.)

'Self-expression good. But has an alcohol fixation. Always on the drink. Able executive, I dare say,' the Doctor concluded grimly, 'but I should *not* like to see a daughter of mine at work in the same room.'

(Peach lay back again, and rolled over, spluttering and hugging herself in a fit of mirth.)

'I think you may be right. Number Ten?'

(*'Jacaranda!'*)

'A bad type – Paranoid? Neurotic? A bit of both. Sullen, suspicious, dislikes authority. Some Polish blood, I believe. The odd thing is that her paper-work is by no means bad. As for sex – she oozes it. Her Word-Association was positively shocking. Nymphomanic, without a doubt, and not, I should say, much use to the public service.'

'Good.' And, indeed, Miss Slice was glad to hear her Doctor speak in such contemptuous terms of the sultry tropical beauty.

'Number Eight?'

(It was Anthony's turn to stare and grin, and Miss Meridew's to blush.)

'Cycloid, syntonic,' said the Doctor professionally: but, against his will, there had crept into his voice already a tenderer tone. Miss Slice looked sharply at him. Yes, there was now a softer expression on the face, like haze descending on a hard horizon.

'Another difficult one,' he went on. 'Extrovert, cheerful, gay, healthy. Written papers good enough. But in Group discussion a sort of aphasia, like Number Thirteen.'

'Sex?' inquired Miss Slice innocently.

The soft haze dispersed.

'Difficult, again. The Word-Associations were – disconcerting. But the Principal and I have a theory about them. As a matter of fact, the Principal has asked me to have a private word with her. I thought perhaps – some time tonight.' He turned and beamed upon her, a gentle, deprecating smile. In the round yellow mirrors of Doctor Maple's face Miss Slice saw all: nor did she need to be a psychologist for that.

'Heriot!' she said excitedly. 'But this is wonderful. We have found the missing factor. I won't have it that you're a cyclothymic even now – look at that long thin body! But something's out of gear – just a temporary psychosexual disrhythmia – and this girl can put the rhythm right again. It will not take long, I know. It's all a fantasy, and it will fade back into its place; but we mustn't repress it, must we? Go to her at once, Heriot – go and get well. And then, Heriot – come back to me.'

With a beautiful smile, half scientific faith, half Christian forgiveness, Miss Slice departed round a hedge of yew. Round the corner she almost collided with Sir William Blant. He apologized testily, and sheered off into the jungle.

'So, you see,' said Anthony, 'you'll be a public benefactor.'

'Mr Bass, I *can't* do it!'

'Please, Miss Meridew. The Evolution is in danger.'

'But I'm almost *sorry* for the rat.'

'The more sorry you are, the more glad you should be to comfort him – for ten minutes, or so.'

'You're a cold-blooded monster! – If you're not careful, I shan't come back!'

'Don't go too fast. I have to put another tape in.'

She put a little tongue out at him and flounced out of the pavilion.

'The gods' thought Doctor Maple, 'must be on my side,' for he had hardly left the Three-Cornered Hat when he beheld his target, walking alone among the fantastic yew-men.

'Good-evening, Doctor Maple,' she said very sweetly. 'Isn't it a magical evening?'

Doctor Maple spent so much time inquiring into the insides of men that he could not spare much for the surface beauties of Nature: but he agreed that the night was magical.

Side by side, they gazed at the valley and the stars.

'That's Arcturus,' said Peach, 'the orange one.'

'Is it?' breathed the Doctor, amazed that so much knowledge should be packed into that little head.

'You wanted to talk to me, Doctor? Shall we sit down?'

She led the way to the predestined seat, and they sat down, a yard apart. The Doctor found that he was trembling. Whether the right word was love or *libido*, Spring-fever or psychosexual disrhythmia, he did not know. But this young person had affected him more powerfully than anything in his experience.

'Have you heard the nightingales?' she said, in that sweet friendly voice, that reminded him somehow of honey.

'No.'

'Let's listen,' she said, and put her finger to her lips and looked bewitching.

They listened.

'This' she thought, 'will annoy Mr Bass.'

The nightingales performed obediently: and, the two humans listened like the devout at a religious ceremony. Anthony listened too, in his ear-phones, cursing slightly, as Peach had expected, while the precious tape ran through the machine, recording nothing but these ridiculous birds. She could not have said clearly why she was annoyed with Mr Bass and was willing to annoy him: but she was. Words like 'stool-pigeon' rambled angrily about her mind: but she had no notion what a stool-pigeon was. How many of us have?

'It's practically' she thought, 'like living on my immoral earnings.'

Peach looked at Arcturus. Doctor Maple looked at Peach. He said to himself: 'I am a member of the Senior Staff. This is a young candidate. It is disgraceful.' But it did not seem to matter. Disrhythmia and the Spring prevailed. He moved a little nearer.

'Number Eight?' he said at last, in a gentle modest voice which would have startled his colleagues, accustomed to harsh assertion.

'Don't call me that *tonight*, Doctor Maple. My name is Peach.'

'Peach.' Wonderful name! How it fitted her – the bloom, the colouring, the soft surface – and, he was sure, in spite of everything, the sweet inside.

'I was rather worried about your Word-Associations. Would you like to tell me about them?'

She looked at him with wide innocent eyes. 'Oh, that? It was just my little joke, Doctor.'

'I'm very glad – Peach.'

'Glad, Doctor?' How surprising!

'I was afraid, perhaps, there might be some fixation.'

'Fixation? What ever's that?'

'Never mind now.'

'Was it naughty of me, Doctor?'

'It was a little naughty. But don't be alarmed. All this is unofficial.'

'Still, if it was *too* naughty, Doctor, I ought to apologize.'

'Don't call me "Doctor" – tonight,' he said gently. 'My name's Heriot.'

Peach giggled. (Anthony guffawed.)

'I'm sorry. But what a funny sort of name!'

'It is, rather. But please don't laugh at me, Peach. I'm very serious – about you.'

Tentative, terrified indeed, he moved a hand round her waist. But he was still at an inconvenient range, and the hand could not get farther than the hip.

Peach stiffened. 'This is rather ill-making,' she thought. It was odd how the touch of one hand could be electric and another like the touch of a slug. But this sort of thing, after all, was the whole point of the Operation, and she did not stir or speak.

'I'd like to hear you call me Heriot,' said the mind-man hoarsely. 'Just once. It's silly, perhaps, but – '

Peach turned her head and regarded him solemnly. 'He looks' she thought, 'like a sentimental cod.' But then her charitable little soul remarked: 'That's not quite fair.' Certainly the pale, anaemic face was new and different. The Principal, Miss Slice, Fantom, would hardly have recognized it. But the change was an improvement. Instead of the cold, suspicious, smug, self-contented expression they knew so well, the face wore a glow, the glow of worship. It is no small thing for any girl to be the cause of such a glow, even if the fires that feed it be fleshly, improper, and inimical to the traditions of the Civil Service. The sense of power is seldom unwelcome, whatever dangers may be ahead. Peach looked solemnly at her lover, and thought again that she was almost sorry for him.

'Thank-you – Heriot,' she said.

The Doctor reduced the range.

Sir William Blant, still on his lonely prowl, heard queer sounds coming from that absurd pavilion. He went up the steps and looked over the wall. In the moonlight he saw a young man sitting on the floor with a box beside him and those ear-phone things over his head. He recognized him as the young man who had handled that body-business so capably. Fishy affair that: it was nothing to do with him, perhaps, but he didn't know what to make of it. But what was the matter with the sensible young man? He wore a frown of intense concentration: but now and then he opened his mouth and laughed; then there would be an angry scowl. Sir William was more and more inclining to the view that he had come to the wrong mansion and was in a madhouse: and here, it seemed, was a little more evidence.

Anthony looked up and saw Sir William with dismay. As he expressed it later: 'If Lot's wife had been salted in a sitting-position she would have been an *exact* sister-ship to the Viscount Anchor. But I went to action-stations, pointed to the machine – and hissed like a stage burglar: *"Recording the nightingale."* '

'The nightingale?' thought Sir William. 'This is better.' Though why the song of that bird should provoke the young man to such queer grimaces he could not tell.

'Could I listen?' he whispered loudly.

'Again' Anthony said later, 'the young mind moved like a rocket. This might be the best end to the whole Evolution. It seemed pretty heaven-sent.'

So he picked up the other pair of head-phones and with them beckoned to Sir William. Sir William knelt and adjusted them eagerly. Never, to his knowledge, had he heard the nightingale.

Immediately he heard a sweet voice say:

'You mustn't put your hand on my bosoms.'

As the first utterance of a nightingale, Anthony would have readily admitted, this was enough to startle any man: and he thought that Fate, as usual, had failed to time things well. But his hope was that Sir William, who seemed a human sort of chap, would be interested, and hear some more. If only the girl would say 'Heriot' once or twice, or even 'Doctor', with special reference to bosoms, or worse, the Evolution was almost complete, the stag was at bay, the Civil Servants were out, the Admiral back on his 'bridge'. All the anxious planning and subterfuge would be over, – though, of course, he would still have to do his best for Bass. It was like the end of some great cricket-match when 70 runs are still required and the last man comes in, a mere bowler who can hardly carry a bat the right way up. For the attacking side the thing is done, the match is in the bag. They crowd like hungry confident vultures round the doomed and dying man. One tiny flick, one infinitesimal error, is all that is needed. And then, damn it, he stays in, and the other fellow gets the runs.

For the workings of rational Man are as unpredictable as those of crazy Fate. Sir William, when he heard the nightingale's remark, made a sound like the snort of an apprehensive horse, tore the ear-phones from his bald pink dome, and flung them to the floor.

'My God, it *is* a mad-house!' he exclaimed. He stood up, dusted his knees, and glared angrily at Anthony.

'As for you, young man – !'

It was in his mind to rebuke the young man for listening to such a nightingale. But he remembered that the candidates were supposed to be free and unmolested in their spare time, he had no official position, and perhaps it was nothing to do with him. And, for all he knew, it was some sort of private theatricals. He said 'Good-night', and stamped out.

Anthony sighed. The Evolution was still on his hands. And he thought: 'Not, perhaps, a very good mark for Stanley Bass.'

The small snake of magnetized paper whirred softly round and round: and he resumed his listening.

Peach had put in the nightingale's remark for Anthony's benefit. He was not, she reasoned acutely, equipped with television: and the kind of evidence he wanted must be in words. She was not so sorry for the Doctor now: he had really behaved very badly – too fast, too clumsily and rudely. But now he took his hand away as if it had been stung by a wasp; and she said:

'The little waist is approachable, Heriot – but *not* bosoms.'

'Thank-you so much.'

Anthony, hearing the grateful voice, and imagining the readjustment, scowled. He was beginning to be fiercely jealous of the Doctor. He much regretted that he had put Peach into the Plan. It should have been Jacaranda. She might have bitten the brute.

The Doctor said, much easier in tone, 'Of course, my dear,' ('My *dear*!' muttered Anthony) 'your Short Stories were even naughtier.'

'Were they, Heriot? But it was all such a rush. What did I say?'

'You don't seem to think very much' said the Doctor, almost jovial now, 'of what you call the "trick-cyclists".'

'Well, I don't think I do. They are rather rancid, don't you think?'

'Oh, come – '

'You're not a trick-cyclist, are you?' said the innocent child.

'Well, I used to do that kind of work. Psychiatry is perhaps the word you mean. Psychotherapy is better.'

'Oh, dear. I am sorry.'

'You mustn't be too hard on us. We do discover things the other fellows can't. We get under the skin.'

'Like ticks,' said Peach impolitely. 'Oh, Heriot, I didn't mean that. Do forgive me.'

'That's all right, my dear.' He could suffer almost any insult now from this adorable creature.

She asked anxiously: 'But will my Words and Stories let me down, do you think – in the exam?'

'They might have. But, after our little talk, I don't think you need worry.' He pressed her arm, comfortingly.

'O Lord,' she thought, 'this is the end. Now I shall pass.'

'I say,' she said, 'how would you like somebody to get under your skin?'

'I shouldn't mind. As a matter of fact, we often analyse each other.'

'What about hands on young girls' bosoms?'

'A perfectly healthy psychosexual instinct.'

'Golly!'

'Besides – '

'Yes?'

'I love you, Peach.'

'Gosh!' she thought, but did not say a word.

'I've been mad about you, ever since I saw you the first evening. I thought I was. Now I know.'

'But you don't mean – you'd like to marry me?'

'Yes.'

'Where *are* we getting?' Peach thought helplessly. She wanted to shout into the microphone 'Mr Bass, what does A do now?'

'Is there anyone else?' the hoarse voice whispered.

'Not particularly.'

'I'm glad. I thought perhaps that Number Nine – '

'Number Nine!' Peach gurgled scornfully. At least she would punish Mr Bass for putting her in this hole. 'He covets me, I dare say: but what a hope!'

The Doctor was delighted. 'A bit conceited, isn't he?'

'Conceited? Nelson and Napoleon were country mice compared with him. His head's so swelled, you wonder the bones hold together.'

'Does he make love to you?'

'He tries. But I wear barbed wire when he's about.'

'This is wonderful,' thought the Doctor. 'There's no barbed wire for me.'

Suddenly Peach thought, 'Oh, dear, I may be damaging Stanley Bass.'

'Mind you, that's only a girl's-eye-view. There's no doubt he's wildly clever, and *exactly* the type you want.'

('Thank-you,' said Anthony, licking his wounds.)

'That remains to be seen,' said the Doctor darkly.

'I say, we ought to go in, shouldn't we?' All the tape in Caraway must be finished now, and she was getting into far too much of a muddle. 'I'm forgiven, am I, poor suffering trick-cyclist?' she said, with a radiant smile.

'Of course, my dear girl. But you haven't – you haven't given me an answer yet.'

'About – ?'

'About marrying the trick-cyclist?'

'But you can't be serious? Little me?'

'I am.'

'Are you sure it's not an endocrine anomaly?'

'What' said the Doctor, staggered, 'do you know about endocrine anomalies?'

Oh, dear, she had put another foot wrong.

'Not a thing. But I couldn't marry anyone.' Lavinia Gable opportunely popped into her mind and gave her a brilliant notion.

'You see, there's my *career*. If I get through they may send me anywhere.'

'*If*,' said the Doctor.

'Oh, goody!' thought Peach. 'Now I shan't pass after all.'

'Even if I don't pass,' she said, 'I want to go out in the world and do things' – she waved her arm across the wide open spaces of the valley – 'before I lapse into matrimony.'

'Well, will you think about it?'

'I'll think, of course. But it's *too* unlikely. I hardly know you by sight, Doctor.'

'Heriot.'

'Heriot. – And on Monday I walk out of your life.'

'No, no,' he said quietly, 'I shall follow you about the world.'

'I am mad,' he thought, 'I must be mad.'

'Gosh!' she thought, 'what won't I do to Number Nine!'

'Peach?'

'Yes, Heriot?' He seemed pathetic again.

'Will you give me a kiss?'

'Yes, Heriot.' Now, she thought, Number Nine shall suffer. They kissed. She did not like it: it was like kissing a snail, she thought. But she said, for Anthony's benefit, 'And I'll give you another!' This she made as brief, but as loud, as possible. 'And another! and another! and *another!* And I wish that Number Nine could see us!'

Ten times she kissed the astonished man, each time swiftly, with an emphatic sound that alarmed the Doctor, and infuriated Anthony, who had already got all the evidence he wanted.

Sir William Blant, drawn back by some fatal fascination to the Queen's Corner, heard far off across the monstrous yew-men the smack of these noisy embraces. He shook his white, pink head, turned about, and, repeating himself, said:

'My God, what a place!'

The Doctor, unaware that any ear had heard those brief but blissful salutes, stood breathless, dazed, but delighted.

Peach, a little surprised to find that she had enjoyed the outrageous performance too, said to herself that she was *not* going back to Mr Bass.

'We must go in,' she said. 'I say, *have* you seen Leda and the Swan?'

'No.'

'Come on – I'll show you.'

The psychologist followed meekly, thinking that perhaps he had something still to learn about the psychology of golden girls.

Anthony, as Sir William had done, dashed his ear-phones to the floor.

CHAPTER XIII

Love, that night of Spring, stalked the Spanish Garden in various guises, sacred, silly, and profane.

Number Fifteen (Captain Cosmo Lennox-Edwardes) and Number Ten (Miss J Daly) came out later than the others. They had sat in the Bar and had coffee and a brandy. Indeed, since it was Saturday night, the Captain, a frugal, temperate man, had ordered a second brandy. One brandy (after some red wine at dinner and some gin before) was quite enough for him. When at last they walked out into the balmy air he felt unusually free from care, and full of force. He could have instructed a Field-Marshal in the Principles of Battle, or pushed over a motor-'bus, if anyone had required it. He had begun by thinking that Jacaranda was rather heavy work. Indeed, she was glum tonight. She found that she had warm fond feelings for Number Nine; and well understood why her sister Olga had fallen. She was hotly jealous of the fluffy little blonde, Number Eight: but she no longer wanted to ruin Stanley Bass, and was sorry for what she had done to him. At the best, Jacaranda would not have been the perfect companion for Number Fifteen. He was accustomed to conversation that ran on smoothly, like a river or road, from one point to the next. Jacaranda's talk – perhaps it was the Polish blood – darted here and there, inexplicably, like a swallow in pursuit of gnats. When he said 'That's a nice dress you've got on,' she did not say, shyly, as she should, 'Do you like it?' She stared at the wall over his head and said with venom: 'I *hate* that picture.' When he said 'Have you done your Short Talk yet?' she said, broodingly, 'The food in this place is *uneatable*.' When he said 'It's a fine evening,' she muttered angrily 'What does it matter?'

Jacaranda thought that Number Fifteen was a great bore. But there was a hunger in her heart and he was the only man in range. Number Fifteen thought that Number Ten was a little mad: but after the second brandy he didn't mind, and out they went. Certainly she was a fine woman to be walking out with on a warm Spring evening. She was a head taller than he, and carried herself like a Princess. There was no 'dressing' at the Hall, and no one else was so near to evening-dress that night. Over her shoulders she wore a yellow silk Spanish shawl. (Peach had thought her 'overdressed'.) Her long black hair, in sinuous coils, shone in the moonlight like a well-kept horse. He wondered if she could sit on it, a thing, he understood, it was important to be able to do. He wished he could hug her, and wondered if it would be safe.

He explained with lordly sweeps of the hand what he would do if he owned the estate – 'cut down all that yew-stuff and give a vista of the hills'. She said savagely 'All these statues are vulgar and bourgeois.' Number Fifteen could not have told a bourgeois statue from one that was not; so he rashly said again that it was a jolly fine evening. She stopped and stamped one foot on the gravel path. 'This is three times you have told me it is a nice evening. I cannot endure it!' She marched on. 'I'm awfully sorry,' he said. She said, still suffering: 'In Russia they do not talk always of the weather. Sometimes there is snow – sometimes there is not. It is all the same.'

'I say, are you a Russian?'

'My mother was a Pole. But I like the Russians.'

'Then why on earth are you here?'

'My father was a British Consul – Murmansk, Gdynia, Dubrovnik; everywhere. I am a British subject like you. What is that star?' she said, with angry eyes on Arcturus.

'Venus, I expect.' Venus, was, in fact, to the South-West, sinking. But the poor Pongo knew no better.

'It is too yellow,' she said. 'I do not like yellow.'

'But you're wearing yellow.'

'That is different. I did not want to look well tonight.'

He gave up.

So she liked the Russians, he thought. The man of action, the good soldier, bubbled up at once in Number Fifteen. What was she doing here? Russia was defeated, in the dust. Young Nicolas Kerensky, of the Middle Way, was at the top. Stalin was dead, and the other leaders were at the School of Citizenship at Ashbridge learning the blessings of true Parliamentary democracy. But there were bound to be some of the Old Gang who were nursing revenge – and planting spies in good time. There would be nothing very surprising in a Russian spy floating into the Foreign Office through the usual channels. In the old days, when the Atom Bomb had been thought important, the Atom Research Station had been thickly peopled with Russians and their friends. Perhaps there was here something even more subtle. The Russian bureaucracy was notoriously cumbrous and ineffective. The British Civil Service, it was thought by many, had done even more for Victory than the fighting Forces. A study of the Civil Service might be as useful as facts about military training. Perhaps the spy was after the secrets of Hambone Hall, the great incubator of the governing class. Perhaps this popsie popped spare copies of the examination papers, the test Words, into her shapely bosom. Perhaps, in a month or two, young Russians, hiding in caves, would be asked to write down their reaction to such words as 'Mother' and 'Steep'. Number Fifteen had not a strong sense of humour; but at the thought he smiled wanly under the moon.

What was he to do? Instinct, training, urged him to prompt action, as they had when he saw the Body in the Hall. That experience had damped him a little. Should he report his suspicions to the Principal? The Principal had not encouraged him before. Perhaps he should wait for stronger evidence. Anyhow, his suspicion was a good excuse – a good reason – to 'get next to her', as the Americans said. Somehow he must soften the wild girl's heart, and secure her confidence.

They had passed in silence the lonely Number Eleven (the scholar Adrian), who was gazing in profound thought at a nude marble figure with a broken nose and wondering who it was. At the border of the Forest of Yew Number Fifteen stopped and said earnestly: 'I say, I do apologize. Will you forgive me?' though what he was apologizing for he could not have said.

The incalculable creature smiled suddenly upon him, a lovely smile: the glorious eyes were tender and glowing: she took both his hands and clasped them; her hot-blood system was in action at once, and she said: 'But of *course* I forgive you. It is I who am so silly and cross.'

This is more like it, he thought. Without a word, without premeditation, as if beckoned and bewitched by Pan, they walked into one of the remnants of the Maze, a long, dark, twisting lane of yew, at the end of which they came upon a blank wall and a bird-bath, half-full of dirty water and dead leaves. Still without a word, Jacaranda turned at once and, back to the bird-bath, embraced her prey. The Captain counted himself a strong fellow, but those long enveloping arms made him feel like the helpless victim of a boa-constrictor. Her kisses lashed, and splashed, and staggered him like sudden spray coming over the foc'sle head. 'Well,' he thought, so far as he could think at all, 'no nonsense here.' No 'May I?' 's or 'will you?' 's, no tentative hand on waist or knee. Bang! – you were in action! He liked it so. He met the attack with certain rough military intimacies which had better not be described. At last, whether in anger or affection he could not tell, nor did he care, the frantic creature savagely bit him, as she had bitten the young lord, and in about the same place. The effect was much the same – but worse. Number Fifteen stepped back, beside himself with rage and pain, and gave the tempestuous lady a stinging slap on the cheek.

She uttered a small yelp and dropped her head defensively, fearing another blow. A piece of blue paper peeped from her bosom. 'Documents!' thought Number Fifteen. He plucked out the paper and marched away down the alley, feeling no gentleman but an effective patriot.

Jacaranda, alone with the bird-bath, cried bitterly, holding her poor face. Oh, why were men so stupid and cruel? Why did they resent her tender bites, the extreme expression of her love and rapture?

Anthony, on his way back from the pavilion, was well content with the night's work, though not with Peach, who had, he thought, behaved barbarously. He heard the small yelp and the sound of weeping. Peach, the little fool, had probably gone too far with her infamous Doctor. With some difficulty he found the entrance to the right alley and strode along it in alarm. It was a shock to find the tough Jacaranda in tears. She came towards him wailing, 'Oh, Stanley Bass! He hit me!' Warily he sidestepped and passed her, but this was a mistake, for now she was between him and the only way out. She threw herself on, or rather at, his breast. He stepped back, his legs against the birdbath, and fended her off gently, a hand against each shoulder, holding away those terrible teeth.

'Oh, Stanley Bass! He hit me – he hit me!' she moaned.

'Who hit you, Jacaranda?'

'I don't remember – his number. That thick one. I hate him.'

'Number Fifteen?' Anthony thought. 'I bet you bit him,' he said.

The tears had stopped.

'I expect I did,' she said sadly. 'I can't help it. But why are they so *cruel* to me?'

'I like that,' said Anthony to himself.

'I hate him,' she said. She looked at him, straightly, and the hunger came back to her eyes. 'But you, Stanley Bass,' she purred, 'I *like* you – I like you very much.'

'No, no!' he muttered, in terror. 'For God's sake don't!'

'I have forgiven you' she cooed, 'about my poor sister Olga. Kiss me, Stanley Bass.'

'No, no, I mustn't.'

'This' he thought, 'is the most extraordinary situation. Here is the most seductive female, it may be, for hundreds of miles, inviting me to embrace her. And here am I resisting, and trying, politely, to push her away!'

'You *must*, Stanley Bass.'

'No, no, you'll bite me,'

'I will not bite you. I promise.'

'You will. You can't help it. You said so.'

'I will not bite you very much. Stanley Bass, I love you. Kiss me.

'No, no.'

'If you do not kiss me, Stanley Bass, I will bite off your ear! I will bite you all over!'

As he afterwards described the scene, 'She surged upon me.' He backed like a boxer 'riding his punches', and suddenly he found himself sitting in the bird-bath.

The water was cold; the posture was undignified. But – worse than all that – he could not get out. He struggled, but Jacaranda was upon him. He was alone and defenceless with the human jaguar. Just before he went whirling down in the cataract of her embrace, he had time to think: 'This, at least, will teach me not to impersonate anyone in the public interest.'

Fate, for once, did a good piece of timing. After they had inspected Leda and the Swan (rather dim in the dusky alcove which the moon had left) Doctor Maple and Peach discreetly said Good-night, and they headed for the Hall by different ways. But Peach heard, behind her, a voice like Anthony's in the jungle of yew. She also heard, she thought – and this sent sparks through her – the voice of a woman. She turned back. She felt a bit beastly: but, after all, Mr Bass had been a bit beastly to her (how, she could not have explained very clearly). Like Anthony, she found, at last, the entrance to the alley and stole along it between the walls of yew. The voices were louder. It sounded like 'a scene'. She crept round a corner and saw in the dim light the man whom she loved (and now she realized that she loved him very much) in a close embrace with that luscious, repulsive creature, with a 10 on her back. A maid of 1855, perhaps (and let us not be too sure about this), would have swooned at once, or tip-toed softly away, gone into a decline, and perished without a cross word to anyone. But Peach Meridew belonged to 1955: and her small breast heaved with anger and the urge to action. She remembered what Anthony had told her about his first encounter with Number Ten. It might be that he was more kissed against than kissing. Whatever the facts, she hated violently this interloping female with the lustrous coils of rich, black hair. She darted forward a few paces and clutched the rich black hair, and gave it a sharp malignant tug.

And it all came off.

It all came off – all the lustrous coils of rich black hair. They left behind them a rather small head thatched rather thinly with black but unattractive hair. Peach gave a shake to what she had in her hand, and the coils unfolded, so that she now held something like a long mane of hairy seaweed, with a light but solid something at the end of it.

Peach gave a little whoop of triumph, turned, and darted away down the alley. Jacaranda yelped, abandoned Anthony, and galloped after her.

The Viscount Anchor, to his great relief, was alone; but in the bird-bath.

Sir William Blant was walking alone on the north side of the Garden. The moon was over the meridian, and all the shadows thrown by trees and urns and statues on the lawn pointed at an exact right-angle to the wall by which he walked. He noted this, and it pleased him, though he was not sure how it was done. He was not there to 'snoop'. He was enchanted by the night, by the moon, by the stars, by the camellia blooms, by the Spring and the spacious Garden. He was excited by the view over the valley from the end of the Garden beyond the Queen's Corner. But whenever he went that way he saw or heard some frightful thing: and, not wishing to snoop, he was keeping away from the dangerous area. But he was worried, nevertheless. He had to make a report – confidential, yes, but still a report. The taxpayers' money was being spent in this place. He was no kill-joy: he had had some fun himself. These young folk were free and unofficial now. The examiners and psychologists and so forth could be trusted to find out what they were worth in office hours. All the same… It all came back to that old question he had heard discussed in one of the Groups the day before – 'Public Service and Private Life'. He didn't quite know what was the answer.

Then, in the moonlight, to his right, he saw, or thought he saw, two nymphs, like the Cloud-Maidens, scudding westward across the lawn. The one ahead was small, with golden hair. She sped with small swift steps, like a gazelle. She flourished above her head, as she ran, something that looked like a horse's tail, and she made in a small voice such sounds as huntsmen make while they pursue their prey. The nymph behind her was taller and moved like a leopard with long and graceful leaps. From her lips there came – or seemed to come – hoarse cries and words of abuse that were clearly incompatible (*a*) with a warm Spring evening and (*b*) with any institution provided by the taxpayers. Sir William shut his eyes and put his fingers in his ears. 'It can't be true,' he moaned. 'I must go to bed.'

He turned on his heel. He saw, or thought he saw, the second nymph disappear at the west end of the Spanish Garden. He winced, but marched ahead, alone at last. Then he heard, or thought he heard, a male voice cry softly 'Help'. He halted. At least, it was a male.

No one who has never found himself sitting in an ornamental bird-bath, half-full of water, and exactly fitted by Fate to the dimensions of his iliac-sacral and lower spinal regions, can fully understand the Viscount Anchor's distress. The bird-bath was narrow and absurdly deep (for what ordinary birds would wish to dive so far beneath the surface?). Anthony had sunk so far that his thighs were almost parallel to his chest; and, try as he would, he could not get out. He put his hands on the sides of the bath and thrust: but he was so low that he had no leverage. The water sucked and gurgled about him, but did not much assist him, he thought, and was damnably cold. He was like a large cork in a small bottle, and what was needed was one of those patent corkscrews: even an ordinary corkscrew might do. A helpful pull from almost anyone and he would be out.

He was reluctant to cry for help. For one thing, he did not think that he looked at his best; and he did not like the notion of any casual passer-by – Number Fifteen, for example – finding him in his present posture. For another, he did not wish to do anything that might draw Jacaranda back to the bosom of a defenceless sailor. Half-drowned by her embrace, he had seen nothing of the rape of Jacaranda's locks. He did not even know that Peach had been about. But Peach was his principal hope. Surely she would not desert him? Surely, having got rid of the odious Doctor, she would come back and look for him?

But then, unless he yelled, a little, how was Peach, or anyone else, to know that he was imprisoned at the end of that blind alley? He might be there all night. He recalled, as he struggled again in the gurgling water, stories of friends who, after sitting for half-a-minute on a cold stone in a garden, had contracted at once 'a painful but almost universal complaint' and spent the rest of their lives having expensive operations. What would be his fate if he passed the night in a bird-bath? He called, *diminuendo*, into the darkness, 'Help! – Help!'

The rescuer, finding at last the lonely outcast on whose behalf he has much endured and dared, may well expect some small sign of gratitude from (let us coin a filthy word) the rescuee. No such sign could Anthony give when, in the dim light, he perceived the form of Sir William at the corner. All he could do was to sit up respectfully, and the water about him made a sucking sound like that of the water running out of a bath.

'Hullo!' said Sir William. 'You again, young man? What are you up to now?'

Anthony stared at him. It was the kind of moment familiar to any Member of a Legislative Assembly. The legislator is making an airy speech, confident in the justice of his case. Suddenly, some inhuman beast on the other side pops in a question, or an interjection, of shattering force. For a moment the speaker, though still persuaded of his general rectitude, cannot think of the right reply. If he cannot devise some smart answer, he will be sunk for ever, however strong his general case may be. He stares. He thinks. And, as a rule, in no more than a second, the god of public-speakers sends him something sufficient to say. So, this night, to the aid of the Viscount Anchor there came the god of worthy liars.

'Oh, Sir William,' he said, 'we've been having a Treasure Hunt.'

'A Treasure Hunt? But how did that get you here?'

'This was the last clue, Sir. It said – it said –

"Where the song-birds find their pleasure
Sit, and you shall find the Treasure." '

('Gosh, that's good!' he thought proudly.)

'Unfortunately, Sir, I took it too literally. I sat too seriously – and here I am.'

A great weight was lifted from Sir William's mind. A Treasure Hunt? That might account for a lot of things.

'I see. That explains, I suppose, the two young women I've just seen tearing across the lawn?'

'No doubt, Sir. Of course, I don't know which clue they were after. This one, I dare say.'

'And all those antics in the pavilion?'

'Yes, Sir. That was all part of it. It's rather difficult to explain.'

'Never mind. What can I do for you now?'

'If you could give me a bit of a lift under the arms, Sir, I might emerge, I think, and claim the prize.'

Even with Sir William's aid, the extraction was not easy: but it was done. Anthony walked back to the Hall with Sir William and discoursed learnedly about the statues, the Garden, and the history of the Hall. Sir William was interested, said 'Good-night' warmly, and put Number Nine even higher in his unofficial ranking.

Meanwhile, in the straggling wood across the stream, two young women were fighting a bitter battle about a wig, and using language which cannot be repeated here.

Venus went down behind the wood, as if ashamed of her sons and daughters.

CHAPTER XIV

Sunday morning was wet. Straight hard rain splashed a pattern of white spots on the moat. In the Spanish Garden the nymphs and warriors looked like anybody under a shower bath. Some of the Intake had gone to the little church in Caraway village. The rest were reading newspapers, or considering the tests of the morrow, smart answers for the Interviews, subtle manoeuvres for the Mutual Ranking.

Anthony was coaching Number Thirteen in a Short Talk.

Jacaranda, enraged and wretched in her room, was doing what she could for her hair, and other damage that Number Eight had done. She had a mind to pack her bag and leave the hateful place. But she did want to get to South America, and this seemed the only honest way to a free passage. The strong, brown men there would not mind how much she bit them. They would like it. These Englishmen! Bah!

In the Great Hall someone was making a hideous noise on the organ. 'That squeeze-box,' grumbled Fantom in his pantry. 'Worse than his lordship.'

Peach, alone in the old drawing-room, sat with her feet tucked under her in a corner of the spacious leather sofa. The standard of dress, after the first few doubtful hours, had descended sharply, and she was wearing cherry-coloured corduroy trousers, with a white sweater. She was making her first attempt at the Self-Analysis Test, and found it difficult. She was clear in her mind about one thing only, that she must do this exercise seriously and well – or as well as she could. Her 'little jokes' with the Words and Stories, she felt, had gone too far: and after Doctor Maple's kindly forbearance she would not like him to think that she had wantonly kicked over the traces again. But this was an odd thought. She sucked her pencil and stared at Ely's *Matthew Flinders* over the fireplace. Doctor Maple, after all, was Enemy Number One. As a member of the Staff, he had really behaved disgracefully. Why should she care what he thought? Somehow, somewhy, she did. She was also feeling a little bad about Number Ten.

Then there was the problem they had all discussed so often. If the Stern Critic was allowed to say too much, would the examiners swallow it whole? If the Kindly Friend was too polite, would they think one blind to all one's faults? At every turn she longed for a consultation with Mr Bass. They had been so happy together two days – was it only two? – ago. But now she had scratched Mr Bass out of the book of life.

She began to write, very slowly at first, but gathering speed:

NUMBER 8

(By a stern critic)

There is hardly *any* doubt that Number 8 is *rather* a bitch, which is *most* unsuitable and bizarre because she is the daughter of the sweetest old Civil Servant, when I say bitch I do *not* mean anything in the sex-context, I think in fact she is pretty monogamous by nature and *quite* virginal *so far*, though she tells me that she does have the *most* degrading *dreams* and everything and to judge by her conversation you'd think she was *Cleopatric* in practice, but that is so like *life*, don't you think, you can't tell a thing from what people *say*, what I do mean is that she does perhaps have a *slight* trend towards hatred malice and all uncharitability, I mean she harbours suddenly the *most* acidulous dislikes for male and female, *which* having done she pursues the same with absolute blithe ferocity, sticking at *quite* nothing, only of course it *too* often

> happens that having *flung* the dagger so to speak it *dawns* upon her that the original hate was utterly erroneous, which must show a faint lack of *equilibrium* don't you think, on the other hand once the warm little heart is attached and magnetized you'll find it's practically a record for *fidelity* and

She paused, sucking her pencil. Anthony came in, from the Bar door, flying signals not of distress but of distraction.

'I've found you at last,' he said.

'Go away!'

'Peach!'

'My number is Eight,' she said savagely. Not the hint of a smile. He had never seen her so.

'Well, Number Eight, what's the matter?'

'I'm not speaking to you. I won't say a word. How dare you? It's *utterly* nothing to do with me, and *if* you prefer black women with *no* hair, carry on, Number Nine. Proceed, by all means, Mr Bass. And *if* you're good at needle-work, as I think is *too* likely, I should proceed at once, because you may be needed.'

'What – *what* did you do to her, Peach?'

'I tell you, I'm not speaking. I practically *unfrocked* her. And' she added, with sudden mildness, 'I'm *nearly* sorry.'

'You left me in the bird-bath.'

'I'm sorry I missed that.'

'Where is her hair?'

'She's got it. I thought she had to wear something.' She flared up again. '*You're* the one I blame, you promiscuous pest!'

'Peach! Number Eight! I swear to you – I told you before, she is the human jaguar. She takes one leap and you're in the jaws.'

'Do you call that the utterance of a Viscount?'

'Perhaps not. But – ' Appalling discords rolled in from the organ. '*Who*' he said, in a frenzy, 'is making that un-Christian din?' He marched to the door and slammed it.

'I think he plays rather well,' Peach said smugly.

'Oh, do you? And I suppose you think you've behaved like a perfect lady?'

'I'm not speaking.'

'You and your trick-cyclist!' Anthony was becoming angry now.

'Who sent me? Who suggested it?'

'I did. And I apologize.'

'Oh, goody!' The grim girl relaxed a little at last.

'But I didn't suggest your flinging yourself at his head like a custard-pie.'

'Try not to be *too* rude.'

'Ten kisses! I counted them.'

'I'm glad. So did I.'

'Leda and the *Swan!*'

'Who showed me that?'

Anthony side-stepped that. 'Of course, if he's your kind of chappie, carry on, Number Eight. It's nothing to me. The thing that matters is that you've messed up the Evolution. He's prancing round like a peacock this morning.'

'Any chap who kisses me ten times is *quite* likely to feel pretty well in the morning,' Peach said with maddening contentment. 'What did you expect?'

'I expected you to sock him on the jaw.'

'Very lady-like, I'm sure.'

'Peach, we can't go on like this. The Admiral says, will you come down to lunch?'

'Will you be there, Number Nine?'

'Of course.'

'Then I refuse duty. My regrets to the Admiral.'

'Peach!'

'I'm not speaking… I'm working, can't you see? I'm self-analysing. Go away, Number Nine.'

He went.

'How do you spell "promiscuous"?' she called sweetly after him.

He slammed the door again.

Peach did not look so much distressed as might have been expected after so distressing an encounter. Indeed, for a moment, she wore a tiny smile.

She tore off the top sheet of her pad and wrote again:

NUMBER 8

(by a fairly good friend)

I *won't* agree that Number 8 is rather a bitch, I think it's the *grossest* exaggeration, though I know in some quarters it is the said thing, it's *too* evident why, because she believes in being *utterly* natural, the frank thought simply *gushes* from the little bosom with *quite* no let or hindrance, whereas in most folk it's *suppressed* and sultry, leading to *fixations* and the *unconscious* and all that abysmal mess, the trouble is of course that all *septic* minds in range suspect the worst at *once*, it's like laughing in *church*, you haven't a *hope*, so my verdict if you ask me is that Number 8 is the *most* misunderstood female since *about* Joan of Arc, with whom as a *matter* of fact she has *quite* much in common, being deep down a cosy little virgin whose *one* idea is to benefit the world, of course in the *far* future it's too true I think she would like to be the mother of *six* boys why not?

Peach read this through with apparent satisfaction, and finished her 'Stern Critic' with a single line. Then she cried a little, quietly.

Viscount Anchor wore no tiny smile as he strode into the Great Hall. His main purpose was to murder the person who was murdering *his* beloved organ. It might relieve the feelings roused by his row with Peach. He would have had no jealous feeling if the player had been *good*. But the person was simply excruciating. Anthony's instinct was to go up to him and say 'For God's sake stop that *noise*!' as the Pongo had said to him. But when he saw that the player was Number Fifteen himself he halted and restrained himself: for now the Pongo and he were friends. He stood behind the soldier, watching, and suffering. Compared with the Pongo, he modestly thought, he, Anthony, was Sir Arthur Sullivan. The Captain would have been rated as a bad piano-player in a dockside bar, and he had never attempted the organ before. All the stops were out, and all the key-boards coupled. To these tremendous forces he applied the technique of the dockside bar. It was not sufficient to play the air in crotchets, or single notes: he thumped it out in a succession of quavers and chords of dubious validity. The left hand (as a rule, fortunately, a single finger or thumb) descended rhythmically in the bass, sometimes, by Heaven's decree, in the proper key. The Captain had not the same respect for the pedals as Anthony. The pedals were common land, without rules or regulations. The large left foot (the right being firmly stationed on the swell) ranged over the pedals like a rogue elephant, slaughtering four or five deep moaning notes at a time. In the long history of Noise there can seldom have been anything like it. But he was enjoying himself: and Anthony, with a kind of fellow-feeling, said nothing.

Presently, Number Fifteen saw a face in the little mirror, and stopped short in the middle of a cruel rendering of *Rule Britannia*. He took a blue letter from his pocket.

'Hallo, Number Nine. I think perhaps you ought to see this.' He spoke rather sternly and stiffly, Anthony noticed, and wondered why. It should have been the other way. But then, everything was upside down this morning.

Before he read the letter, he glanced at Number Fifteen's face. 'I see' he said, 'you have been in action with Number Ten. Shake hands.'

Number Fifteen looked sheepish, but he shook hands.

'Tough customer,' he said.

'The Ayes Have It,' said Anthony. 'If this course went on for a week there would not be a man unwounded in the place – She says you hit her,' he added.

'I did,' said Number Fifteen shortly.

'Generally a mistake.' He read the letter:

> MY DEAREST JOY,
>
> It was good of you to telephone. I am glad you bit him. But I have been thinking, from what you say, he does not sound like my Stanley Bass. For one thing, my Stanley Bass had a beard. In any case, bite him again.
>
> Your loving
>
> OLGA

Anthony shuddered slightly.

Number Fifteen, the man of action, said strongly: 'What does it mean?'

'Nothing, old chap. We do wear beards in the Navy, as you know. But not all the time. The only thing that matters is the bit about biting me again.'

'I have an idea' said the Pongo heavily, 'that she's a Russian spy.'

'Maybe,' said Anthony lightly. 'Though I doubt if even the Russians would employ anyone with Jacaranda's PQ.'

Number Fifteen had intended to be very stern. He had been going to ask Number Nine to explain how he came into a correspondence between two Russian agents. But somehow the damned fellow always took the wind out of your sails. He said, mildly:

'I thought of searching her room.'

'Did you?' said Anthony solemnly. 'You're a brave man. I shan't be there. I say, let's have some more music.'

'You have a go.'

'No, you go on. I hardly play at all.'

'I only strum.'

'You're jolly good, old chap. Play *Rule Britannia* again.'

'Oh, well.'

To Anthony's dismay, the soldier consented. And even those first few bars, which, someone has said, express in less than fifteen notes the whole of the British character, were agony.

Anthony, as he stood behind the soldier, suffering, thought: 'Somebody like me should be officially inserted into every Intake. I know the PQ of the Pongo from A to Z. But he'll probably get through.'

At the end of *Rule Britannia* there was another polite argument, each imploring the other to make music. Once again, it ended with Number Fifteen at the instrument. After a little of *Tea for Two*, unable to suffer more, Anthony stole out into the garden. At least, the Pongo had forgotten about the spy.

Doctor Maple came into the Great Hall as Number Nine went out. As Anthony had said, the Doctor was looking, and feeling, as perky as a peacock on a fine June day. Eleven times he had been embraced by the delectable Peach. He had held her in his arms; she had received his guilty secrets kindly, and made them innocent. True, she had said by the Swan that it was good-bye for ever: but faith, or indomitable conceit, told him that he would wear her down. For the first time devotion reigned in his heart, and he cared nothing for psycho-somatic reactions, or endocrine anomalies. But he had not forgotten the fishy Number Nine. To expose Number Nine, who had dared, though vainly, to make love to *his* Number Eight, might put him finally out of court and would be a satisfaction anyhow. He was determined to get to the bottom of that body affair. He sat down now in an arm-chair in the corner, and as the best detectives did, he knew, began to 'reconstruct the scene'. He was so elated and eager that he hardly flinched from the discordant boomings of Number Fifteen. He had so little music in him that the discordances did not affect him as they affected Number Nine. He thought merely that they were a lot too loud. That gave him an idea. Number Nine had been too loud that Friday night. Cover for some dark deed? The screams of the strangled might well be drowned by such a noise as Number Fifteen was making now. The Hall itself was shuddering with screams, with female squeals and unearthly groans. So far, so good. Assume there was a body – he had to believe his own eyes, even in that dim light. Where had it gone? If it had gone out into the grounds it would surely have been found by one of the innumerable gardeners. It could not have gone upstairs, for it would have met the Principal and Sir William Blant. Through the north door – into the Candidates' Wing? No, it would have encountered one of the Intake – the delicious Peach, for example, who had come in just before the police. Down the passage to the drawing-room and the Bar? No: for according to Number Fifteen he had come straight back that way after his telephone-call. The only other way out was through the swing-door in the passage to the kitchen quarters. But Fantom and his Irish maids were out there. And the police had searched every room on the ground-floor at least.

But the police search had not been very serious – partly his own fault, no doubt. So the conclusion was that the body was somewhere in the house, but not in any place where the police had looked. Cellars? In an old place like this there must be leagues of cellars, acres of cellars. Dungeons. Trap-doors. Secret passages.

'Secret passages?' The Doctor marched to the Bar, where were most of the important books. He found *Hambone History* and turned to the Index.

There was nothing about secret passages. He looked at 'Cellars' – many references. Then, below that, his eye caught, 'Concealed spaces 71, 253, 489, 508.' Charles I, it seemed, had spent most of his life in hiding at the Hall. There was a false roof to the Long Hall where he had 'lain' for some time (also, at an earlier date, the Three Bishops). There was a passage under the moat by which he had escaped (also two burglars in 1849). There was a hidden cellar below the old Buttery, with a trapdoor under the Vat (Charles I had been there too – and the Sheriff of Winchester, 1673). There was an oubliette in the Rogues' Dungeon (but they had never put King Charles there). And – what he wanted at last – there was the King's Stairway. This led from the Armoury Room on the first floor to cellars below ground: and it could be reached through a sliding panel in the wall of the passage between the Great Hall and the drawing-room. 'Six feet from the Hall, six feet from the door to the Servants' Quarters, a projection in the shape of a rose, when pressed, releases a spring, which... Here Charles I...'

The Doctor, bored with Charles I, but wild with excitement, went back to the passage. There was no one about, and Number Fifteen was deep in his blissful din. But there were scores of projections in the shape of roses – each one carved as carefully as if it were to be the only rose in the world. Doctor Maple pressed dozens of them, but nothing happened. At last he had his will. The panel slid back a little, he gave it a push, and stepped cautiously inside. He slid the panel back and lit a match, feeling a little like Aladdin at the entrance to the Cave. On a small table the match showed him, miraculously, a small electric torch, left, no doubt, by Charles I. The torch showed him a lot of dust, some foot-marks, and a spiral staircase, up which, rather nervously, he went. At the top it was easy – the panel slid back at a pull on an obvious knob: but this one squeaked a little. He stepped out into the Armoury Room. Here he was, back in civilization again, and, it seemed, no nearer to the object of his quest. The long low room had a smell of old battles. At each end arrow-slits commanded the moat. The walls were lined with suits-of-armour and ancient weapons, pike and pistol, halberd and arquebus, musket and powder-flask, even a battering-ram. But, dotted about among the armour, were four or five shapes that were draped in dust-sheets. The Doctor idly pulled one of the wrappings aside. It revealed, he supposed, some sort of 'classical' figure with a broken nose and only one arm. The next was a wooden figure of the Virgin and Child. The third – and when he had seen only a little of it he began to tremble with excitement – was *Susanna Resenting the Elders.*

There was no doubt he had seen that figure before. And now he had seen the face, which was beautiful, though there was a small chip out of her forehead – a pity. She reminded him of Peach. Reverently, he covered Susanna again: triumphantly, on air, he marched down to the Great Hall by the stone staircase. On the way, he remembered something – a small white speck of plaster? stone? – he had noticed, but then thought nothing of, on the dusty floor of King Charles's Chamber. He went boldly back to the panel – for what did it matter now who saw him? – and pressed the varnished rose again.

Fantom, coming out through the swing-door, saw 'the perisher' disappear into the Chamber, and the panel slide back. He returned to his pantry, shocked and sweating, and poured himself a generous sherry. Doctor Maple! This was terrible. Where was 'Mr Bass'? Mr Bass, he remembered, was lunching with the Admiral. He must ring up the Lodge. He did. But the Admiral had switched off the telephone, for he was preparing to get his noon position: and nothing could be allowed to interrupt that. Fantom poured out more sherry, and sat worrying about his pension.

Doctor Maple came out, with his chip in his pocket. He thought he could find a resting place for that. He put a firm hand on Number Fifteen's shoulder, and said in a masterful manner:

'Stop that.' ('That' was *The Old Folks at Home.*)

'Yes, Sir?'

'I know all.'

Cosmo simply stared at him.

'I know exactly what you did on Friday night – you and Number Nine. I have found the secret passage. I have found the statue – '

'But, Sir – ' began the astonished soldier.

'If you have anything to say you can say it tonight to the Principal. He will be back at eight. I must ask you to be here in this Hall at 9.0. is that understood?'

'Yes, Sir.'

'And please tell Number Nine the same.'

'Very well, Sir. But, Sir – '

But the gay, inflated psychologist had marched off, humming. What a triumph! What a sell for that smug old Principal! He would have to admit that there was 'something in psychology' after all.

The rain cleared, the hazy sun appeared just in time for the Admiral to get his Sunday latitude. Lady Primrose had gone to Church; Potter was cooking: and Anthony was glad to serve as 'Tanky' again. He stood over the chronometer and shouted 'Bang!' at the exact moment of Apparent Noon, which, that day, was at 11h 55m 55s by the clock (Summer Time had been sensibly abandoned after the war). At noon the two Admirals signalled their positions by flags, and Anthony bent on the bunting and hoisted it. His father's latitude was about a quarter of a mile out – too far to the Northward. They gazed anxiously through the glasses when Admiral Mole's flags went up. Anthony interpreted them, and the Admiral stood by the chart with his dividers. Admiral Mole was half a mile to the Southward. This put the Earl in fine fettle for the rest of the day.

'Ha!' he roared. 'The old boy's losing grip.'

He carefully put his sextant to bed in its box. 'Well,' he said, 'sun's over the yard-arm. Hoist the Gin-pennant! And then we'll have an Appreciation of the Situation.'

It took several gins to carry them to the end of Anthony's Report. The Admiral was saddened by the mutiny of Peach, to whom he had taken a fatherly fancy.

'Parted brass-rags, eh? Well, never mind. Brass-rags can be shared again.'

For the rest, he seemed fairly content.

'You've done very well, my boy. The Body Operation was brilliant. A nice tidy little engagement. Lucky, of course, but there you are. And mind you, boy, it's all round the Fleet. Potter tells me they're talking in the village. "No smoke without fire" and so forth. That's what we want. Get these flumbusterous Dagoes a bad name. A stinking name. A name like a French latrine. All very well, you know, for Sergeant What-name to talk about practical jokes. But practical jokes in the nude don't sound like good order and discipline – hey?' he roared. 'And then there's this Whitehall wog, you speak of, this perishing politico. I bet he's taking a note or two. I'm sorry about the Treasure Hunt, though. You threw away, it seems to me, some good stuff there – spiked your own guns.'

'I know, Sir. But I was thinking of Stanley Bass.'

'Quite right. Never mind. You've done well, Anchor. You're promoted.'

'Thank-you, Sir.' Whenever his father addressed him as 'Anchor' he knew he had won a really good mark.

'But what's the course now, Sir?'

'Hard to say. What baffles me, my boy, is why the action isn't over already. This Jacktree – '

'Rackstraw, Sir?'

'This Racksaw, this – this Maple! Both of 'em have got dirty marks in the log. Cowardice in action. Failure to take charge in simple emergency. Lying to superior officer. By God, if it had been me, they'd have been ashore that *night*, and out of the Service the next. Not fit to command a canoe. But here they are, you say, still strutting the quarter-deck and lecturing the young idea. What sort of a ship is that? And what sort of a Captain? Give me a gin.'

'Aye, aye, Sir. May I switch on the 'phone, Sir?'

'Infernal gadget. Why?'

'I thought perhaps that Peach may – '

'Oh, aye, yes, certainly. I hope she comes. By the way, I ought to tell you that your sister Prim is sailing tack for tack with young Bass. Sits on his bunk all day.'

'Good show.'

'Hope so. Well, boy, where are we? By rights the enemy should have struck their flag long ago: but they ain't. They flourish like a blasted baytree, armour-plated. As for you, my boy, I don't like the look of it. The Pongo suspects you. Maple is after your blood. The Racksaw and the Whitehall wog can't think a lot of you. At any moment the Polish bat may bite you again. This Peach, it seems, didn't do you much good in action and now is in a state of mutiny. The Bass stock does not seem high – '

'Oh, Sir! I've done wonders for the lad.'

'I was thinking of the Evolution. What shot, if any, have we got in the locker now?'

'We've got the record, Sir. The tape.'

'Ah, yes, the nightingale nonsense. That was stout stuff too. Submarine-work, possibly, but with an enemy like this we can't be too scrupulous.'

'I wish you'd explain that, Sir, to Peach.'

'I will, boy, I will. Now if I were you, I'd take that record up to the Hall and play it to this unseaman-like Principal-fellow tonight.'

'Isn't it a bit too soon for that, Sir? I mean, I should have to explain myself and everything. And that would be the end of Stanley Bass.'

'Damn Stanley Bass. I always forget him. Well, where are we now?' The Admiral mused.

'All I can see for it' he said, at last, 'is a mass court martial.'

'Sir? A mass –?' Anthony faltered.

'Arrest the whole damned afterguard up there, bring 'em down here, and play the record. That should finish 'em, from what you say.'

'I'm not quite sure, Sir – '

'Very well, boy,' said the Admiral testily, 'if you know better than I do, carry on.'

Anthony was silent. Then, fortunately, the telephone-bell rang, a harsh, rural ring.

Anthony said 'The Lodge' and listened with an expression passing from serious to solemn.

'Thank-you, Fantom,' he said at last. 'Well done! Fantom' he reported, 'says that the Maple has discovered the secret passage. "Walked in" he says, "as natural as if he was going to the heads." '

'What does that mean?'

'Might mean nothing, Sir. It might mean a lot.'

'Well, I told you, court martial the lot of 'em. Bring 'em down about six. Star-time's about eight tonight. You'd better have a Circumstantial Letter ready.'

'Lunch, Father! Oh, *Anthony*!'

'Hullo, Prim. The sailor's joy. Or so I gather.'

Lady Primrose blushed, but fondly embraced him.

'What have you done to your lip?'

'I bit it – thinking of you.'

During lunch Anthony explained to the Admiral the theory of the Parliament Pools.

'Good notion,' said the Admiral. 'Potter, we'll start that tomorrow. Pass the word to the Paymaster-Commander.'

'Aye, aye, Sir.'

After lunch the weather was wondrous again. In the Spanish Garden peace and warmth had won, and Doctor Maple strolled alone in the sunshine, thinking blissfully of Peach.

Towards him, on the north side, came slowly Number Ten. He had noticed at lunch how woebegone the long and lustrous lady looked. Now, too, she seemed to droop a little and her eyes were fearful. He felt sorry for her. Also, though his private soul was full of Peach, he remembered professionally that he had promised to keep a special eye on the queer Number Ten. But he had been too much occupied with Number Eight.

So he smiled (as benignly as that face could smile) on Number Ten.

Number Ten was moved to see a kindly, smiling man, in this little world of brutes. She said, like a very old 'cello, 'Oh, *Doctor!* What a *lovely* day!' He turned and they walked together. Slowly they walked towards the Queen's Corner. They disappeared from sight into the dark jungle of yew.

Anthony, returning from the Lodge well-fed and battleworthy, but sad about Peach, found Number Fifteen prowling round the Spanish Garden in search of him.

'Thank God!' said Number Fifteen, true to his part, as usual. And he plunged into an excited account of the strange words, and peremptory commands, of Doctor Maple.

'He burbled' Number Fifteen concluded, 'something about a secret passage – and a statue.'

'Did he?' said Anthony. 'Then this is fairly serious.'

'Is there anything in it?' said Cosmo anxiously. 'I'm a bit worried. As you know, it's my second go, and I don't want to fail again.'

The sailor regarded the agitated soldier. He thought: 'Stanley Bass, are you a judge of character? Number Fifteen is either (*a*) entirely the pompous prig he looks, in which case, if I tell him all, he will canter to the authorities: or (*b*) he is more human than he seems, and quite a nice kind of snob, in which case all will be well.'

He betted on (*b*) and said: 'Number Fifteen, in confidence, I am not the man you think me. I'm…' and he told him all.

He won his bet. Number Fifteen, of course, had to be right: so he said: 'I always thought there was something phoney about you, Number Nine.' But he was delighted to strike an alliance with the heir to Admiral of the Fleet the Earl of Caraway and Stoke. They shook hands.

'Good,' said Anthony, thinking aloud. 'But now what? What, in other words, now? The only real rock in this morass of uncertainty is that the proposed encounter with the Principal must *not* take place. The Admiral is right, as usual, I suppose. A court martial is the thing. But how do we arrest this wasp? How do we transport him to the place of justice? Yesterday, I should have said that Number Eight would be the active lure. But Number Eight has gone soppy and mysterious. She wouldn't do it. Number Ten?' he mused. 'Number Ten might do. But Number Ten, at the Lodge, might find the original Stanley Bass and bite him to death. No, I don't think – '

'By the way,' said Number Fifteen. 'I ought to have told you, perhaps – I fancy Number Ten has – got Maple – '

'Got him? You don't mean – "bit him"?'

'Yes. He came out of the yew-stuff looking wild and wounded like – like – '

'Like you and me?' said Anthony firmly.

'Yes.'

'Good Lord! What a leopardess! I have a sort of respect for that young lady. But I wish you'd told me before. It cuts her out as a lure, I fear. On the other hand – I have an idea! Yes, – *Yes*! This alters all. This makes all plain. We will arrest him – you and I – together. Come!'

The bewildered soldier followed him into the Hall: and there the young lord wrote his first anonymous letter, in block capitals, of course:

MEET ME AT THE SWAN 5.30 – 8

'There is something to be said for these numbers,' he thought.

CHAPTER XV

'Did she bite him badly?'

'Worse than us.'

'Poor brute. Still, I suppose, for a practising trick-cyclist, it's all in the day's work.'

The two men were waiting in Leda's alcove. Number Fifteen said: 'I say, Number Nine, about this Mutual Ranking. Have you thought about it at all?

'A bit,' said Anthony cautiously.

'I thought, perhaps, we might help each other there.'

'Yes?'

'Most people seem to think that it's the "official" list that matters – I mean the ranking for appointment. As a matter of fact, I believe the other one counts quite a bit – the "How d'you like him?" list. It shows, you see, what people think of you outside office-hours, so to speak.'

'I see.'

Number Fifteen stared at the Swan. 'They say they're not bad eating,' he said. He cleared his throat.

'I'd like to tell you, Number Nine, that I've put you pretty high in both my lists.'

'My dear old Pongo, I call that pretty Christian of you.' This is hideous, he thought This is bribery, corruption, log-rolling, back-scratching, simony, or something. But what else can you expect if you put the young through squalid cross-examinations about each other's capacity and charm?

'Thank-you, old chap,' he said. 'I'll – S'sh! I hear the hooves of the beast.'

Doctor Maple came round the corner cautiously. He was much less perky than the peacock of the morning. The end of his professional interview with Number Ten, though clinically instructive, had upset him. He was conscious of adrenal maladjustment. He hated to think what Peach might think about his appearance. But, at least, he was going to see her – at her own invitation too.

Instead of Peach, he was shocked to find the two candidates he proposed to haul to justice that evening.

'Hullo,' said Anthony with a charming smile. As one intent on putting a good chap at his ease, he stepped forward and held out his hand. 'You've joined the Jacaranda Club, I see. I'm so sorry.'

Number Fifteen shook his hand too and said: 'Bad luck, Sir.'

Doctor Maple, bewildered, said: 'The Jacaranda Club?'

'Number Ten. We've both been through it.'

'Number Ten? That? Oh? Yes,' he faltered sheepishly. But a faint current of sympathy passed inevitably between them, as when two foxes meet during a hunt.

'I hear' said Anthony pleasantly, 'that you're interested in the secret passages. As it happens, I was lunching with the Admiral – he owns the Hall, you know – and he said he'd like to tell you all about them. Care to come?'

The Doctor hesitated. He could hardly tell them that he had an assignation with Number Eight: and there was something compulsive in the friendly gaze of these two strong young men. And, of course, the Admiral might have some useful information. He could not have explained it, but he felt he had *better* go. He did.

Peach, sitting alone and mournful in the valley side of the Three-Cornered Hat, heard voices behind her, and, peeping, saw the strange trio go by. They walked very close to each other, the Doctor in the middle, like two gangsters 'crowding' a third, like a new Member being steered up the floor of the House of Commons. They all looked solemn, and, at the sight of the three, each with the Mark of Jacaranda on him, Peach giggled suddenly and was happier. If the black cow had got one of the Staff, no wonder her poor Number Nine had fallen. She was sorry for the Doctor no more. The other two had a perfect right to expose themselves to man-eating females. But only last night the Doctor – 'Heriot'! – had asked her to marry him. He was 'waiting for her answer'. Ha! And before he had waited a day he had flung himself into the arms of a vampire. She felt herself a woman scorned, and did not care what injury was done to the yellow rat.

But what were they up to? She watched them dwindle down the middle of the avenue, then followed, keeping close to the trees.

Near the gate of the Lodge garden, behind a hedge, stood Chief Petty Officer Potter in uniform. He wore brief greeny gaiters, for shore-duty, and a belt which carried a revolver in a holster. He held the lanyard of a small gun, such as is used for starting yacht races. As they stepped into the garden he pulled the lanyard and the gun discharged.

The psychologist leaped a foot and put his hand to his heart. Even Number Fifteen, the iron-nerved soldier, said angrily: What the Hell?

'One Gun Salute, Sir,' said Potter saluting, 'prior to court martial.'

'Of course,' said Anthony. 'The Rogues' Salute. Come along, Doctor.' He firmly clasped the Doctor's arm and steered him into the house. The prisoner was too shattered by the gun to apprehend his doom. He did not start protesting till he found himself locked in a small cloak-room. But then it was too late. Potter, now Master-at-Arms, paid no attention to his just complaints.

'Pipe down, Sir,' was all he said.

The psychologist, being a sea-lawyer, as Fantom had pronounced, made mention of writs for assault and false imprisonment.

'Pipe down, *please*, Sir,' said Potter gently.

The Admiral (he had been warned by telephone) was waiting in the study. He was in full uniform, a cocked hat upon his head, the colours of a sunset in the Indian Ocean on his breast. The King's Regulations and Admiralty Instructions were before him.

An empty chair was on either side of him, but in front of each chair were foolscap, blotting-paper, ink, pen and pencil, as if the chairs were full. In a corner sat the nightingale box, plugged in to the electric supply. Anthony solemnly handed to him his 'Circumstantial Letter', the basis of all Naval courts martial, relating the horrid charges in detail. The Admiral read it through, underlined a passage here and there, and made some notes in the margin. He looked round the little dingy room to see that the Court was ready. But it was not a little dingy room. It was a great place, full of high officers, and gold braid, and bright ribbons. Some of them were wearing their swords. There were Masters-at-Arms and Chief Petty Officers, sturdy magnificent men, and rows of 'square-rigged' sailors in the blue jean collars, the black silk scarf, the blue tapes, the white triangle under their chins, the tight jumpers and inconvenient trousers, that ancient, absurd, but glorious uniform. And a few smart Marines.

'Bring in the prisoner,' he said.

'Three paces forward, march! off cap!' said Potter.

Doctor Maple – he could not have said why – found himself standing as nearly to attention as an untrained psychologist can. But he began to splutter: 'May I ask the meaning of this outrage?'

'Pipe down!'

The Admiral surveyed him with distaste.

'Is this the ullage mentioned in the Circumstantial Letter?'

'Yes, Sir.'

'I am the President of this Court,' he said more kindly. 'Also, as we are short-handed, I am the Deputy Judge-Advocate. Irregular – but can't be helped. On my right, Captain Tantrum' – he bowed to the empty chair. 'On my left, Commander Rummage. Prosecutor – Mr Bass. Friend of the Accused – Mr – Mr Damn it – '

'Lennox-Edwardes, Sir.'

'Exactly. Thank-you. Have you any objection to make to any of the Court?'

The Doctor, despite his bewilderment and alarm, was beginning to take a professional interest in the proceedings. This gaudy Admiral, with the imaginary officers at his side, was evidently suffering from grandeur delusions. It was a very common compensatory mechanism – a psychotic way of attaining in phantasy what cannot be achieved in reality. As for the young men, this was, he supposed, another of their 'practical jokes', for which they would pay. But perhaps it would be best to humour the old fellow.

'Yes, Sir,' he said mildly. 'I object to the whole Court.'

'You can't do that, you know. I said "any of the Court" – not all the Court. You can't object to me because I'm Deputy Judge Advocate. One moment.'

The Admiral conferred with Captain Tantrum and Commander Rummage.

'The Court is unanimous. You can object to Captain Tantrum, or you can object to Commander Rummage. But not both. And not to me. Do you still wish to object?'

'No, Sir.'

'Very well. Try not to make frivolous interpolations.'

The Doctor saw himself reading a learned paper on this case to an eager audience of mental therapists.

'Prosecutor, what is the first charge?'

'Sir, that the accused person did falsely and maliciously insult and vilify one Private Adley.'

'AND SENT HIM TO HIS DEATH,' the Admiral roared.

'What is all this?' thought the Doctor. The Admiral was rather terrifying now. But he was not going to show fear to a madman. '*Do* you remember one Private Adley?'

'I seem to remember the name,' said the Doctor jauntily. 'But, you know, a good many young men have been through my hands.'

'Poor devils. Recollect. Some damned Pongo-performance at – where was it?'

'Watney, Sir,' said the Prosecutor.

'Do you remember Private Adley *now*?'

He did. A very rude young man. He had disliked him and given him a bad report.

'Yes, Sir.'

'You told him he was not fit to take command of men in the field.'

'Maybe, Sir. If so, I believed it.'

'But you *told* him – you told him to his face.'

The Doctor was silent. That, perhaps, had been a mistake.

'AND THAT WAS MY SON,' the Admiral bellowed, 'MY ELDEST SON!'

The old eyes flashed, the old hands thumped the table: the mind-man, queerly, was not quite so sure that the man was mad as he had been. 'What have you to say?'

'I was only doing my duty, Sir.'

The Admiral snorted.

'What is the next charge.'

'On the evening of Friday the 29th inst. – '

'You mean "ult.".'

'Last Friday, Sir, – April 29th.'

'That's "ult.". Why not say April?'

'I beg your pardon, Sir.'

'Go on.'

'On the evening of Friday the 29th April, skulking from duty, and, while in the position of officer of the watch, failing to take charge in an emergency.'

'That's the body, isn't it?' said the President, consulting the Circumstantial Letter.

'Yes, Sir.'

'Did you see a body in the Hall from the gallery that night?'

'It wasn't a body.'

'No prevarication, please. Did you *think* it was a body?'

'Yes, Sir.'

'What sort of a body?'

'A female body, Sir. Unclothed.'

'What did you do?

'I did nothing, Sir. At least, I kept an eye on things – from where I was.'

'Did it occur to you that the young woman might have been murdered?'

'No, Sir, I didn't think that.'

'You thought she was alive?'

'It was a statue, Sir. A practical joke.'

'Never mind. At that moment you thought she was alive?'

'I think I did.' He had to admit that.

'So your evidence is that you stood in the gallery and "kept an eye" on a nude female body?'

The Admiral might be mad. But he put things very acutely and awkwardly.

'Do you think' he went on, 'that such conduct is compatible with the position of a member of the Senior Staff at that damned institution up there?'

There would be no more humouring. 'May I ask, Sir, what the Hell all this has got to do with – '

'SILENCE!' the Admiral thundered, and the table shook again. 'I'll tell you. The answer is that you, who have just confessed to incompetence and cowardice, had the infernal nerve *to tell my son that he was not fit to command troops in the field!'*

He glared. The Doctor felt far less jaunty.

'Have you yourself, by the way, ever commanded men in action?'

'No, Sir.'

'Next charge?'

'Prevarication and lying to superior officers, Sir.'

'Oh yes,' said the Admiral. 'Having, no doubt, for reasons that seemed good to you, done nothing – did you report what you had seen to your Principal?'

'It's nothing to do with you, Sir, what I said or did. You'll kindly let me go.'

He turned and stalked to the door.

But Potter was at the door. And – good Heavens! – yes – he had a revolver in his hand.

'About turn!' barked Potter. 'Three paces forward – march!'

The Doctor returned to his place, trembling with rage and sweating slightly with apprehension.

'This is too much,' he gasped. 'I'll take you into Court for this.'

'Perhaps, perhaps,' said the Admiral quietly. 'Next charge?'

'Conduct to the prejudice of good order and discipline, Sir. To wit – '

'To what?'

'To wit, Sir, that the accused person, being one of the persons responsibly in charge of young persons at an instructional establishment, did corruptly force his attentions upon one of the young female persons before-mentioned, the same being *in statu pupillari*, approximately,' Anthony concluded, proudly.

'It's a lie!' said the Doctor, nettled at last.

'I'm glad to hear you say that,' said the Admiral. 'You would agree, would you, that it would be grossly improper for an officer in your position in that Hell-vessel up there to make love to one of the ratings, so to speak, he was instructing, examining or what-not?'

'Yes, Sir.'

'To be fair to the accused person, Sir,' said the Prosecutor, 'the evidence is that he did propose marriage to the young person.'

'Propose marriage?' said the Admiral dubiously. 'I don't see that that improves things. The duty of the accused person is to examine and make reports upon the candidates. How can he make a fair unprejudiced report if he has just proposed marriage to one of them? – Don't you agree?' he said, almost gently, to the prisoner.

'Certainly, Sir. And, of course, I didn't.'

There was a knock at the door. Potter opened it. A small voice said 'May I come in?' – and there was Peach.

'Come in, come in, Miss – Clerihue,' said the Admiral.

'Meridew, Sir.'

'That's what I said. Take a seat, young lady.'

'Oh, Admiral, what a gorgeous get-up! Hullo, Doctor! What's going on?'

'Be seated,' said the Admiral, not much amused by 'gorgeous get-up'. Potter showed her to a seat by the door.

The prisoner smiled wanly at her. Why on earth had he answered all those perilous questions? Outside, he would not have said a word to any of them. But there was something paralysing in this court martial masquerade, the roaring Admiral, the official language. It seemed to have weakened his wits. The 'mad Admiral', he thought, must be a pretty subtle psychologist. And now, here was Number Eight. Surely, surely, his little Peach would not give him away?

The Admiral said kindly (and his coo, the Doctor realized, was as dangerous as his roar):

'Well, here, by chance, is one of the young ladies in question. You wouldn't think, would you, Doctor, of making love to her, or proposing marriage, while under your supervision at the Hall?'

'Of course not!' It was quite true. He had never thought of such a folly before. What special devil had been about to make him do it?

He did not look at Peach: but Peach looked at him with cool contempt. The little rat! Why couldn't he answer 'Of course I did! And proud of it!'

'Have you anything to say, Miss Clerihue?'

'No, Admiral. Not a thing!' said the innocent child. 'What is it all about?'

'Prosecutor, I understand you have some other evidence?'

'Yes, Sir.'

'Let the Court have it.'

The Admiral sat back. Anthony went to the box and pressed things. But he had picked the wrong reel. Into the little room, rather tinny and remote, the voice of Miss Slice said:

'*...a case of pituitary deficiency. You seem to me to have a split libido.*'

'I beg your pardon, Sir. That's the wrong – '

'No, no, go on. I like it. Who is this?'

'Another member of the Staff, Sir.'

'This is monstrous!' the Doctor hissed.

'I find it amusing. S'sh!'

The Doctor, at the first sound, had gone dead-white. Now his face was flooding red, a colour it had seldom worn before. He took a threatening step towards the machine, but Anthony stood in front. He darted for the door, but Potter was there.

'Quiet!' roared the Admiral. 'I can't hear.'

'*Our egos were a perfect blend. Our ids made rather a cosy pattern.*'

The Admiral chuckled. 'Sit down,' he said kindly. The prisoner sat and stared at the floor.

The Admiral much enjoyed the love-making of the psychologists. He chuckled. He laughed. He rolled about. Now and then he shared his pleasure with his two colleagues. 'Hear that, Captain Tantrum?' 'A lesson for *you*, Rummage.' He listened solemnly to the summing-up of Stanley Bass, and shook his head at the Prosecutor.

The Doctor was thinking: 'This, after all, doesn't matter much. Let the old fool laugh. – But is there any more?'

At the end, there was silence in the room while Anthony changed the reel. Slowly, hoping against hope, the Doctor turned his head, to see what the fellow was up to. Yes, evidently there was more to come.

'Have you heard the nightingale?' came Peach's voice.

The Doctor hid his face in his hands. Peach gave a little yelp of surprise and dismay. This was genuine enough, for she had never heard her own voice recorded before, and the first hearing is a shock to everyone. Others, they say, hear our voices as they leave our mouths: we hear them through the bones of the face. But the yelp was a small comfort to the Doctor: for it showed, he thought, that she, at least, was not a party to this wicked plot. 'What shall I *do*?' he thought. 'What shall I *do*? They can do this anywhere. The Principal... Whitehall, a Court of Law... the BMA...' He was ruined.

The Admiral laughed no more, though once he threw a monstrous wink at Peach. But Peach was giving a display of embarrassment which was by no means all acting. Apart from the sound of her own voice, which she thought was dreadful ('Have I been speaking like that all the little *life*? It can't be!'), the whole scene distressed her, the wretched fellow cowering in the chair, the crazy, shaming things she had made him say. When she heard:

'You mustn't put your hand on my bosoms,' she gave another little yelp and rushed to the door. Potter was not sure whether she should be allowed to go: but the President nodded, and he opened the door.

At the end there was no sound but the heavy breathing of the prisoner. 'Was that your voice?' said the Admiral, in a very deep, but gentle voice. He had to sink the stricken enemy: but he did not expect to enjoy it.

'Yes, Sir,' the prisoner whispered.

'So you lied to the Court – as well as to your own superior officer?'

The prisoner merely nodded.

'You plead "Guilty"?'

'Yes.'

'Stand up, then, and hear the sentence of the Court.'

The prisoner could hardly stand: but he did.

'The Court' said the President, after a short conference with Captain Tantrum and Commander Rummage, 'desires to be merciful. The evidence you have just heard could be reproduced anywhere – in any place, that is, where there is a supply of electricity. If you obey the instructions of the Court, it will never be heard again: and these young gentlemen will undertake to be mute and dumb about what we have seen and heard this evening. If you do not —— Is that understood?'

'It's blackmail!' whispered the prisoner.

'I'm no lawyer,' said the Admiral comfortably, 'but, technically, I doubt if it is. However, let it be blackmail, if you like that kind of manoeuvre. Whatever it is – is it – understood?'

After a slight pause, the Doctor bowed and whispered, 'Yes.'

'The instructions of the Court, then, are as follows: One! You intended, I understand, to go to your Commanding Officer with some foolish foc'sle chatter about secret passages and statues. You will forget all that. You will not blow the gaff about secret passages or statues – or about these two young gentlemen. Understood?'

'Yes.'

'Two! Tomorrow morning you will resign your position at the Hall, lash your hammock, and take your dunnage ashore. A sudden sickness – anything you like – but you'll go ashore. You will not even leave any reports behind: for in the present weather your reports, it's clear, would be as fair and unprejudiced as a Dago's salvage account. Understood?'

'Yes, Sir.'

'Three! You will tell your Commanding Officer that, as an ancient mariner, and, after all, the rightful owner of the ship, I should like to be invited to the farewell feasting tomorrow night. Since your lot came aboard I have never set foot in the old ship; and I take it rather hard. Understood?'

'Yes, Sir. I'm sure they will be glad.'

'Very well. I think that's all. Except – this is not an order, but a recommendation. Why don't you give up this perishing trick-cyclicism and earn an honest living? It seems to me that you have dishonoured the good name of "Doctor". How did you get it?'

Stuttering, the Doctor told his little life-story. This was the kind of impression it made on the Admiral's mind: Qualified in medicine not long before the war. After the minimum of postgraduate training ('Twelve months in a mental hospital – I gather,' said the Admiral, afterwards) he was 'conscripted' into the Army as a 'graded psychiatrist' ('Whatever that may be!'). Spent the war at military depots, sorting recruits – and, in the end, candidates for commissions – into sheep, goats, and what-not. End of hostilities – demobilized. By then, having had a high tyrannical time with would-be officers, thought quite a lot of his powers. Saw himself as a famous specialist ('Commander Mind-Sweeping – ha!'). Unhappily, after the war, not so easy to get a hospital appointment. Glut of specialists – especially in psychiatric waters. So – very glad to get the offer of 'psychological' job at Hambone Hall, though this meant a break-away from medicine.

'Orphan of the War, of course,' said the Admiral, sardonic, at the end. 'But what it comes to is (*a*) too many damned mind-sweepers? and (*b*) you didn't feel like going back and doing an honest job as a doctor? – Any complaints?'

The Doctor had nothing much to say to that: but he murmured something about 'the study of the mind'.

'The *mind?*' said the Admiral. 'The human mind? If you live to be a hundred and fifty-three, you fraudulent fellow, you will not know as much about the human mind as I do. Very well. You have leave to proceed.'

The Doctor, humble and yellow and bent, proceeded.

'Well done, Sir,' said Anthony, shaking the Admiral's hand: and Number Fifteen, making his first utterance for a long time, said the same.

Peach pranced in, blushing no more, and put her small arms round as much of the Admiral as she could. 'I *still* think it's a gorgeous get-up – however much you scowl at me.'

The Admiral embraced her fondly. 'If you're not careful, hussy,' he said, 'I'll place my hands on your bosoms. Ha!'

'Oh, goody!'

'I tell you what,' said Anthony, elated, 'let's take some rum up to Prim and Stanley Bass, report progress, and celebrate Victory!'

'Avast there!' said the Admiral. 'Navigate with caution. What have we got? The word of a rat – a tough rat too – and those damned discs of yours. Have you any spares for those contraptions, Anthony?'

'No, Sir.'

'Could dummies be arranged? Potter?'

'Yes, Sir. I could fit two of the old nightingale records, Sir.'

'Do that, then. And put the others under your pillow.'

'Aye, aye, Sir.'

'Why so, Sir?' asked Anthony.

'Because, my boy, I expect a burglary in this small ship tonight. And let it be a good burglary – a good, successful, quiet burglary – I don't wish to be disturbed. Master-at-Arms, leave this window open, and the front-door on the latch. Order understood?'

'Aye, aye, Sir.'

'Make it so. And now, if it's an order from their Lordships, we will celebrate Victory.' They did.

CHAPTER XVI

The Admiral, indeed, was no mean psychologist. Doctor Maple, tottering into the dusk, was beaten, bewildered, broken in spirit and body. As he stumbled up the avenue of limes, his skin felt queer, his inside seemed to have floated away, and his body was as light as a feather, and accordingly difficult to manoeuvre. He was a stumbling skeleton of shame and rage, thinly covered with goose-flesh. As he rested against a great tree, he muttered 'adrenalin-deficiency'.

But the night air filled his lungs and freshened his blood: and, free of the Admiral's overpowering personality, his mind began to work again. At the top of the avenue he felt better. He stopped at the Three-Cornered Hat, and sat down in the seat he had shared with Peach that fatal night. That was something, at least: Peach had not gone against him. Indeed, she had as much right to be as enraged as he. How disgusting they had been!

But what, after all, had they got, the devils? Only those horrid records, or whatever they were. Without those, he could laugh at them. And those, surely, they would never dare to use in public. Was not Number Nine rather keen on Peach? The brain-tester began to feel that he had allowed himself to be bluffed. But, of course, with such brutes, you never knew. They had got the records: and, while they existed, he would never know peace. But why should they exist? He walked more firmly through the Spanish Garden, thinking. He went to the Staff Common Room and had a large whisky, with not much water. He was quite sure then that he had absurdly allowed himself to be bluffed and bewildered by a lot of theatrical make-believe. He had another large whisky. After that, he felt that he had got his persecutors on the run. The room, after all, was on the ground-floor. He still had the electric torch he had found in King Charles's Chamber (it would serve them right if he used *their* torch!). He had seen no signs of a dog at the Lodge.

So, just after midnight, Doctor Maple went down the avenue of limes again. It was his first burglary, and, in spite of the whisky (he had had one or two more), he was, very properly, nervous. But, as it turned out, the thing was ludicrously easy. The garden gate was not latched, and he got in with no noise at all. The silly fools had even left the study-window (an in-and-out affair) open, and it was the easiest thing to step inside. He then knocked over a chair and thought he heard a dog bark (it would be just like the treacherous brutes to have a secret dog). He stood with thumping heart for five minutes, but all was quiet (upstairs, the Admiral was almost throttling the old dog, Beatty). He found with his torch the mysterious box, still in the same corner. Inside, at the top, were two metal reels. Round one was wound a mass of brown paper, about the width of a typewriter ribbon. The other was empty. But by the side of the machine lay another reel with coils of paper round it. Presumably, the papered reels were what he wanted. He took them both, and stealthily made off. Back in his room he lit a fire, and spent a long time feeding the brown paper from the reels to the flames, and happily burning the song of the nightingale. He did not know what to do with the metal reels: but that could wait. It might not be a bad idea to send them back to the Admiral – with his compliments. That would be funny! He laughed into the fire. What was funnier still, perhaps, was that all this care and toil had been quite unnecessary. He had only to press a button on the machine at the Lodge, and whatever was on the tape would have been quietly rubbed out. But that the scientist did not know.

In spite of his triumph, he thought he had better lie low, perhaps, about the statue and the secret staircase. After all that had happened, it would be wiser not to attack in the open. The great thing was that the brutes could not now attack him, while there was much that he could do – his reports, for example, on Number Nine and Number Fifteen. And somehow, one day, he would be even with that king-devil, the Admiral. Doctor Maple was well pleased with Doctor Maple: he thought he was a very remarkable man.

The Admiral was flashing 'A' 's across the Lake. He wanted to signal:

BURGLARY SUCCESSFUL AAA MAN THE GUNS. But no steady 'T' came back to him. Anthony was asleep in 'Blanket Bay'.

Monday was the Last Day – some thought the worst day. The Day of Interviews. Each candidate was interviewed thrice – by the Chairman, the Observer, and the Psychologist of his Group. All day the 'STOP' young lady was coming and going with discreetly whispered summonses. As she carried off each victim to some new inquisition in a private room, Anthony was reminded of those stories of the prisoners of the Gestapo or the NKVD and the torture of a hundred cross-examinations. Some interviews lasted an hour. Meanwhile there were two 'mass-meetings' of the Intake, presided over by Mr Rackstraw, one for a General Discussion, and one for Short Talks by those who had not already performed. Also, they wrote an essay on the wisdom of giving full adult suffrage to the coloured inhabitants of the redundant Island, of which all were thoroughly tired. In the intervals, any who were behind-hand had to do their 'mutual ranking' lists and self-analytical essays. Altogether, a testing, exhausting day.

About half-past ten Number Thirteen came back to the mass-meeting looking strangely white. As he sat down, Anthony was astounded and horrified to hear him whisper to his neighbour:

'Been with Maple. *What* a bastard!' Anthony had to stop himself from calling across 'But surely he's *gone*?' Maple still here – and in wicked action! He had imagined the fellow on his way to London. But soon there was a short break and Fantom brought him a signal from the Admiral:

NAVAL MESSAGE

TO: LIEUT. BASS FROM: FLAG OFFICER IN CHARGE

HOUSE BURGLED NIGHTINGALE RECORDS GONE MAN THE GUNS RUFFIAN MAY BE DANGEROUS

'Good Lord!' thought Anthony. 'But where are we *now*?' What a tough, indestructible rat it was! He showed the signal to Peach.

'Oh, baddy!' she said. 'But what does it mean?'

'I suppose he thinks he's got the record and is in the clear. Anyhow, he's here still. He's interviewing.'

'But why did they *let* him?'

'I can't quite make out what's in the old man's mind. I wondered last night. But you know how he is – you don't argue a lot. And there's generally something there.'

'All very well,' said Peach. 'But here we are. And I don't think I can face an *interview*.'

'After last night, I doubt if *Maple* can. Anyhow, he won't send for me – or Fifteen.'

'I shouldn't be too sure. It's a case of baddy, Bass – indubitably baddy.'

If anything had been needed to warm the heart of Number Eight towards her old friend Number Nine that nervous, nagging day, it would have been the trouble he took to help and fortify the shy Number Thirteen, Tom Crawley. The subject tossed into the arena for General Discussion that morning was 'Discipline and Freedom'. A nice theme, some of them thought, for a number of young folk who were just about to be hauled before an inquisition, or had just escaped from one! But it was a gift to anybody who had served in the fighting Forces. Anthony was one of the few who seemed alive and alert, and made many contributions. But, before he finished his remarks, he always made a point of drawing in the shy young warrior. 'I feel' he would say, 'that our good friend Number Thirteen, with all his experience of handling men…': or, 'What do you say, Number Thirteen?': or, 'I expect that here Number Thirteen will disagree with me – it's only my own personal…'. Thus cued and stimulated and drawn out, Number Thirteen did talk – and talked well: about drill, and discipline, and the human touch; about the relation between smartness on parade and courage in the field. It was during one of his little speeches – modest but compelling – that the 'STOP' girl summoned Anthony away. 'Mr Egerton,' she whispered.

This interview went pretty well. The cosy Mr Egerton never asked so many questions as his two colleagues, being content with a general picture: and, in spite of everything, he was inclined to approve of Number Nine. His favourite question (beloved by many of the Staff) was: '*Why* do you want to go into the Foreign (or Civil) Service?' It sounded simple, but few candidates had come out quite sure that they had given the right answer. If you said 'I think it would be fun', with a jolly smile, you might mean to be brave and gay, but you sounded frivolous. But if you said 'I wish to serve my country' you could hardly fail to sound the dismal note of the prig. The subject had been much discussed in the Bar, and even Number Fifteen had been able to offer no confident advice.

Anthony said simply: 'Well, Sir, that's rather difficult. All I know is that I want to do a good job – and this is the sort of job I should like to do – if I'm good enough.'

Mr Egerton nodded comfortably. It was his habit to pick one subject mentioned in each candidate's Interest Form, and, as he put it, to 'call a bluff'. Now he said:

'I see that you are interested in sun-dials. How would you go about setting up a sun-dial in – the Spanish Garden?'

'I shouldn't, Sir. There's one there already.'

'Of course,' the Chairman smiled, 'I forgot.'

'But there's room for another, Sir. And if you want another fixed, of course, you must…'

He explained so eagerly, and in so much detail, how he would set up a sun-dial in the Spanish Garden that the Chairman wearied of the theme and, satisfied, kindly sent him away.

'I hope' thought Anthony, 'they all ask about sun-dials.'

Peach followed him: and her interview was shorter still. When the Chairman put his favourite question, she said:

'I don't,' and told her little story.

Mr Egerton mildly reminded her that she was wasting public money, but said that he understood, and sent her away. He was sorry. He would have liked more talk with the little daffodil.

In the Bar before lunch, she said: 'You've done wonders with Number Thirteen, Bass, bless you. After you went he simply scintillated. If you weren't such a beast I'd like to bite you.'

'*Please*!' he said with a shudder. 'The next thing is his Short Talk. After lunch we'd better meet here and stoke him up a bit. Any news of the Maple?'

'Not a word,' she said, frowning.

It was a most extraordinary thing: he realized that they were both afraid. But of what?

It was a nice question, after lunch, how much to give Number Thirteen to bring him to the pitch of his Short Talk. It was like bringing a Derby favourite or a Boat Race crew to the start in just the right condition. Anthony's prescription was risky – but, as events showed, right: a large port after lunch, creating contentment and calm; then a short rehearsal or 'pep-talk'; and then a medium whisky and soda, for fire and effervescence. It was a gamble. It might have been fatal. But, as things turned out, it was fine.

The young hero, when he was called upon, rose up as straight as a lamp-post, as proud as a swan, fearing nothing. The subject handed to him had been 'Nationalization'. But Anthony had told him to ignore that ('The Staff are cowed. They won't stop you.') and speak about 'The Infantry'. The theme was that the Infantry was the indispensable arm, come sea, come air, come tank, come atom-bomb. This was something the lad knew something about; and what he knew, released by encouragement, port-wine and whisky, he said with grace and gusto.

But Anthony was not to hear his pupil. As Number Thirteen began, the 'STOP' girl whispered: 'Doctor Maple, please. Will you come with me?'

'What a nerve!' thought Anthony. Should he go – or not? He had more than half a mind to refuse. To be summoned like this. by the little rat he had helped to trample upon last night was simply grotesque. He was still, of course, doing his best for Bass, but nothing he could say to the Maple could win any marks for Bass tonight. On the other hand, he thought, he might do still more harm to poor Bass. Refusal to attend an interview would be a legitimate black mark, and the Maple could record it without any revelations embarrassing to himself. Number Nine found himself following the 'STOP' girl – and feeling absurdly uneasy.

'Good-afternoon, Number Nine. Sit down.'

'Good-afternoon.' (He was damned if he would say 'Sir'.)

'What a nerve!' thought Anthony again. Doctor Maple, though of course 'no oil-painting', showed no signs of last evening's harrowing scene – or his late night of crime. He sat in a small room, at a large table, on which were neat piles of examination papers, Interest Forms, Short Stories, all the accumulated evidence against Group A. His amber spectacles were tilted upwards, aimed, as usual, half-way up the wall: and he peered downwards at his prisoner through the lower half of his glasses. There was no expression on his face. But Anthony felt himself in the presence of evil – and, strangely, of power. Here was the psychologist's own familiar environment, his own apparatus of intimidation: and, though the young man might despise it, its effect upon him was strong and disturbing. The trick-cyclist was the Admiral today. 'It gave me quite a turn,' he told Peach later. 'Here was the King of Slugs batting on his own ground – and looking like the Lord Chief Justice.'

Doctor Maple took up a form from one of the piles and laid it before him. Anthony thought 'My Interest Form. What the devil did I say in it?'

'Number Nine, I should like you to tell me the story of your life. You can either imagine yourself as a fashionable biographer, or you can be giving an interview to the *Daily Express*. Begin at the beginning. You have an hour.'

'It was then' said Anthony later, 'that I began to sweat in my stomach.' It can never be great fun to tell the story of your life to unsympathetic ears. How much more trying to have to tell the life-story of someone else – with which you are imperfectly familiar!

The ordeal was not entirely unexpected. Number Fifteen had whispered that the 'life-story' was a favourite trick. Anthony, from the old days at sea, ward-room chatter and reminiscences on watch, knew a good deal of the Bass background, and the night before he had extracted a few more details from the injured man. He felt he could do a plausible general picture of the Bass Career. But a whole hour!

'I was born at Ashstead, Surrey…' he began. He described the old house at the corner of the Common, where, fortunately, be had spent a weekend during the war. He described the Bass *père* and *mère*. He thought he was not doing badly.

('I felt I'd been talking for twenty minutes. But when I looked at the clock it was only four. Gosh!')

His spirit sank again.

He plunged into an absurd story Bass had told him about his childhood. Every day the child Stanley had been sent to a small school in Epsom by pony-trap. One day the trap had been halted outside a large baker's and confectioner's shop, in the window of which were many shiny penny buns. The boy got down, went into the shop, and said simply: 'May I have a bun?' 'Certainly, my little man. How is your mother?' She gave him the bun, and put it down to the Bass account. Stanley thought this was a good arrangement, and the morning bun became a routine affair. Later, an afternoon bun was added as well. Everybody remarked how much the little fellow enjoyed going to school. But when a bill for 315 penny buns came in, the Bass parents had not been amused, and sternly stopped the supply.

Anthony thought it was a funny story, well told. It showed, he thought, the sturdy spirit of Bass. He thought it must have taken him ten minutes to tell. But the clock showed that he had done only seven minutes in all. *53 to go!*

Doctor Maple noted idly that the deprivation of the buns had probably set up a persecutory delusion which would account for the young man's rebellious attitude to authority. But he said nothing.

'I went to a private school at – ' Where the Hell was it? – 'Worthing.' Anthony's own school had been at Folkestone, so he was on fairly easy ground, but barren. He could think of little to say about his private school, except that he disliked it: and that perhaps would not be for the best. 11 minutes.

Doctor Maple listened in lofty silence, sometimes staring at the wall, sometimes turning his amber lamps on his captive. He was enjoying himself. He always enjoyed this performance. He loved to see the young folk floundering and squirming under his cold gaze in the silent room. The silence was the big thing. They made jokes and you did not even smile. They poured out their enthralling talk and you showed no interest. They grew more and more uneasy. You could almost see them tucking away their perilous secrets in the backs of their poor little minds. Then, when they had got used to the silence, you suddenly shot a question at them – quite an innocent question, perhaps, but it staggered them, threw them off their balance. After that, sometimes, the secrets began to leak out.

How wonderful, how delicious it was to apply this refined torment to the conceited, impudent, brutal, Peach-pursuing, intolerable Number Nine! *He* was in the dock now, *he* was the wretched wriggler – with no bullying Admiral to help him, Doctor Maple felt a warm glow of power – and rectitude – within him.

'About this time' said Number Nine, 'I was very fond of sun-dials. There was a small sun-dial on the lawn at the old home at Ashstead. I used to say it was too small, because you could not read the time from a distance. "Can't we have a big sun-dial, Daddy, so that we can see it from the bath-room?" ' ('This is fun,' thought Anthony, 'I can keep this up for hours!') 'Daddy said "You shall have a big sun-dial if you can make it." He lent me some books and I learned how to make sun-dials...'

He went on to describe how he had made the big sun-dial, with nothing but a long pole and some marks on the lawn, how Daddy had been able to see the time from his bed-room and was delighted. ('Your dear Dad, Bass,' he said later, 'jolly nearly made me cry.')

Anthony – or Fate – had chosen the subject well. For Doctor Maple had no notion how sun-dials were constructed, and could not have called the bluff, if it had been a bluff.

But then the young man put a foot wrong.

'All this' he said – he thought that the relevance of the sun-dial should be explained – 'led me to the study of navigation. Of course, I'd done a bit of sailing in small boats on the lake – '

The torturer sat up and spoke for the first time.

'The lake? I thought you said it was a small house with a small garden?'

'This was a lake, Sir, at the house of a friend.'

It was then that Anthony began, as he put it later, to 'sweat seriously'. All the time, he had been afraid of letting some of his own 'background' creep into Stanley Bass's. This horrid fellow suspected something. Bass was in danger. And, damn it, he had called the rat 'Sir'. Doctor Maple, in fact, had merely thought it was time he asked a question: for Number Nine was becoming a bit too comfortable. He could not understand, for all his experience, why the question had caused such marked unease. Surely the young man was sweating a little? He was. Excellent. But why?

Anthony had been going to explain how the sun-dial had introduced him to the mysteries of the Equation of Time, Apparent Time, and all that, and so to the movements of the heavenly bodies. But all this had gone out of his head.

He said: 'So I made up my mind to join the Navy.'

'But you didn't. You went into business.'

'Yes, Sir. My father was against the Navy.'

Once more, as far as Doctor Maple could tell, a perfectly good answer. But Anthony was dismally conscious that he had put another foot wrong. He had forgotten that he was Bass. He must pull himself together. Thirty-five minutes to go.

'When the war began I did join the Navy. I had six months in the ranks, and – '

'One moment,' said the cold superior voice. 'You've only just left your private school. What happened next?'

He fumbled through another pile and produced another form – the candidate's 'pre-record'. 'O Lord!' thought Anthony. 'He does suspect!'

Doctor Maple suspected nothing in particular: but he was wondering what Number Nine had to hide. Had he been expelled from his Public School? No sign of it in the form. But you never knew. 'Superannuated', perhaps, for stupidity.

'You went to Eton?' he sharply said.

'No – yes.'

'You did go to Eton, didn't you?'

'Yes, Sir. Of course.'

Some strong suppressive mechanism here, thought the expert. This is the second time he has shied away from Eton.

'Then why not tell me about it? How long were you there?' he snapped.

'Four years.'

'Why did you leave?'

'To join the Navy.'

Oh, Lord, wrong again! Anthony himself had been a 'Public School Entry' to the Navy and had spent nearly four happy years at Winchester. But that did not fit in with Bass. This hound would be after him again. He was.

'But you didn't join the Navy till the war – 1953. You left Eton in 1951.'

'Yes, Sir, I told you – my father changed his mind.'

('Well done, Bass.')

Doctor Maple looked at him. Something fishy here – but what?

While he looked, a grim thought now alarmed Number Nine. Perhaps, in spite of the Admiral's beard, the hound had smelt some family likeness – something in the eyes? He looked away – a mistake – and began to sweat again.

'You don't like talking about Eton?'

'Oh, yes, Sir. Rather, Sir.'

'Tell me all about it.'

'That's it,' thought Anthony. 'He doesn't think I ever went to Eton.' Fortunately, there is a close link between Winchester and Eton. Every year one school visits the other for the 'Eton Match'. Anthony had made many friends at Eton, and had walked all round the College. He knew the names of the Head, and some house-masters, and how to say M'Tutor. He could talk about 'Pop' and 'Athens' and Agar's Plough and the Wall-Game and the Fourth of June.

'I was a Wet-bob,' he began, and continued confidently. He did pretty well, he thought.

But Doctor Maple had no doubt about Number Nine's having been at Eton. He was seeking only a clue to something discreditable.

'In my last year' Anthony concluded proudly (he had almost forgotten this), 'I was Captain of the Boats.'

'As an Old Etonian,' said Doctor Maple, 'do you go down to the old school much?'

'No,' said Anthony, without sufficient thought.

'Why not?'

'Because' he nearly said, 'I'm nearly always at sea.' He stopped just in time, but the slip had shaken him, as Doctor Maple saw. He said, lamely: 'I don't know. Don't feel like it very much.'

'Ha, ha! Left under a cloud,' thought Doctor Maple.

He said: 'Is that the whole truth?'

Suddenly Anthony lost his temper. He could stand no more from the amber insinuator. 'Of course it is! How dare you sit there and call me a liar! And, after last night – '

'*Please*, Number Nine,' said Doctor Maple, delighted, 'please, please control yourself.' He peered at his prisoner with half-closed eyes. This was how he liked to see his enemy – this was better than he had expected.

'*Quite* calm now, Number Nine,' he said, soothingly, like a dentist saying 'Open, please' or a Nurse 'There, ducky'.

'We don't like Eton very much, do we? Some memory, no doubt. Never mind. The next thing, we went into business. Tell me about that.'

Anthony, angry with himself for being angry, had to hold himself tight against another outburst. 'I've hardly ever before' he told Peach, 'actually wanted to throttle a man – not that he is.'

'Yes,' he said at last. 'Well – ' But the voice squeaked, so high was his rage: and that made things no better.

There was a knock: and kindly Fate sent in the 'STOP' girl with a message for Doctor Maple. 'The Principal would like to see you as soon as it's convenient.'

Doctor Maple coolly surveyed his victim, still sweating, still flushed, and now ashamed of himself. He could hardly hope for a better end to the interview. Better leave him in that condition before he could recover himself. He would be on his best behaviour now, anxious to make a better show. But he would not get the chance.

'Very well, Miss Plumly,' he said, 'I'll come now. Thank-you, Number Nine.'

Anthony was left alone, muttering to himself a great many old-fashioned words.

CHAPTER XVII

'This' said Peach to herself sadly, 'is *not* how I thought it was going to end.' But she cracked another walnut, and enjoyed it.

Of old, at the end of the Day of Interviews, the Intake had packed their bags, shaken off the dust of Hambone Hall, and scuttled back to London by the 6.15, in which they compared notes, gay or grim, about the indiscretions and agonies of the weekend, and gradually returned to the characters they had left behind at Victoria.

Sir Gilbert (bless him!) had thought that this was a sour, unsatisfactory ending. Whether the young folk had done well or not, whatever they thought about 'TPQ', it would be sound, he thought, to send them away with a friendly taste in the soul. And the Hall, after all, needed good word-of-mouth publicity as well as any other institution. So much of TPQ must seem inhuman and harsh to the young. Why not show them that, beneath its rugged exterior, the State, which they aspired to serve, had some warm blood too?

So, with Treasury sanction (not easily obtained), he had instituted the Farewell Dinner. The food was a little better, and there was wine (Government Hospitality Scale B, but not more than one bottle per three personnel).

After the Dinner there was coffee and port (Scale C) in the Great Hall, and the Staff and Intake joined together for unofficial gossip and good-bye. Evening dress was not compulsory, but was approved.

Peach, looking round, thought well of herself in her modest velvet dinner dress of midnight-blue, with twinkling silver buttons.

The evening was not always as gay as Sir Gilbert had hoped. The Intake chattered about their trials and errors: the Staff fretted a little because they could not get on with their Reports. But a certain merriness generally emerged in the end, and Sir Gilbert always enjoyed it. It was his baby, this party. He saw the young folk, in his mind, pulling Treasury crackers, a pleasing image.

Sir Gilbert, of course, did not know about the special trouble in Peach's heart – and Peach's camp. Number Nine had come out from his interview with Doctor Maple looking like a ghost; and two generous gins had been required to extract the story from him. When it came, it was not clear. He seemed to think that Maple had guessed the guilty secret. Yet he was not sure. Maple, it seemed, hadn't said so. Anyhow, her beloved Bass – she was sure about that now – was depressed and deflated, and that was a monstrous thing to see. Even the rugged Number Fifteen confessed that he had had a nasty time with the Maple – and even he could not explain the how and the why.

(Peach had not been summoned by anyone after her interview with the Chairman, for he had passed the word to his colleagues that it would be a waste of public money and time.)

Number Fifteen, the Maple let loose again, was justifiably anxious about his 'career': but unjustly, Peach thought, was inclined to blame Number Nine for everything. Peach herself was inclined to blame the Admiral for letting the burglar do his work without 'let or hindrance'. Why not catch him and put another nail in his coffin? The Admiral, she thought, had been 'too clever by half'. Secretly, though he would never have said it, Anthony thought the same. He had had no more signals from the old man; he did not know what he was up to: but he suspected that Papa had made a bloomer.

They were quite right, up to a point. The Admiral had made one miscalculation, at least. The Admiral thought that, whatever else Doctor Maple did or did not do, he would carry to the Principal the Admiral's desire to attend the Farewell Dinner. Doctor Maple, the Admiral thought, having secured as he, Doctor Maple, would suppose, the incriminating record, would think he had nothing to fear from anyone. He might even get a good mark – and enjoy a big laugh – for being the man who had got the Admiral invited. All this was rather subtle – too subtle. The psychologist, thinking simply, for once, had said to himself: 'I'm damned if I get that old devil asked to dinner here.'

So the Admiral had waited all day for an invitation that never came. And he fretted severely. For he realized that he had exposed his patrol-forces to undeserved dangers. He had planned to extricate them by an advance of the Grand Fleet: and now he could not get near them.

The Forces of Right, then, were everywhere divided and dubious. It was all very well to say, as the Admiral had said, that 'the village is talking'. Possibly. It was all very well to hope that Sir William Blant (now back at his duties in the House of Commons) would send in a 'stinking report'. Possibly. But 'the *central* thing', as Peach said, was the 'presence and prevalence of the Maple in *mass*!' There he sat, the main target of the Forces of Right, pierced by a thousand arrows, but showing not a sign of woe. There he sat, at the Staff Table, two places from the Chairman, looking like a camel but laughing like a bilious clown, laying down the law about something or other – and being listened to. 'The entire Evolution' Peach thought, 'is the *most* utter *flop*.'

Peach had her private troubles, too. Tomorrow morning, rejected by the State (thank God!), she would go back to her worthy Daddy and cook and wash-up for him until she could decently escape to a better job. Much as she hated 'TPQ' and all its works, it had been an interesting, exciting weekend; and she found herself sorry that it was nearly over. The end of a party was always sad, somehow, even if it had been a dubious party. And Number Nine? Nobody could tell what was in the mind of that wild lovable creature. Tomorrow morning he might ask her to marry him. Or, just as likely – far more likely – she would never see him again.

Anthony was deep in gloom and self-accusation. He would have applauded, if he could have heard them, almost all the thoughts of Number Eight. He could not imagine what the Admiral was up to: but who was he, the wretched Anthony, to complain? He had let the side down pretty badly, he thought. To take on an impersonation-job without notice or preparation was, at the best, he realized, a crazy impertinence. Up against trained trick-cyclists like the Maple, it was madness. They could read you like a book. The Evolution had fizzled out. He would not have minded so much if he had kept the flag of Stanley Bass flying high. He had done his best: but now that flag, very soon, might have to be struck. There, at the next table, sat the King of Slugs, triumphant: and here was he confessing to himself that, after all, there might be something in trick-sluggery. Not that that mattered. He still hated their guts. As the American said before a Picasso: 'I shouldn't like it even if it was *good*.' But they had *won!* And Peach – dear, golden, gurgling Peach, how could he expect her to think seriously of such a dismal failure?

But when the company moved out into the Great Hall for coffee and port, Peach gave Anthony's arm a comforting little pinch, and the two flew their flags bravely enough. The chatter was loud, and as merry as could be expected. Fantom moved about with his tray of glasses, like a battleship among a fleet of trawlers. Anthony had noticed that he was wearing his evening dress, a pleasant touch of the old times. Peach looked round the lively scene, and wondered for a moment what it would be like to be the wife of an Earl (she was not quite sure what the wife of an Earl was called), to be the mistress of a great house like this – with, of course, six boys. It would be nice, she thought, to give gay parties – real parties – here. She would have this floor polished, and they could dance. But Anthony would hardly ever be allowed to play the organ. She blushed inside her at her presumptuous dreams, and moved across to Jacaranda, with charity in her heart.

Jacaranda was looking luscious, in a severe black dress with a *corsage candide* (as they called it then), and dangling ear-rings of shiny jet. She was feeling better. Doctor Maple had not summoned her. The Chairman and the Observer had interviewed her kindly, and nobody had asked about those horrid Words. Perhaps she would get to South America after all. Anyhow, tomorrow she would be free of this dreadful place, where no one cared for warm-blooded love.

Peach said softly: 'I do hope you've forgiven me, Number Ten?'

'You must call me Joy,' said Jacaranda graciously. 'It is all right. I should have done the same as you. But you must *never* tell.' She patted her lustrous locks as proudly as if they had been her own.

Peach promised: 'I'll be *too* reticent.'

Anthony too was soothing the sores of Number Fifteen. 'I'm sorry about the whole thing, old boy. But don't you worry. You'll be through. I've put you top of both my lists.'

'Thanks, Number Nine,' said Cosmo, remembering uncomfortably that he had not done the same for Bass. Doctor Maple sat in a corner, in stealthy talk with Elinor Slice. Sir Gilbert moved among the company, distributing cheery words to all, contented with his party.

Someone said 'What about some music?' Number Fifteen cried loyally: 'Number Nine, give us a tune!' 'Number Nine! Number Nine!' cried many, and Anthony, much astonished, found himself being gently propelled to his own organ. 'This is moving,' he thought. 'Old Bass must have scored a mark or two after all.'

While the organ was warming, Number Fifteen muttered behind him: 'Not *too* loud, old chap.'

Anthony nodded. This must be good – and another mark for Bass perhaps. He would give them Handel's *Largo,* the one piece he was fairly sure about – and he would let them off with one verse.

He didn't. He thought he played the first verse so well, so softly, that he deserved a second. And, after all, he was the heir of the Adleys, this was *his* organ: and perhaps he would never play it again.

Even in the second verse, by a stern effort, he restrained himself, and used no more than half the artillery at his command.

Peach, proud of her Number Nine, would not have cared much if he had played *Knocked 'em in the Old Kent Road*. But the simple, noble, flowing tune seemed to fit the high Hall, the ancient house, so well, and all her dreams and all her secret serious thoughts so well, that small tears crept into the corners of her eyes. 'All will be well,' she thought. And it seemed to fit the last notes of the song. 'All sha – a – all be well!' Anthony was only human, and, for the final repetition of the principal phrase, he did let the thunder have its way: and very fine it sounded. But during these last bars, by chance – or what? – Peach turned and saw Doctor Maple in his corner. He was staring, like everyone else, at the back of the amateur organist, who was doing so surprisingly well. But, on his face, and in his eyes, was more malignity and hatred than Peach had ever seen: and in her faithful little soul she shuddered.

There was loud (and genuine) applause at the end of the *Largo,* and cries of 'Encore'. Anthony, pleased with himself, was wondering whether he would risk *Annie Laurie,* the Russian National Anthem – or what? But strange and thrilling music from another quarter took all eyes and ears away from him.

At the entrance to the passage on the south side stood ex-Chief Petty Officer Potter (for the moment converted into Bo'sun's Mate). He was in uniform (gaiters and all), and he was blowing vigorously into his bo'sun's whistle. Anthony, alone of the company, recognized the call for Piping an Admiral Aboard.

It was a wonderful cue. But what was he to do about it? He could think of many tunes suitable for 'playing-in' an Admiral of the Fleet. But none of them had he ever attempted on the organ.

The others stared, amazed, at Potter. The Staff thought it must be another practical joke by the craziest Intake in the history of TPQ. The candidates thought it was, perhaps, part of the kind Sir Gilbert's farewell treat. Whatever it was, it was fascinating, as is any performance of technical perfection. At the end, now thoroughly warmed by the carnival spirit, all applauded, which seemed to Potter to be most improper (though it pleased him). Then the great figure of Fantom appeared beside him.

Fantom, in a sepulchral voice, like that of the Messenger of the House of Commons announcing the approach of 'Black Rod', intoned:

'Admiral of the Fleet the Earl of Caraway and Stoke!'

Suddenly, the Admiral emerged from the dusky passage into the light. He was in full uniform. Under his left arm he carried the cocked hat. He wore his sword. He looked magnificent.

Everyone who was sitting, obeying some deep, respectful instinct, stood up – even the Maple and the Hen: and Anthony, daring greatly, played *Hearts of Oak* on the organ.

During this suitable but uncertain 'voluntary', Sir Gilbert went to meet the Admiral and led him to a chair. Fantom gave him coffee and a glass of port. Sir Gilbert said how glad he was to see him, how sorry he was not to have seen him there before. He had thought of inviting him many times, but they were always so busy. 'You know how it is, Sir. As soon as one Intake has gone, another comes in. It's a treadmill.' This was true enough; but not, the Admiral thought, a very good excuse. Nor was it. The truth was that Sir Gilbert had heard from many mouths that the Earl was a testy, eccentric, rather terrible old man: and Sir Gilbert had quite enough troubles of his own.

Tonight, however, the old boy seemed gracious enough. A genial beam on his face, he looked slowly round the room, like a lighthouse searching the sea. He found Anthony, and the other fellow, the Pongo, and Peach – and very nearly winked at Peach. The Intake stared back at him, quiet and expectant. All had a proper respect for an Earl. All had heard of the hero of Bornholm and other battles. And, after that dramatic 'entrance', there must surely be something coming.

Doctor Maple, after the first surprise, did not look at the old man. Who was he, anyhow? There were better brains than his about.

Sir Gilbert, sensitive man, had the same thought as most of the Intake. He said: 'I wonder, Sir, whether you'd care to say a few words? It's their last night, you know.'

'Well,' said the Admiral readily, 'if it's an order – aye, aye, Sir Gilbert.'

He rose: and, such was the impact of his personality, that even the rising to his feet of this short, sturdy old man commanded silence everywhere. Only Doctor Maple continued muttering something: and the Admiral discharged so fierce a glare into that corner that Miss Slice quailed before it, and nudged her love, and he was silent too.

The Admiral raised his glass of port.

'First,' he said, 'Ladies and Gentlemen, – I give you – the King!'

There was a startled shuffling of chairs and feet – and then a solemn hush, as they drank to the King's health. Only poor Number Four, at the end, said 'God bless him!' though not an officer in His Majesty's Navy. The Admiral sank him with a fifteen-inch glare.

'Forgiven, I hope, Sir Gilbert?' the Admiral went on, when all were seated. 'That was the custom when I was in command of this ship. My patrols tell me it's *not* the custom now. Funny thing – ' he gave a booming chuckle, like a quick touch on a pedal of the organ – 'half of you are in the service of His

Majesty: the other half are trying to creep in through the hawse-hole. Yet you don't drink "the King". Ain't that extraordinary, Sir Gilbert? Ain't that as funny as a Swiss battleship?'

The voice was severe. But the smile, and the bow to Sir Gilbert, were disarming: and the Swiss battleship had everybody laughing. Sir Gilbert gracefully nodded agreement. As a soldier, he had often had the same thought: but the Treasury had reasoned acutely that the King's Health every night would mean port-wine every night and (even at Scale C) that was too much.

'Well, Intake!' the Admiral roared – and the young folk roared as well. 'Intake! What a misbegotten, Irish pennant of a word! Reminds me of the Civil Servant who said that something or other opened a "serious door". Ha!' (This allusion was wholly innocent. The Admiral had no notion that he was addressing the celebrated 'SD'.) Poor Mr Rackstraw smiled ruefully, and Sir Gilbert frowned a little. The Intake laughed.

'I'm glad, I must say, Sir Gilbert, to be back in the old ship. First time since the King took over. And, from what I've seen, she looks all snug and Bristol-fashion. Decks clean and paintwork bright. I wish the young folk well – I beg your pardon, I wish the Intake well.'

They laughed again. They loved him. Peach said to herself: 'If Anthony won't have me I'll marry the Admiral.'

'I hope you all make harbour and find a snug berth. But, by God, if you do, you'll be a damned fine lot! I've had my patrols out, as I said, and, let me tell you, Nelson himself would never have got through this course! Wellington would have been turned down! Napoleon would have been sent away the first day! How old are you children – 21 – 24 – 26 – 30? Nelson was a post-captain at the age of twenty. What d'you suppose Nelson would have said,' the Admiral roared, 'if anyone came up to him and shouted "MOTHER! What are you thinking of, dear boy?" '

The Intake had been alert and silent up to this point: but now they collapsed in laughter. They laughed and laughed and laughed. Sir Gilbert laughed too. He rather agreed.

'Wellington, at your age, was in command of a brigade. What would he have said if you'd put up "BAYONET" in front of him? He'd have said "Stick 'em in the guts!" Quite right, too. But how many marks would he have got at Hambone Hall?'

They roared.

'Napoleon was a general at the age of twenty-four. But now, they say, his glands were all wrong. A mass of – what-is-it? – "endocrine anomalies". God knows what he'd have said about "MOTHER",' he bellowed, 'but two minutes with a trick-cyclist would have been the end of him.'

The Staff were no longer so much amused as the Intake. They thought the Admiral was being unfair, even in jest, to their devoted labours: and they were not quite sure about his history.

'However, they don't want Admirals or Generals, I know. They're after Whitehall wogs. Well, take Gladstone. At the age of twenty-two he didn't know where he was. Thought he wanted to be a Bible-puncher. Wasn't sure. Read the letter he wrote to Papa (Morley). Wrote like a crocodile. You can read for miles before you get to the meaning. To say what he thought about "MOTHER" would have taken him two days. Ask him something about your old Island, and he'd have preached a sermon. I don't suppose you'd have got him here at all. But, if you had, he'd have been flung out and become a Bishop. Ha!'

No one laughed now. It was clear that the Admiral, however unfair, was out for more than a frolic. The Staff were shocked and the Intake intent.

'Take Mr Churchill. At the age of twenty-three he was shooting Dervishes at Omdurman. I wonder what he'd have said when he came back if anyone had tried "MOTHER" on him – or even "BLOOD". He knew no Latin or Greek. Never went to a University. He'd never have made the Civil Service *this* way.'

A general chuckle.

'Just as well, perhaps. But that ain't the point. Some of you lads have been shooting Russians. Well done. You're too good, and you're too old, to be put through all these nursery hoops by a gang of mind-sweepers, talking a lot of mumbo-jumbo about their slimy souls. I tell you, if I had ten minutes with each of you, I'd know what you were fit for: and I've never been shipmates with an endocrine anomaly yet.'

The Admiral turned to Sir Gilbert, who was still trying to look the dubious but forbearing host. All felt that he had but fired his sighting shots, and now the bombardment was to begin. There was absolute stillness.

'Sir Gilbert, I'm sorry for you. You're a good man in a bad command. I dare say you think I'm talking out of turn. So I am. I dare say you think I'm abusing your hospitality. Well, I ain't. You're abusing mine. This is my ship, my house, my home, as you know, Sir Gilbert. If I'd known there'd be all these Dago antics I'd never have let Whitehall come aboard. I know now. Tomorrow, Sir Gilbert, I resume possession – and Whitehall can do what it likes about it – '

'But, my lord – ' Sir Gilbert protested at last.

'At 12.30 on Wednesday, having established the position of the ship, I shall hoist my flag again. Tomorrow morning, early, I believe, the "Intake" return to London. Tomorrow, before sundown, the Staff will go too – '

'My lord!'

The Admiral made a kindly suppressive gesture.

'All must be ashore by sundown. *The man called Maple,*' the old man thundered, 'who has treacherously betrayed his word, will go ashore *tonight*. He will lash his hammock now. I will not have that skate under my roof another night.'

All stared at a single corner. Doctor Maple sprang to his feet spluttering and trembling.

'How – how dare you, Sir? I – I defy you – you – you silly old man.'

The Admiral glared.

'You defy me, do you? You refuse to leave the ship tonight?'

'I do.'

'Then you will leave at once. You will not even pack.' He waved a hand at Potter and roared 'Bandmaster!'

Potter had never been 'Bandmaster' before: but, still unshaken, he stepped into the passage. All stared, fascinated by the queer proceedings. From the passage emerged a hoarse male voice:

'Go on.'

'I deliberately release the dream-mechanism,' said a cooing female voice, *'with you at the centre of some appropriate fantasy. This, I find, gives me considerable relief. It keeps the endocrines fully charged, and offsets any tendency to over-sublimation.'*

Few of the Intake recognized the voices: but the words seemed funny, and they laughed uproariously, glad of any relief in this mystifying, uncomfortable scene.

Poor Miss Slice gave a small yelp, put her fingers into her ears, and hurried out.

Doctor Maple stood irresolute, his assurance gone but some of his devil alive.

'AVAST!' cried the Admiral: and Potter stopped the tape-machine.

'Now – you! Get out! The second barrel, you may remember, is more deadly still.'

Doctor Maple gave him a look which, as Peach said, 'would have made an elephant feel *too* small'. But he went. He went with his head up, with his glasses high, with a certain dignity. At the entrance to the passage he turned and bowed a farewell to Sir Gilbert.

'Now, boys and girls,' said the relentless mariner, 'we must say Good-night. I wish you well in your examinations. I wish you well in the world. Always remember you belong to Britain, the best thing God ever made. Fear God. Honour the King.

Don't let the trick-cyclists get you down. And now – dismiss. I have things to say to the Staff. Good-night.'

The Intake departed obediently: but, as they went, someone cried 'Three Cheers for the Admiral!': and these were heartily given.

'Now, Sir Gilbert, let's keep this friendly, shall we? Let's have another glass of port. Would you like to hear my records?'

'I should be interested, I must say, to hear what caused those two unpremeditated exits. Fantom!'

When all were served with port, the Admiral called 'Bandmaster! Perform!'

'I see,' said Sir Gilbert, at the end. 'It's blackmail – isn't it, Admiral?'

'Call it what you will. But call it a day.'

CHAPTER XVIII

Whatever it was called, whatever it was, it worked. All men know that the Civil Service, the pride and glory of Britain, are impervious to reason, unmoved by humanity or loving-kindness, blind to the tears of widows, and deaf to the cries of the oppressed. Not even the threats of ridicule can shake those tough horsemen in their eternal saddles. They parry or ignore the spears of buffoonery and wit as easily as mothers-in-law, plumbers, poets or politicians. But now and then – not always: rebellions must not be encouraged – some rude eccentric fellow with a huge illicit bludgeon does bait and even turn them back, where all the ancient and proper weapons have failed. The retreat is never admitted (they had always intended to alter course at that point); it is soon forgotten, and may never be repeated. But it has happened. At all events, that was the last Intake to be tormented at Hambone Hall.

Sir Gilbert (bless him!), having heard some fragments of the goings-on of his psychological assistants, for whom he was responsible, handed in his resignation. Publicly, he gave no reason: but, privately, he said a lot. The Admiral would have agreed with much of it. Sir William Blant, who had gone back to the House on the Monday, said one or two things too. No Questions were asked in Parliament: but the whispers of Whitehall roared round the world.

Anthony, of course, had to go up to London with the rest of the Intake by the 9.15. All were chattering about the tremendous evening in the Great Hall; and all but one, he was glad to hear, commended his father. The exception was poor Number Eleven, who said (as usual, to an audience of one) *'Non tali auxilio nec defensoribus istis.'* Anthony had no notion what he meant: but he judged, from the tone of voice, and the 'form' of the speaker, that the intention was hostile.

Peach sat beside him, happy but sad. Happy? It was wonderful the way the tricky play had ended. The Admiral, of course, had stolen the stage; he was *quite* miraculous, and she loved him. But, looking back, she did feel that her Anthony had sown the seed, taken the risks, made 'the crooked straight and the rough places plain'. She thought she might have helped a little herself. But now, she supposed, all was over. At home she would find the kitchen in the *most* insanitary state, and no food anywhere. So she was sad.

At Victoria, after the general good-byes, she found herself clutching sturdily her tiny grey bag, alone with Anthony.

'Well, good-bye, Number Nine,' she said. 'It's been bliss. You did marvels.'

'Where are you bound?'

'Home. There'll be five days' washing-up.'

'How long will that take us?'

' "Us"?'

'Us. I have some time on my hands.'

'How much?' she said, bewildered. 'What are you going to do?'

'I'm going home. By the 4.33.' He held up the return half of his ticket.

'But then you'll collide with the Staff, coming away. And all will be out.'

'By no means. I shan't stop at Hambone Halt. I shall go on to Caraway Station, and walk back across the fields. So will you.' He held up a second return half.

'I can't imagine what you mean.'

('Actually,' she told her numerous grand-children, 'at that point my heart was *utterly* static.')

'Tomorrow' he said, 'the Admiral hoists his flag again. You, as the spear-head of the whole attack, could hardly be absent from *that* parade.'

She liked that. It was just what she had been thinking about him.

'I see the point: I like it,' she said. 'But what about Dad? I can't leave him again – so soon.

'I tell you what. We'll take Dad out to lunch at the Savoy and fill him so full with food he won't have to eat again for four or five days.'

'We might try that.'

They did that. Then they did the washing-up.

At 4.34, incredulous, Peach found herself alone with a Viscount in a first-class carriage, returning to the Caraway country.

'You know,' she said sleepily, 'I *can't* imagine what all this is *about*.'

'The fact is, Number Eight, I rather think I rather love you.'

'Oh, goody!' said Peach. 'What a coincidence!'

Pleasant things took place.

'You gave us the devil of a day, Sir, on Monday.'

'I know, Anchor. My compliments, and my apologies. But, you remember, I was always for a mass court martial?'

'Yes, Sir.'

'Blowing up the one fort was a worthy operation. But it might have left the stinking citadel intact. See what I mean?'

'Yes, Sir.'

Hambone Hall was still, technically, in the clutch of Whitehall: but, in fact, it was occupied by that cantankerous old Admiral, the rightful – well, not the rightful, but the original – owner. 'This' all the wits of Whitehall giggled, 'has opened A SERIOUS DOOR!' But 'TPQ' had surrendered: and other Government Departments, Boards, Corporations, Commissions, Committees, gathered in a monstrous queue, competing for the body of Hambone Hall. Down the queue came worrying whispers. That awful Admiral! You might get him out of the Hall: but he would still be at the Lodge by the lake, and there, who could tell what he would be up to next? He had guns trained on the Hall. At any moment he might roar into a committee meeting, a lecture, or a party, with a platoon – or whatever it was – of Marines, all heavily armed. Worst of all, as the Treasury reminded them, he had those *ghastly* records – officially known as 'The Nightingale'. There was nothing to stop the Admiral from playing 'The Nightingale' at Number 10, or (though there might be technical difficulties) in the House of Lords. While 'The Nightingale' existed in the Admiral's possession the Treasury was *not* prepared to enter into any negotiations with anyone, even if it was a branch of the National Coal Board. So the queue dwindled, and, at last, disappeared.

'Not six! Not *six*!'
'Yes, darling – six.'
'Why *six*?'
'Why not?'
'Why not five? Or four, perhaps?'
'No, six. Just six. Don't you see what I mean?'
'A woman of one idea?'
'No, six.'

Before the hoisting of the flag the Admiral, back on his old bridge again, got his noon position, with particular care and solemn ceremony. Peach, for whom he had already a warm affection, was allowed to stand by the chronometer and say 'Bang!' in a sharp (though still sweet) voice when (assisted by Anthony) she judged that it was Apparent Noon. Nor, like the wretched Primrose, did she fail him. He embraced her.

Then came the business with Admiral Mole. It was quite a thing, this first time, to be signalling a new position to that silly old sailor in the woods, especially as the new position was Hambone Hall, and the Admiral was only 300 yards out. Admiral Mole was five cables out. The Earl of Caraway embraced Peach Meridew again.

The Admiral, not being a ship or Naval Establishment, could not, to his great regret, hoist the White Ensign. But he could send up, beside the Union Jack (which all Britons, on land, may fly), the flag of the Caraways, the Anchors, the Adleys. This, with proper ceremony, was done. It was a small company, but a great occasion. There was no band, but Potter did what he could with his whistle. Peach, very proud, hauled up the flag, saw that it was 'chock-a-block', and carefully made all fast. The Admiral, Anthony, Lady Primrose, stood to attention. The flag of sanity was up again. The Admiral embraced Number Eight.

'The Nightingale' was discussed 'at the highest level'. One Cabinet Meeting discussed nothing else. No Government, it was felt, could count itself safe, while 'The Nightingale' was about, alive. It was decided, at last, that something special must be done about the terrible Admiral. The Treasury proposed that there should be a kind of unique and unprecedented *ad hoc* (and, of course, 'once for all') joint ownership of Hambone Hall, shared between His Majesty and the Earl of Caraway and Stoke (and his heirs, for two generations). The Earl (and the said heirs) should have the right to tranquil possession of the premises, subject to the right of the People to visit the grounds on Mondays, Wednesdays, Thursdays, and the living-rooms on Saturdays, Sundays, Good Fridays and all Bank Holidays. In compensation for any unavoidable disturbance, the Treasury would finance (through the National Trust) an annual grant towards (repeat *towards*) the upkeep of the Hall and grounds. But all this was conditional on the immediate surrender of 'The Nightingale' to the Treasury, for destruction by fire (or otherwise).

The Admiral agreed, under protest, to all this, except Clause 473, which dealt with 'The Nightingale'. 'Cut that out,' he boomed. 'You can trust me – but I can't trust *you*.'

The Treasury, to everyone's astonishment, said: 'Very well.'

'Have a look in here.'

'Why?'

'If you're going to be the Countess (I hope that's still in the air) you ought to know your way about the place.'

'But I think I've been here before.'

'It's just possible. This is King Charles's Chamber. This is, more or less, where everything began.'

'Oh, goody! I remember now. Kiss me.'

Pleasant things took place.

But the Earl was not content with Treasury grants, here today and gone tomorrow – and subject, it seemed, to the un-Christian income-tax. In the name of Potter, who did the work, he entered each week for the Parliament Pools.

The Earl's Matrimonial Causes Bill was very short and simple. Its only clause provided that in Section 2 (*b*) of the Matrimonial Causes Act 1937, or rather, Section 1 of the consolidating Act of 1950, the word 'three' should be replaced by the word 'two'. The effect was to reduce the period for 'desertion' from three years to two.

When the Bill was read a first time and printed there was the usual stir in the Press. But the Admiral, unlike most fathers of Bills, seemed to desire no publicity for his child. He refused to be interviewed. He made no reply to indignant letters in *The Times* which accused him of wishing to tear up family life by the roots. Weeks passed. For a week or two a few acute observers risked their shilling in the Ten Bishops column (Bishops, by the rules, included Archbishops): but nothing was heard about the Second Reading of the Bill, and it was generally forgotten, and those who thought about it at all supposed that the Earl had abandoned his nefarious project.

In the Bishops' Pool you could bet on any number of Bishops being present together in the House on any particular day. But the more Bishops you went for the more it cost. Few punters, therefore, risked more than four, the minimum bet. Whenever there were fewer than four, the money was set aside for the next occasion. Ten Bishops (considered about impossible) scooped the pool.

Most of the population 'did their pools' on Thursday evening, after the Leader of the House of Commons had announced the 'Business' for the following week. On the last Thursday in June the Earl went quietly to the Clerk of the Parliaments and put down the Second Reading of his Bill for the following Tuesday. But this was not announced in the papers till the following day, and all but a very few of the acute observers were caught napping that night. Potter invested heavily.

During the weekend the Forces of Right massed vigorously against the measure: and on Tuesday, when the Admiral rose, both Archbishops and seven Bishops were on the episcopal benches. Nine. This was disappointing, and the Earl was worried. Many punters would have betted on eight on this occasion: and some might have gone as far as nine. He had very little to say himself and was far from sure that he would get any support. The debate might well collapse before the tenth Bishop came in. But, while on his feet, he had an inspiration. He observed that the venerable Bishop of Paddington was not in the House. The venerable Bishop had attacked him hotly in a letter to *The Times*. The Admiral now expressed strong surprise and displeasure at the Bishop's absence. He had refrained, he said, from replying in the public Press to an attack which he bitterly resented – 'rightly resented, I think, my Lords – I preferred to meet my assailant face to face in your Lordships' House, and little thought that he would keep away.' He did not like, he said, an enemy who fired a single shot from the horizon and then turned tail. He developed his attack with a wealth of marine metaphors, and worked himself into a state of indignation which was almost genuine. A friend of the Bishop's hurried out and telephoned to the old man, who was suffering from lumbago and intercostal neuritis. He was bundled into a car and hastily carried to the Lords.

It was a near thing. The Archbishop of Canterbury made a powerful speech, with every word of which the Admiral agreed. Nobody would support him now, and there was really nothing else to be said. Still no number ten. But, as the Archbishop's peroration began, the venerable Bishop of Paddington limped in, to a generous murmur of applause. He rose immediately, expressed his regret, and said that only his infirmity would have kept him from hearing the noble Earl's motion. The Admiral charmingly accepted his apology, and apologized himself for his unfair attack, in excuse for which be could only plead ignorance.

He then said that, shot out of the water by the Archbishop's speech, he would withdraw his Bill.

Potter's 'dividend' was £43,000 8*s.* 2*d.* – free of tax.

'Anthony, I think you're pretty supreme.'

'I can see a good many good points in you.

'Oh, darling, then why not six?'

'Six, I feel, is just about two too many.'

'But why?'

'I don't know. That's how I feel. Why six, for that matter?'

'I don't know, darling. It's just a thing of mine. Six. Of course, if you don't feel it – '

'I feel four, thoroughly.'

'Darling, I do think you're being a little unreasonable. I think I shall cry a little now.'

'Oh, darling! The point is, we haven't any mon."

'You must get some mon.'

Oddly enough, the Admiral professed to be shocked by Anthony's success in the Pools. In July, Anthony had weekend leave from his new ship (*Gadfly*), and his old friend, Lieutenant-Commander Pope, now the Member for Hewsham, stayed at the Hall.

One of the most difficult prizes to win was the Fifteen Divisions (in a day – or rather, sitting). An all-night debate in Committee on the Finance Bill was about the best chance, and even that, this year, had done no better than fourteen. But every Thursday evening the next week's Business was shrewdly scrutinized, and, though a far chance, it was a popular bet. In the third week of July, that particular bet seemed hopeless. It was the fag-end of the Session and hardly anything remained except the Third Readings of some not very controversial Bills – and a Third Reading, of course, meant a whole day's debate and a single division. There was still the Nationalization of Land Bill which had recently come out of Committee. But the guillotine had fallen on the Report Stage of that: and after that, by the Standing Order of 1947, any remaining amendments or new Clauses were put to the House without debate. The Speaker said, 'Will those of that opinion say "Aye"?' If the Government had agreed to it, a Whip said 'Aye' and it was so. If they did not, he said 'No' and the amendment was rejected. There was no debate, and no division. Far back in 1947, when the Standing Order came in, a handful of Conservatives, stampeded by a rogue Independent, had protested against this queer method of legislation by challenging a number of divisions. But the procedure was now accepted as normal and proper. Great was the surprise, then, and indignation, and many the mutters of 'Bad Form' that Thursday when the Member for Hewsham, supported by some young members of the Opposition, began challenging divisions.

They kept it up. For nearly two hours they made the Government supporters tramp angrily through the Lobbies.

After the thirteenth division they suddenly stopped. There had been two divisions already that day.

As in the Bishops' Pool, money had been accumulating for some time: and a man called Meridew, a Civil Servant, won £22,000.

The Member for Hewsham was called before the Committee of Privileges. But he was able to show that he had not himself invested in the Pools (this was forbidden to a Member of either House). Nor did he know Mr Meridew.

But it was observed by some that a few months later he had a nice new Humber Hawk.

'Six, now, darling?'

'Six, of *course*.'

One sad note has to be struck. Stanley Bass was gently transferred to Hambone Hall and, though still in slight dudgeon about the whole affair, enjoyed his new quarters. The sad note is that, after one week of devoted care by Lady Primrose, he decided that Lady Primrose was too much of a mouse, and after two weeks he sighed for livelier stuff. She started using lipstick for his benefit: and that was the end. Stanley Bass is unmarried still. So, alas, is Lady Primrose. She has still no notion what her latitude is: but she runs the Hall very well.

The mystery of Olga's twins is a mystery still. Bass remained indignant: but not so indignant as to risk going to see Olga about them.

'But, darling, why not announce it? I want the planet to know.'

'No, you don't.'

'But I *do*! The cosmos! Even the Russians!'

'Bass has still to get through his Final Board. Do you want the Maple to see large Press-photographs of Number Nine and his betrothed one?'

'Oh, I do follow now. Not yet, you mean?'

'Not yet. But meanwhile...'

Pleasant things took place.

Single too is Elinor Slice. She abandoned mind-sweeping, and became an ordinary bureaucrat. Old Boys of Hambone Hall who meet her by chance at conferences or committees are astonished to remember the mystique with which she was surrounded at the Hall.

Dr Maple roamed the town like a mad thing, ringing up Peach at every call-box he passed. Mr Meridew, at last, though it was against his principles, resigned from the National Telephone Club altogether. The mind-man had himself psychoanalysed by a fellow trick-cyclist who found that he was a perfectly normal trick-cyclist. At last he abandoned the pursuit of Peach and looked up, in the records he had taken away, the address of Jacaranda. He married Jacaranda and took her to South America, where he had secured a post as Personnel (Vocational) Consultant to an American firm of stocking-manufacturers. On his third night in Rio he flung himself from a fifth-floor window. The papers said that the English scientist was not merely dead but formidably devoured.

One queer fact remains to be recorded. Some of that Intake climbed into the public service in the end. Lavinia Gable did, but not, alas, her handsome boy. Number Four did: but not poor Number Fifteen (he joined a firm of Sports Outfitters). Number Eleven, the Oxford lad, got through at last, and shot up the slopes of Whitehall like a rocket.

But the only one who came out successful from that last, famous Intake was Number Nine, a man called Stanley Bass.

A P Herbert

Topsy, MP

Fresh from 'Earth's *rosiest* honeymoon since Adam and Eve', Topsy returns to a life of marital bliss, and finds herself '*too* unanimously' elected a Member of Parliament. Social functions and parliamentary and wifely duties aside, she somehow still finds time to pour out her thoughts on her new life to the devoted Trix. In this latest collection of letters, she remains as endearing as ever and her deliberations, preoccupations and observations retain their candid freshness – and make hilarious reading.

'my dear you know I'm a *comparative* fundamentalist in dogmatological matters' [Topsy on principles]

'he was so beflattened that the little *feminine* heart was *totally* melted, and besides it's *quite* my policy to conciliate rather than *inflame* the foe' [Topsy on the Opposition]

Honeybubble & Co.

Mr Honeybubble proved to be one of A P Herbert's most popular creations and avid readers followed his progress through life in A P H's column in *Punch* where he first appeared. Here his exploits are collected together with a cast of other colourful characters from the riches of their creator's imagination. *Honeybubble & Co.* is a delightful series of sketches revealing some of the more humorous aspects of human nature.

A P Herbert

Light Articles Only

In this amusing collection of articles and essays, A P Herbert ponders the world around him in his own inimitable style. Witty, droll and a respecter of no man, the admirable APH provides a series of hilarious and unique sketches – and gently points the finger at one or two of our own idiosyncrasies. Such comic dexterity and inspired versatility is beautifully enhanced by a string of ingenious illustrations.

The Old Flame

Robin Moon finds Phyllis rather a distraction in the Sunday morning service – after all her golden hair does seem to shine rather more brightly than the Angel Gabriel's heavenly locks. His wife, Angela, on the other hand, is more preoccupied with the cavalier Major Trevor than perhaps she should be during the Litany. Relations between the Moons head towards an unhappy crescendo, and when, after an admirable pot-luck Sunday lunch, Robin descends to the depths of mentioning what happened on their honeymoon, the result is inevitable – they must embark on one of their enforced separations. Finding his independence once more, Robin feels free to link up with Phyllis and her friends, and begins to dabble in some far from innocent matchmaking.

This ingenious work brilliantly addresses that oh so perplexing a problem – that of 'the old flame'.

Printed in Great Britain
by Amazon

24344778R00149